The Art of the Creative Commons

Studies in Critical Social Sciences

Series Editor
David Fasenfest
(*Wayne State University*)

VOLUME 214

New Scholarship in Political Economy

Series Editors
David Fasenfest
(*Wayne State University*)
Alfredo Saad-Filho
(*King's College London*)

Editorial Board
Kevin B. Anderson (*University of California, Santa Barbara*)
Tom Brass (*formerly of SPS, University of Cambridge*)
Raju Das (*York University*)
Ben Fine ((*emeritus*) SOAS *University of London*)
Jayati Ghosh (*Jawaharlal Nehru University*)
Elizabeth Hill (*University of Sydney*)
Dan Krier (*Iowa State University*)
Lauren Langman (*Loyola University Chicago*)
Valentine Moghadam (*Northeastern University*)
David N. Smith (*University of Kansas*)
Susanne Soederberg (*Queen's University*)
Aylin Topal (*Middle East Technical University*)
Fiona Tregenna (*University of Johannesburg*)
Matt Vidal (*Loughborough University London*)
Michelle Williams (*University of the Witwatersrand*)

VOLUME 16

The titles published in this series are listed at *brill.com/nspe*

The Art of the Creative Commons

Openness, Networked Value and Peer Production in the Sound Industry

By

Miłosz Miszczyński

BRILL

LEIDEN | BOSTON

Cover illustration: Bust of Karl Marx, 1939, by S.D. Merkurov, at the Fallen Monument Park (Muzeon Park of Arts) in Moscow, Russia. Photo courtesy of Alfredo Saad-Filho.

Library of Congress Cataloging-in-Publication Data

Names: Miszczyński, Miłosz, author.
Title: The art of the creative commons : openness, networked value and peer production in the sound industry / by Miłosz Miszczyński.
Description: Leiden ; Boston : Brill, [2022] | Series: Studies in critical social sciences, 2666-2205 ; volume 214 | Includes bibliographical references and index.
Identifiers: LCCN 2021061950 (print) | LCCN 2021061951 (ebook) | ISBN 9789004504233 (hardback) | ISBN 9789004504240 (ebook)
Subjects: LCSH: Cultural industries. | Intellectual property and creative ability.
Classification: LCC HD9999.C9472 M57 2022 (print) | LCC HD9999.C9472 (ebook) | DDC 338.4/77–dc23/eng/20220103
LC record available at https://lccn.loc.gov/2021061950
LC ebook record available at https://lccn.loc.gov/2021061951

Typeface for the Latin, Greek, and Cyrillic scripts: "Brill". See and download: brill.com/brill-typeface.

ISSN 2666-2205
ISBN 978-90-04-50423-3 (hardback)
ISBN 978-90-04-50424-0 (e-book)

Copyright 2022 by Miłosz Miszczyński. Published by Koninklijke Brill NV, Leiden, The Netherlands.
Koninklijke Brill NV incorporates the imprints Brill, Brill Nijhoff, Brill Hotei, Brill Schöningh, Brill Fink, Brill mentis, Vandenhoeck & Ruprecht, Böhlau and V&R unipress.
All rights reserved. No part of this publication may be reproduced, translated, stored in a retrieval system, or transmitted in any form or by any means, electronic, mechanical, photocopying, recording or otherwise, without prior written permission from the publisher.
Authorization to photocopy items for internal or personal use is granted by Koninklijke Brill NV provided that the appropriate fees are paid directly to The Copyright Clearance Center, 222 Rosewood Drive, Suite 910, Danvers, MA 01923, USA. Fees are subject to change.

This book is printed on acid-free paper and produced in a sustainable manner.

To Emma and Max

Contents

Acknowledgements IX
List of Illustrations X

Introduction
The Art of the Creative Commons 1
1   Creative Industries: Opening Copyright with Open Licensing 3
2   Creative Commoning: Commons-Based Peer Production and Networked Value of Objects 8
3   Sound Industry and FreeSound.org 12
4   Studying the Art of the Creative Commons 15
5   The Structure of the Book 18

1 Managing and Organizing Openness in the Digital Economy 22
1   Openness in Business Strategy and Operations 26
   1.1   *Open Innovation* 26
   1.2   *Open Business* 31
2   Participatory Cultures 33
   2.1   *Open Capital* 33
   2.2   *Open Production* 37
3   Openness in Public Policy 41
   3.1   *Open Data Movement* 42
   3.2   *Open Scholarship* 43
   3.3   *Open Government* 47

2 Cultural, Legal and Organisational Foundations of Digital Commons and Peer-Production 50
1   Culture of Resistance and the Roots of the Digital Commons 52
2   Open Licensing: The Legal Foundations of Digital Commoning 56
3   Principles of Digital Peer Production 60

3 Creative Commons
Political Economy of Creative Peer-to-Peer Production 65
1   The Basic Framework of Copyright in Creative Industries 66
2   Creative Industries' Crisis in the Digital Era 70
3   Opening Creative Industries: Creative Commons as a Remedy to Restrictiveness of Copyright 74
4   Creative Commons: Alternative Production and Distribution in Sound Industry 80

4 Creative Commons
Peer-Production and the Quest for Networked Value 84
  1 Metadata and Content Annotation 87
  2 Sound Scenes and Their Cross-Fertilisation 92
  3 Growing Commons: Providing Representation for Underrepresented Sound 94
  4 Sharing Building Blocks: On a Search for Use Value of Content 101

5 The Art of Commoning and Content in Context 107
  1 Technical Quality and Context 111
  2 Openness and Artistic Experimentation 117
  3 Sound Commoning and a Sense of Community 121

6 Acknowledging Authorship
Attribution in the Market Context 127
  1 Attribution and Reputation 130
  2 Waiving Attribution 134
  3 Violation of Creative Commons License 138
  4 Public Domain (CC-0) as a Response to Limitations of Protection 145
  5 Conclusion 149

7 Art for Art's Sake? Commodifying the Commons 152
  1 Symbolic Unity of Creative Commons and Creative Industries 154
  2 Multiple Channel Content Sales 159
  3 Freemium Mode of Sound and Related Products 163
  4 Exclusivity of Access and Intermediation 166
  5 Curation and Automated Integration 170
  6 Conclusions 173

Conclusion
The Art of the Creative Commons 175
  1 Creative Commons and the Opening of the Creative Industries 176
  2 Networked Value and the Commons 179
  3 Artistic Work through Commons-Based Production 180
  4 Creative Commons in the Political Economy of the Creative Industries 182
  5 Future Research on the Art of the Commons 184

Bibliography 187
Index 214

Acknowledgements

The research for this book was realized as a funded project "The Open Licensing Model and Re-organisation of the Creative Industry" of the National Science Centre, Poland (no. 2017/26/D/HS4/00183). I would like to express my gratitude for the financing as well as constructive support of reviewers of this grant project.

This book would not have been possible without the help of Frederick Font from the Music Technology Group at the Pompeu Fabra University (UPF) in Barcelona. I am grateful for access to the respondents allowing me to study FreeSound. I would like to also thank all participants of our earlier project in which I worked as a Research Fellow: "AudioCommons", funded by the European Commission through the Horizon 2020 programme, research and innovation grant 688382. The early, theoretical work on this book, was done during my Fellowships at the University of Oxford's Institute of Social and Cultural Anthropology and University of Surrey's Centre for Digital Economy (2015–2017). I would like to thank all their members for unforgettable experience and exposure to a variety of perspectives and approaches to academia.

I would like to express special gratitude to European Group for Organizational Studies' research groups. They discussed my manuscript during a number of sessions focusing on open innovation, peer production and creative industries. Your feedback and continuous remarks supported the development of this manuscript. Similar thanks to all anonymous reviewers who have peer-reviewed my texts on commoning and commons, enriching my work with new perspectives, literatures and creative impulses.

I would like to thank my colleagues at Kozminski University, who have supported me on multiple levels. Andrzej Koźmiński, Dominika Latusek-Jurczak and Tomasz Olejniczak were the readers of the early draft of this manuscript. Their genuine interest and honesty have greatly influenced the quality of my analysis. The research office of Kozminski University was extremely accommodating and supporting, with Anna Tybuś-Kamela Andrzej Krzyżewski, providing a wonderful administrative support of the funded project.

Lastly, I would like to acknowledge the unique circumstances of working on this book. Two pandemic years with a lot of unexpected events produced new types of challenges. I would like to thank my wonderful wife, Emma Greeson for the never-ending love and support and my almost two-year-old son, Max, for the most joyful moments in my life (and making sure all the wheels in our house spin fast enough).

Illustrations

Figure

1   Steps prior to sound upload on FreeSound   86

Tables

1   Five open science schools of thought   45
2   Creative commons license application on major sound and music platforms   82

Introduction

The Art of the Creative Commons

Imagine the sound of your car's engine in neutral. Your car works rhythmically and slowly generating a sound similar to a bass, with a slow rhythm and mechanical quality. Then imagine, you make a recording of it, where all qualities of that sound can be heard. Using your phone, you capture the vibe of your engine. Then imagine you save the file to your computer and decide to share it by specifying what other users can do with the file (for example prohibiting commercial usage) and describing the sound using tags that describe that sound: "car", "engine", "vehicle", "exterior", "noise", maybe the model name: "Skoda Yeti", "1.4 TSI". Then you share that sound, not really knowing what it can be useful for. Then imagine your recording is downloaded more than 5000 times. Your engine sound is used as a sample in a video game, you tube videos, radio plays, and most of the designers place your name in the credits of their work. In most cases you have no way of knowing where your sound was used. Someone even transforms your engine sound into a musical instrument, making it sound like a drum in an electronic piece. This one decision to record, tag and upload, enriches several hundred. With time, this number only grows and occasionally you receive an email from users thanking you for the contribution.

This thought experiment explains the basic idea of participating in the digital commons in the creative industries. The digital commons can be understood as a pool of digital resources shared using an open licensing framework and embedded in a specific community or industry. The objective of this book is to describe the role of the open licensing model in the context of artistic activity in the sound industry. Focusing on the Creative Commons framework (CC), this project concentrates on shifts in the processes of cultural production, distribution and marketisation of works. As of this writing (early 2021), CC is the biggest globally recognised open licensing model, which in the form of a series of legal contracts regulates free access and usage of creative content. Unlike the dominant copyright protection model, the open licensing model does not concentrate on sanctioning the paid usage of works but promotes free, egalitarian access to information and only regulates the scope of this access.

In the creative industries, open licensing has been adopted by both creators, publishers and public institutions. According to 2015 estimations, over 1.1 billion works have been licensed under the CC framework, which has been accessed over 136 billion times (Creative Commons, 2015). With the dynamic increase of content, these numbers might have already increased tenfold. So far, business and management researchers have examined various aspects of the open licensing model, mostly observing changes in the IT industry among software developers (Lerner, 2013), and in the access to scientific information (Eve, 2014). The prevailing interpretation of these movements in the literature has been based on the resistance argument, depicting open licensing frameworks such as CC, GNU or BSD as social movements eroding the vast power of monopolists, powerful corporations and copyright intermediaries (Berry, 2008; Hess, 2007; Holtgrewe and Werle, 2001; Juris, 2005; Tkacz, 2014). This literature has also noted the importance of open licensing in fostering new user-led open innovations or providing technical support, usually in reference to the software industry (Lerner, 2013). However, there is a need of going beyond the IT sector as there are very few accounts that examine the role of open licensing in the creative sector. This project expands the existing knowledge by filling this niche and directing attention to the ways in which the open licensing model informs cultural production processes.

The title of this book *The Art of the Creative Commons* refers to the users' unique ability of relying on the dynamic taking place inside a specific type of commons, the creative one, with a community in search of artistic exchange and collaboration, and by a production method, organisation, and industry that has not previously been described in the literature. This book's main objective is to propose a theoretical perspective on the shifts provoked by the open licensing model of the Creative Commons license in the creative industries. The book posits that open licensing in the creative industries not only proposes an alternative approach to intellectual property protection, playing an important role in resisting current copyright practice, but also and more importantly, it enables new mechanisms of peer production, fosters new ways of achieving artistic innovation, mediated by the digital environment, and creates a path for new, commons-based business models. In other words, this project identifies how the open licensing model contributes to the changes in the ways in which cultural production and distribution occur, which in studies of creative industries so far has not received the same sustained attention as the resistance thesis. Focusing on the sound industry and its potential to cross-subsidise the value of audio/music to emerging industry needs, this project analyses the largest repository of CC-licensed content, FreeSound.org, that contains over 500.000 works shared by the authors in more than 15 years of its existence.

1 Creative Industries: Opening Copyright with Open Licensing

This book expands the knowledge about the role in which an alternative framework of copyright protection regulates peer-to-peer creative production and establishes norms and conventions within the commons. Copyright law was initially intended to protect creators, to prevent commercial distributors from exploiting their works, and to stop then from being plagiarized by other artists. In sociology and social analysis more broadly conceived, copyright law has largely been understood as a social construct created to secure rights to creative works and the economic regulation of their reproduction in a capitalist society. Its creation coincided with mechanical reproduction, which influenced the creative industries with revolutionary inventions such as the machine press, phonograph and cinematograph. These innovations were ground-breaking, transforming the way in which reproduced cultural creations are interpreted (Benjamin, 1998). In effect of the technological changes, music, or more broadly sound, has been decontextualised and made into "an immutable mobile" (Latour, 1986) when it was disconnected from local environments and oral cultures and became a fictitious commodity inserted onto the global market. This has created a market not for the product itself, but for the rights of usage, establishing a copyright trade. In effect, this process propelled the commodification of creations, regulated their usage and purchase, and created the institutional structure governing, regulating and participating in this market. These processes simultaneously constrain creative production and by enforcing copyright limited the scope of material that may be borrowed (Boldrin and Levine, 2002; 2008).

Copyright provided a frame for the trading of cultural works, while the commodification of cultural creations has always been controversial. Discussions of the process brought ground-breaking theorisations in the social sciences. Members of the Frankfurt School showed the deterministic and threatening influence of the market on the creative industries (Adorno and Horkheimer, 1979; Benjamin, 1998), and it has resonated in studies of copyright. Benjamin (1998) wrote of the loss of the aura through the mechanical reproduction of art, which had challenged the existing concepts that governed art. This debate produced a range of critical arguments on the outcomes of art commodification stemming from mechanical reproduction, for example showing how the market influences the type and quality of artistic goods (Griswold, 1981). One of the major results of these enquiries has been the assertion of the deterministic nature of law and the regulations shaping cultural expressions. For instance, Dowd's (2003) study takes on a small number of works that explicitly demonstrate the socioeconomic functions of copyright by showing how the expiry of sound recording technology patents brought new genres in popular music.

Importantly, the literature has also focused on the actors in the industry, who solidified their activity through copyright. It has been demonstrated how the development of music labels and media corporations has been tied to the increasing marketisation of intellectual property, which was linked to changes in global copyright law and increased the power held by copyright holders at the cost of creators (Boyle, 2004; Graber and Nenova, 2008). This link between commercial activity and law has favoured powerful intermediaries, whose business models have relied on speculation of copyright and patenting of sound recording and motion picture technology (Fredriksson, 2014; McLeod and DiCola, 2011; Scherzinger, 2014). In effect, since the early 20th century, major corporations have controlled the global music market and film industry (Negus, 1998, Rayna and Struikova, 2009). In the music industry, they generated profits through the slow industrialisation of popular music (Firth, 2001) and the standardisation of music products (Hirsch, 1972; Weber, 1958). Similarly, the media industry has been dominated by corporations that centralised production technology, distribution channels and erected entry barriers (Kellner, 1995). As a result, the creative industry has become globalised, increasingly homogenous, and major music labels and production companies became key actors by influencing the kind of cultural goods produced and, to a large degree, shaping intellectual protection policy. These processes were understood to be rooted in capitalist accumulation (Coriat and Weinstein, 2012; Fligstein, 1990) and globally regulated by market logic (Griswold, 1981).

In recent work, however, there has been an increasing emphasis on the discrepancy between regulations and the directions of cultural production. Several arguments underscored the legal system's inability to prevent unauthorised use and reuse of cultural products (Marshall, 2005; McLeod and DiCola, 2011). Arguments against the legitimacy of existing copyright regulations have been brought up in the context of technological development. Technological innovations inaugurated a change in the way consumers and producers approached intellectual property, as they, intentionally or unintentionally, started violating copyrights by sharing work to which they did not have rights. Some works trace it back to the popularisation of home recording equipment, which since the late 1960s transformed the ways in which music and video is consumed and produced (Lopes, 1992). Collage-like production techniques became available to anyone who possessed a recording system. This shift led to problematic applications of copyright, for example in bootlegging and copying music at home (Marshall, 2004; 2005). Consequently, creators have changed their ways of production, adopting new remixed techniques that relied on other works protected by copyright (Rodgers, 2003), and bringing out sample-based musical genres such as hip-hop or drum and bass. As this usage needed to be authorised for the purpose of commercial circulation, cultural production using remix techniques started to be accompanied by legal negotiations, which again proved to be a constraint on artistic production (McLeod and DiCola, 2011).

This resulted in a growing resistance, most notably in the underground music scene. Practices like bootlegging have been identified as movements against powerful copyright holders and driven by "people locating their experiences and their selves against the commodification of popular music" (Neumann and Simpson 1997, p. 323). As Lee Marshall shows, even though these underground practices clearly conflicted with copyright, they were not necessarily harmful to the music industry because they promoted participation in music scenes and increased the fan base, in effect boosting sales of records and interest in artists (Marshall, 2004). The resistance to copyright was met with strong counteractions by music labels and production companies, preventing copying without authorisation, for instance by developing DRM technologies to control the use, modification, and distribution of copyrighted works (Sinha, Machando and Sellman, 2010).

The practice of cultural production and consumption is interwoven with the spread of new technologies, which in the last decades has disrupted the intellectual property regime (Caroll, 2006; Goss, 2007). The ease with which a single user can exchange content has transformed the way in which creators and creative producers approach this domain, reshaping industries and transferring the power to digital innovators. These tensions intensified when new digital formats and sharing platforms burst onto the scene (Berry, 2008; Juris, 2005; Tkacz, 2014). Change occurred in the way music and video is stored and consumed with development of easily transferable digital formats such as MP3 and DivX (Haring, 2000). Thanks to broadband internet, copying and sharing content became even simpler (Kretschmer et al., 2001). The creation of peer-to-peer sharing technology has likewise challenged copyright protection (Alexander, 2002; Cooper and Harrison, 2001; Jones and Lenhart, 2004; Ku and Singh, 2002). It has caused the emergence of new legal digital distribution channels, created in collaboration with major copyright owners (Hardy, 2012), such as iTunes or Spotify in music and Hulu and Netflix in the video industry. The literature on this intersection of technology and copyright has so far concentrated on the implications of digital distribution on industry practices, including copyright management (McCourt and Burkart, 2003, Styven, 2007), changing consumption habits (Molteni and Ordanini, 2003) or business models of intermediaries (Fox, 2004, Vaccaro and Cohn, 2004). Studies have emphasised both the extensive success and power of major labels in the industry (Kretschmer et al., 2001; Young and Collins, 2010) and the growing power of small music labels (Furgason, 2009). Research has also theorised on digital commodities (Poster, 2004) or explained the influence of digitalisation on economic value (Oberholzer-Gee and Strumpf, 2007). In many ways studies of internet piracy understand it as a political movement aimed at restoring more democratic ways of private music consumption and challenging copyright institutions (Hann, 2007).

In this landscape, between piracy and restrictive copyright, open licensing models have offered an alternative to traditional copyright practices by providing simple licensing tools, based on "building 'a layer of reasonable copyright' on top of existing law" (Goss, 2007: 977). While traditional copyright law creates the default rule of "All Rights Reserved", making permission necessary for each use of a work, open licensing facilitates an environment in which "Some Rights Reserved" or "No Rights Reserved" become the norm. In other words, open licensing seeks to "use copyright to authorize (rather than inhibit) copying, distribution, modification and reuse of software and other copyrighted works" (Dusollier, 2006: 274). In nearly all cases, the content remains the property of the original creator who is permitted to charge for additional permissions, like commercial application of the material when the CC license allows only non-commercial usage. Originating from the computer software industry, open licensing initially aimed at promoting open exchange of information in user-led development of computer programs, allowing for greater participation among the community of users, stimulating a collaborative spirit of creation, and increasing the supply and stock of knowledge. Numerous works identify the main goal of open licensing as focused on ending imbalances in spheres that rely on restrictive intellectual property, such as the cultural industries (Berry, 2008; Shemtov and Walden, 2013).

While free and open source software (FOSS), has produced numerous specific, project-oriented frameworks (Chapter 2), the Creative Commons framework is the only licensing that was adopted in a non-software context, catering to users who want to upload digital content and information. Creative Commons provided a simple, user-friendly tool that permitted anyone to distribute and build on others' work, without the necessity of contact or legal documentation. This framework relied on a simple set of rules, regulating permissions set by the author of the original work. It responded to the mounting needs of the creative industry, providing a legal alternative to unauthorised usage of others' work. A framework created in 2001 by the Creative Commons initiative has achieved global scope and recognition. Mainstream online platforms that implemented CC and have full support for licensing include YouTube, Flickr and Vimeo (in multimedia content) and Jamendo and FreeSound (in the audio industry). The literature identifies several social functions of CC in the political and ideological spheres (Carroll, 2006), institutional (Elkin-Koren, 2006) or commercial purposes of promotion or recognition (Elkin-Koren, 2006; Goss, 2007). Certainly, the resistance to copyright regimes has its roots in institutional changes involving a wholesale shift caused by the rapid growth of technological culture and the power of new technologies resulting in the extremely high supply and availability of content, the ambiguous situation of licensing of online material, and very few standards concerning online rights management. Open licensing responds to this situation by normalising the legal status of works and facilitating their co-creation and exchange. Carroll names this process "re-intermediation", with open licensing as a movement to liberate creativity from powerful, corporate intermediaries who specialise in rights management and speculation (Carroll, 2006). My project adds to this discussion, by including a theory of social change occurring in the domain of creative production, which has been catalysed by the spread of CC in three fields: subjects of property, objects of property and collaboration and cross-subsidisation patterns.

Open licensing is making significant steps towards having a transformational and universal impact on science, technology and society. As the management and social sciences literature lacks a clear conceptualisation of its role in the creative industry, this project fills that niche by addressing key spheres related to organisation of production, labour of artists, networked nature of objects, ways of collaboration driven by it and emerging monetisation strategies. All these topics fit into the thematic field of opening, which as I show in Chapter 1, is located within the sub-disciplines of organisational studies and work and employment studies. It comprises numerous spheres, touching on open business strategies and operations, creating new participatory cultures in capital and production, and influencing public policy in the domains of public data, governance and scholarship. The findings of this book bring an important voice to these debates and transform the traditional linear value chain of media, in which content is delivered from producer to consumer, to a fully interconnected model that conceptualises and identifies the communication and interaction among all stakeholders. It is also necessary to learn more about the context of open media to build a basis for understanding its dissemination.

There is a promise that the changes described in this project will expand within the next few years. The activities of commercial actors in the sound industry are concentrating on producing innovative new technologies for annotation, access, transformation and licensing. In the future these technologies will play a key role in supporting content reuse in unprecedented and unexpected ways, such as procedurally generated soundtracks, benefiting content creators and content users and erasing the boundaries between them. There are concerted efforts to further strengthen the application and popularisation of open data by institutional actors. For instance, open licensing models are identified as a central element of the Digital Agenda for Europe (see IP/10/581, MEMO/10/199 and MEMO/10/200) and recognised as a key driver to develop content markets in Europe, which could not only generate new business opportunities and jobs but also provide consumers with more choice and more value for their money.

2 Creative Commoning: Commons-Based Peer Production and Networked Value of Objects

This book also contributes to the literature on peer-to-peer production, by providing a unique, often less described model of commons from the creative industries. The concept of peer production in the literature has been popularised by Benkler (2002), who, relying on his analysis of GNU/Linux community, has shown how commons-based production, based on decentralised, multiple co-contributions to one object, show much higher productivity than firms and markets. Commonly, peer production is understood as a distributed network of co-producers and participants who, using computer technology are working on a shared goal. For instance, a common associate in regard to peer-to-peer networks are popular sharing networks such as Napster, Kaazaa or AudioGalaxy, which in the late 1990s and early 2000s allowed for downloading copyrighted content. But, as the literature shows, the definition of peer-production has become a new model of production that is embedded in the idea of asynchronous, technologically dispersed production.

The literature on commons-based production has been slowly expanding. One of the first publications in this field of exploring peer-to-peer networks has been Michael Bauwens' article on peer production (Bauwens 2005), later revised (Bauwens and Kostakis 2021). Both papers allow for understanding the specificity of the model of peer-to-peer production. Bauwens and Kostakis (2021) identify the key characteristics of this model of production, by emphasising the following characteristics: "different from for-profit maximization production or production by state-owned institutions" (p. 22), community-driven governance, "different from market allocation or corporate hierarchy" (p. 22), and emergence of new property regimes, commons-oriented and "making use-value freely accessible on a universal basis" (p. 22). An important accent in this literature lies on use value, which plays a central role, since many of the peer-production projects are non-commercial and separated from the market dynamics. They rely on decentralised networks, that by using the means of technology allow for equal participation in production, as well as accessing its effects. The literature identifies several mechanisms attributed to the specificity of peer-production, such as model of control, modular character of the projects, based on smaller sub-segments, and anti-credentialism, so no a priori selection of participants.

Often the model of peer production is separated, or even opposed to the market-capitalist idea of production (and products), proposing an alternative model, usually less-profit driven, open and transparent – in opposition to closed, proprietary model with products which mechanics and code are unknown. This idea is part of the ethics of early hackers and technology enthusiasts, revolves around the establishment of communities and products guided by the idea of digital commons, digital resources accessible to all members of a society with no explicit commercial purpose. The result of this approach is the emergence of productive communities, such as the one described in the book, donating their work to the community. The idea of the commons, well known to the literature, is updated by the realities of the digital economy, providing a new way of expanding the goods and providing a unique, poll of shared resources that are accessible and can be used by the productive powers of users, but also of capitalist enterprises.

Commons-based production is recognised as a third way of producing that is neither anti-capitalist, nor aligned with capitalism. Its effects often bring productive resources that are exploited by the commercial actors. In this sense, the literature has started to consider the innovative character of this work. Commons and commoners provide attractive resources and customer base to the corresponding industry actors. Free/Libre Open Source Software literature contains several studies on the hijacking of commercial projects. But commons quite often produce communities that are market-active, often even supporting the commons' infrastructure. This book shows this relationship to the industry, outlining the commodification of the commons and tight relationship with the industry, not only in the financial sphere, but also symbolically confirming the suitability of commons-based production to the realities of mainstream media industries.

The book's premise is that commoning in creative industries differs from other forms of commoning. This argument is built on studies that treat commoning as a form of collaboration guided by a goal of either sharing common or proprietary goods (e.g., sharing economy), or jointly producing or working for common goals (e.g., free/libre open source software, wiki projects, co-creation models). In the further chapters I will outline how the model of Creative Commons supports the generation of creative projects and user-led artistic innovations through the model of commons-based peer production. Unlike software models, this production differs, both following fewer structures and less governance, and generating a new format that relies on the commons.

The instance given in this book exemplifies a distinct form of production based on participation of many users. So far, business and management research has examined various aspects of the open licensing model, mostly observing changes in the IT industry among software developers (Lerner, 2013), and in the access to scientific information (Eve, 2014). As I have shown in the previous two chapters, the prevailing interpretation of these movements in the literature has been based on the resistance argument, depicting open licensing frameworks such as CC, GNU or BSD as social movements eroding the vast power of monopolists, powerful corporations and copyright intermediaries (Berry, 2008; Hess, 2007; Holtgrewe and Werle, 2001; Juris, 2005; Tkacz, 2014). This literature has also noted the importance of open licensing in fostering new user-led open innovations or providing technical support, usually in reference to the software industry (Lerner, 2013). However, there is a need to go beyond the IT sector as there are very few accounts of the role of open licensing in the creative sector. This project expands upon that body of knowledge by filling this niche and turning attention to the ways in which the open licensing model informs the cultural production processes.

A key mechanism identified in this book is the co-generation of value that differs from these earlier software projects. The key mechanism of the dynamic generated by the described creative commons rests on the generation of "networked value", a form of dispersed valorisation of content reliant on the on-demand usage of content. In this book I use this term, arguing that its generation is the key factor in facilitating the exponential growth of the commons, providing an unexpected effect of revealing the value of content by the users. In that domain, I employ Aristotelean distinction between use value, embedded in providing components for creative activity; and exchange value, tied to market realities and encompassing attempts of commodification of content or commercial activity of the creators. In the empirical chapters I show how networked value plays a key role in commons-based peer production, attracting users to share creative material and fostering their use in the new contexts. Networked value also refers to the specific model of collaboration, often based on lack of direct contact between creators, with solely the virtual connection provided by that content. In that sense, I argue that the establishment of the commons produces a distinct type of organisation, one that is reflected in a network of content which often cannot be mapped using legal, or interpersonal contacts and tools.

At the same time, networked value normalises the relationships between creators that have been hindered by copyright regulations. Opening copyrighted content responds to the earlier established conventions of collage and the use of other artists' work to generate something new, for instance by combining it. So far, especially in the music industry, which epitomised the highest fortification of content, this has been impossible, in some context prohibiting musicians or hobbyists from using the content, experimenting with it and producing new, unique ideas and aesthetics. Hundreds of lawsuits, typically of sampled music context, only exemplifies the problematic nature of this design. Introduction of commons, freeing content from constraints, and leaving the possibility of regulation of terms of usage, opens new possibilities and horizons for creative industries. At the same time, 15 years after the establishment of the commons, the dynamic inside the commons remains separate, and often reliant on the production in non-commons context.

I also argue that the same network value already functions in the spheres where the provided protection was inefficient, such as in the sound industry. The music and film industries have grown in environments within which their closed content is monitored by external agents, such as collecting societies. For them, any form of reuse is treated like a business loss, hence extensive monitoring for any kind of presence of content: from coffeeshops, to digital platforms and peer-to-peer sharing networks. Yet, there are industries that fail to protect the creations, mainly because their products are not as valuable as mainstream music or film. In such situations, compliance with copyright is quite low, and as with some of the interviewed creators, the prevailing logic of using sound effects is based on ignoring the copyright. In that domain, commons enhance ethical production without the violation of copyright and, by building the networked value, support also non-commons-based production.

Typical of the commons, the dynamic within creative commons, follows the mechanisms of the other industries, such as reputation built on virtue and technical quality of content; it also relies on commons to cater to other industries. This manifests in numerous forms of commodification that rely on the commons, from simple use of a unique sound (such as Tibetan bell) in a documentary to more advanced business projects, with the commons as the display window; sourcing the mass of content; or providing filtering services that support the work of users within the commons. To understand the dynamics inside the commons, I show the market relationships established inside (or with) the commons and draft the political economic analysis of this phenomenon.

This book concentrates on changes in the processes of cultural production caused by the popularisation of open licensing in the digital economy. The analysis proposes a theoretical perspective on the organisational shifts provoked by the open licensing model in the creative industry and verifies the thesis that open licensing serves a dual function: it proposes an alternative approach to intellectual property protection, playing an important role in resisting current copyright practice, and enables new mechanisms of collaboration and fosters new type of artistic innovation, mediated by the digital environment. In other words, this project identifies how the open licensing model contributes to the changes in the ways in which cultural production and distribution occur, which so far has not received the same sustained attention as the resistance thesis. Focusing on the sound industry and its potential to cross-subsidise the value of audio/music to emerging industry needs, the analysis presented in this book is based on the study of the largest repository of CC-licensed content, including research of creators, re-creators and objects of creation to delineate this form of organisational change.

3 Sound Industry and FreeSound.org

This work provides a view on a particular fragment of the creative industries landscape: the sound industry. This industry's products are tailored to multimedia productions, ranging from films, theatre, music video clips, radio plays, loops and instruments used in music production, to video games and YouTube videos. This industry's specificity lies in bridging the technological nature of professions from within this industry with a very narrow focus on creative specialisation. Members of this industry work as sound engineers, for instance in theatres or television networks; do foley recordings, going to natural sites to record animal noises; or mix and master audio tracks in film productions. In other words, sound industry comprises all kinds of sounds used in creative projects. The sound industry's technical character makes its professionals much different from those in the music industry, which concentrates on products related to and centred on musical sounds. Due to its profits, scope and logic, the music industry has its own rules and logic, largely controlled by major music labels. Despite some significant overlaps in the processes of production of components for music production, it remains separate from the sound industry despite some cross-fertalising with its products.

Freesound.org plays a significant role in sound industry, being the largest online platform of open sound. Its origins date to April 5, 2005, when during the International Computer Music Conference, the Music Technology Group of Universitat Pompeu Fabra, Barcelona launched a new platform that allowed its users to share all types of non-musical sound. The site was created by Xavier Serra, a professor of sound and music computing, and Bram de Jong, a developer who created FreeSound's code and administered the site. The site was created based on technologies developed by the members of Music Technology Group, used for enhancing the process of browsing and organising sound on the platform. At the heart of FreeSound is a basic functionality of uploading sound, which prior to upload needs to be annotated using tags that describe the sound. Users can browse the site's archive, use its search engine, and comment on other users' sounds. The site is also equipped with an internal messaging system for private messages, and a forum section. The site offers a range of functions connected to tagging (based on users' manually entered descriptions), geotagging (specifying the geographical location of where the recording was made), and search based on. From the technological side, FreeSound has an API based on RESTful principles through which third-party applications and websites can access and retrieve audio content and its metadata. This access has the possibility of integration with third-party applications and products.

As of 2020, FreeSound was led and administered by Frederic Font. According to the community update published on the site (FreeSound, 2021a), FreeSound comprises 483,213 sounds. There have been more than 171 million downloads from the site. In 2020 alone, its users published 46,441 sounds corresponding to 772 hours of audio recording, wrote 22.000 messages, 1.100 forum posts and made 65.000 sound comments. The platform attracts users who share an interest in sound for multimedia production. The user survey, conducted in 2017 (FreeSound, 2017) and based on 661 responses, found that more than 54% of the site users define themselves as professional, and work on composition, recording, and audio for games (FreeSound, 2019). Almost 85% of respondents rely on other web databases with audio content, such as commercial stock libraries such as pond5 or AudioJungle. Over 85% of the respondents in this survey were male, reflecting the industry's highly masculinised structure. The age of surveyed users ranged from 17 to 80 years old. The survey reflects a truly global scope of the site, with the majority of users originating in North America, Western and Eastern Europe, but also with some users from other regions.

FreeSound is a home to multiple cultural practices, from field recordings (Stanisz, 2018), to music sample sharing, loop building and sound effects. While it is difficult to describe a single user profile, there are two main activities on FreeSound. The first is the uploading of content, typically by users who are either skilled in field recordings or who have an archive that they want to share on the site. Uploading is quite often related to familiarity with studio equipment, experimentation with microphones or a general interest in recording sound. The second and most popular users are people who download content; these users are looking for content that they can use in their creative projects. These users often are less technically adept at recording and working on sound. Their motivation is often tied to a search for components that can foster their production of multimedia projects, such as videos or documentaries.

From the outset, the site has used the Creative Commons Licensing framework which allows users to decide among three permissions: Attribution (any person using the content needs to refer to the original creator), Attribution-NonCommercial (any person using the content cannot use it commercially), and CC-0 Public Domain (the content can be used by anyone in any context with no reference to the original author). According to the official numbers, the site's hosted material is dominated by the CC-0 Public Domain (61%), followed by Attribution (23%) and Attribution-NonCommercial (16%). The propagation of the licensing rules, as well as promoting Creative Commons, is an inherent programme of FreeSound, which facilitates the use of licensing.

Over more than 15 years, Freesound.org has remained independent. It is hosted by the University Pompeu Fabra which regularly makes a big contribution to the site's functioning. According to the published estimations made by Frederic Font, FreeSound's lead administrator, the market value of the University's cost of operating FreeSound exceeds 20,000€/year for only hosting costs, equal to five servers, 4 TB monthly data bandwidth and IT support staff (FreeSound, 2021b). Additionally, research, development and administration of the site that takes place on the platform is performed by the staff hired on by the university on academic contracts. FreeSound also uses donation-based model, that plays a significant role in financing the development. By 2019, the site had received 48,000€ in donations, which was used for development of the website, related to the improvements of site's front-end and optimisation, as well as licensing of help desk services (Zendesk), email services (Amazon), maps services (Mapbox), and site monitoring (Site 24×7) (FreeSound, 2021b). There are no commercial sources of financing FreeSound's activity besides a small stream of licensing of access to content through API. Importantly, the platform does not accept advertising or charge any fees. FreeSound's content has been the basis of scores of academic projects in sound processing, which have analysed and categorised sound or assessed similarities among sounds.

4 Studying the Art of the Creative Commons

This work is a study of the opening and reorganisation of the creative industries. It concentrates on the Creative Commons framework, the world's largest recognised open licensing model, which in the form of a series of legal contracts regulates free access and usage of creative content. Unlike the copyright protection model embedded in the traditional model of intellectual property, Creative Commons licensing follows the tradition of open licensing and abandons sanctioning the paid usage of works in favour of promoting free, egalitarian access to information and regulates only the scope of this access. In the creative industries, Creative Commons provide a framework useful for artists, publishers and cultural institutions.

The empirical part of the book was completed during the qualitative research of the relationship of the CC and cultural production. This project concentrates on the sound industry, comprised of production, circulation and consumption of musical and non-musical sound. This branch of the creative industry underwent a significant change in the wake of open licensing, which started a highly visible reconstruction within the industry; in recent years this segment of the creative industry was transformed in light of increasing digitalisation, widening use of CC content and evolution from saturated, dominated markets into CC-driven industry. This reconstruction has also cross-subsidised other creative sectors, such as advertising, production of computer games and film and video industry, within which CC-licensed sound has been extensively used. The choice of the sound industry is also driven by the type of medium: remix originates in sound works and for decades this branch has informed practices of popular culture.

My chosen research method was preceded by the analysis of my ontological approach, first positioning it among other paradigms of social sciences. This process was meant to inform the researcher about the accordance of research strategy with the type and nature of studied phenomenon as well as a researcher's approach to science (Konecki, 2000. My paradigm choice and following interpretative tradition is rooted in studying the phenomenon through the experiences and relations of participants, grasping meanings and conventions as well as learning about their approaches. The interpretative tradition sees reality as a social construct, based on a dynamic process of assigning subjective and different meanings as well as shared perceptions (Berger and Luckmann, 1966, 54–55). The study uses the principles of interpretative research (Orlikowski, 2000; Olikowski and Baroudi, 1991) and a critical approach (Madison, 2011; Walsham, 1993). In this approach, every action is connected to meanings and there are no meaningless actions (Koncecki, 2000).

Studying the dynamic from the perspective of users is tied to the description of the perspective of actors, which is interpreted by the researcher. For that reason, the approach is often understood as more descriptive than interpretative (Czarniawska-Joerges, 1992; Konecki, 2000).

In this book I provide an extended case study. Extended case studies are best used to study the contextual conditions of social phenomena and to draw a strong connection between on-the-ground data and grand theory. Michael Burawoy sums up the method's ambition and goal well by writing that it is intended "to extract the general from the unique, to move from the 'micro' to the 'macro', and to connect the present to the past in anticipation of the future, all by building on preexisting theory" (Burawoy, 1998: 6). Case studies provide a large quantity of data necessary for the experts in this discipline and for the discipline's functioning. The construction of the extended case study will allow for the evaluation of how theories of relationships apply to developments fostered by the open licensing model. The fundamental question of this work is about the reconstruction of the organisation of cultural production caused by the emergence of open licensing. The mediator in this relationship is the licensing framework, comprising millions of elements that are part of a global value chain. By focusing on content, the creators and the social function of rights of usage, I will explore and improve the understanding of both the form and substance of this reconstruction. The main task of this project will be to understand and to describe how alternative property informs different spheres and influences the way creators and consumers of content manage their work. This investigation will lead to a network-based theorisation of networked objects and innovations, which might improve our understanding of the nature and outcomes of the growth of the digital economy.

The project adopts a qualitative methodology based on 83 interviews, desk research and content analysis. The respondents were subjected to purposive sampling method, based on analysis of their activity and popularity of their sound on the platform. The rationale for purposive sampling to identify and reach core users, who have extensive experience using the platform and whose content is popular. The search for respondents was performed using a script written by Frederic Font, part of the FreeSound team. The respondents were categorised based on the following four factors.

Sound popularity: Respondents were selected based on the number of times their sounds were downloaded. If a sound was downloaded more than 1000 times, we stopped counting at 1000 to prevent one extremely popular sound from sending that user to the top of the ranking. Following that rule, 188 users were selected, and invited by FreeSound to an interview.

Sound quality: FreeSound's rating system allows users to rate sounds using the 5-star system (1 star for the lowest quality and 5 for the highest). In the selection we calculated the average rating of all ratings of all users' sounds. Only sounds with more than 25 ratings were considered, to avoid bias. We also eliminated users who have fewer than 25 sounds with at least 25 ratings. As a result of this selection, we identified 92 users of whom 23 agreed to be contacted by the researcher for an interview.

Forum activity: In this category we selected the 50 FreeSound forum users with the highest number of posts. In this category, 11 of users responded positively to an invitation to interview.

Moderators: We contacted 10 moderators who are experienced and who actively moderate sound. Our selection was based on their number of uploads. In the selection process, many users appeared in more than one category. To eliminate duplication of respondents, our script placed the respondent in the highest category, and removed that name from other lists. For every spot in each category that opened after crossing the user out, the script assigned another user from the bottom of the list. The script manually eliminated users who had been interviewed earlier as experts or who were directly associated with FreeSound's team. The list of users was downloaded by the script on November 12, 2019.

Interviews were divided into two parts. In the first part, interviewees were asked to introduce themselves and discuss their work, narrating their personal and professional trajectory to contextualise their involvement in FreeSound and their professional experience. In the second part, the responded answered specific questions, following a semi-structured questionnaire with open-ended answers. The research scenario was crafted within the three key domains of the creative labour process, regulated by property law, and where the Creative Commons framework model incites transformation: (1) influencing the way in which subjects of law and labour operate (creators); (2) affecting the type and usage of objects of law and labour (creative products), and (3) examining the shifts in the role of rights of usage in the market context, looking at the elements such as source information, patterns of collaboration and ways of marketisation. The main ambition of this work is to put forward a theory that will demonstrate that to view cultural industry in light of the open licensing model means, in effect, to see it in terms of new type of networked collaboration, influencing all spheres of creative production, consumption and distribution.

The selected material was digitally collected. The majority of respondents have used Skype (recommended method of data collection), but also Zoom, Viber, Google Hangouts and Microsoft Teams. Each interview lasted from 20 to 95 minutes and was recorded using portable handheld sound recorder Zoom

H1n. The recorded files were transcribed verbatim and coded using qualitative data analysis software (MaxQDA). From the beginning of the interviews, qualitative and inductive techniques were used to recursively code and identify patterns in the data concerning the role and interpretation of CC content (Coffey and Atkinson, 1996). This stage confirmed that Creative Commons content is interpreted as an alternative instrument of content acquisition and distribution (aside from market transactions), which emerged as a key theme. In the second phase, I modified my code structure to capture more elements of this relationship, following the themes that emerged during coding.

For anonymity of the users, often requested during interviews, this book does not contain user names and personal details. All but three of the respondents were male, reflecting the industry structure. All were between 17 and 81 years of age. Most of these respondents have worked with sound for more than three years, with more than a quarter reporting more than seven years of experience. The largest number of the interviewees lived in the United States, Canada, the United Kingdom and Western Europe (the Netherlands, Belgium, Sweden, Norway, Germany, Spain, France, Italy). About a quarter came from Eastern Europe (Poland, Czech Republic, Russia), Israel and others came from Brazil, Ecuador, Japan, Serbia, Slovenia, Croatia etc. About one-third have also worked in the music industry, either composing or mixing and mastering. Nineteen have worked full-time in preparing audio for multimedia projects such as film, television or videogames. Three were academics in disciplines other than sound and music technology or engineering. Only nine described themselves as amateurs, with no professional involvement in the creative industries.

Twelve interviews were also done with game developers and sound professionals who had been selected through purposive sampling (Teddlie and Yu, 2007). They were either professionally involved in the music industry, or active in Creative Commons communities by regularly uploading their own material or actively reusing that content and publishing creative products (for instance as computer games). The majority of experts have openly relied on CC sound in producing their own products and promoted this activity online.

5   The Structure of the Book

In the next chapters I consider the role of the implementation of open licensing in contemporary creative industries. I understand openness as a paradigm of introducing new, innovative practices, implemented in multiple spheres of society, technology and environment.

Chapter one reviews the literature on the theme of openness and summarises the ways in which the principle of openness has been applied to different spheres of social and business life. This part shows how the open licensing framework influences a transformation of not only technological industries (e.g., open innovation in IT), but catalysed new practices in spheres that were previously neither accessible nor easy to obtain (for instance due to copyright protection). It shows how the adoption of openness influenced approaches to innovation and business strategy; generated new participatory cultures in the forms such as opening of capital and production; and was adopted in public policy, where it influenced open data movement, greater openness of scholarship and transparency of government actions. Presentation of these insights allows a better understanding of the translation of the idea of openness into the creative industries.

Chapter two links the idea of openness in the digital economy to the digital commons and the model of peer-to-peer production. This chapter explores three crucial aspects of the establishment of the digital commons, and which drive openness and new models of production. The first foundation of this processes I attribute to the culture of resistance, dating to the early days of information technology and the emergence of a technological culture, often labelled in the literature as 'hacker ethics' (Himannen, 2001; Levy, 1984). As I show, the ideas of these early adopters, shaped the role of the commons in contemporary technological capitalism. Understanding of these practices, as well as approaching cooperation and elitist perception of production helps to see the relationship between the participants of the commons and contemporary digital capitalism. I then describe the legal aspect of the commons, addressing the legal foundations of open licensing. In a short overview, I outline how open licensing establishes the framework for functioning of the commons by mapping the legal rules and different types and functions of alternative copyright protection frameworks. Lastly, I show the organisational mechanisms typical to the commons-based peer production. Referring to the literature on this phenomenon, I outline the mechanisms such as self-aggregation of the distributed networks (Bauwens, 2009); motivational diversity (Benkler, 2017); heterarchy as well as the specific mechanisms of governance and decision making. The material contained in this chapter discusses the findings of the literature and leads to a greater understanding of the context of commons-based production.

Chapter three addresses the specificity of the creative industries by focusing on the Creative Commons framework. It concentrates on the political economy of creative peer-to-peer production, providing a broader socioeconomic context for this book. It starts with a description of traditional approach to copyright in the creative industries. Then, it describes the crisis of creative industries, caused by the digital era, showing how both emerging models of production (e.g., sampling, bootlegging) and models of distribution (online streaming, piracy), cause controversies and tensions among industry participants. Responding to this conflict, this chapter shows the role of the Creative Commons framework, which after a short introduction, is shown as a remedy to some of the problems of digitalisation of the creative industries, which relies on the principle of openness and provides a framework supporting the generation of the new types of commons. Lastly, this chapter addresses the role of this framework in the current sound industry, the focus of this work, showing the scope of application of Creative Commons, and introducing the studied platform: FreeSound.org.

Chapter four begins the empirical part of the book. It introduces the mechanisms of commoning in the sound industry, by describing the activity of uploaders and identifying the mechanism of sharing as part of the processes of value of activation. This chapter emphasises the approach of creators to the value, manifested in considerations about the properties of work, including specific metadata, containing descriptions and tags of digital objects. I also show how users actively look for small communities inside the commons (similarly to musical scenes), as well as how they look for niches to enrich the commons (for example identifying low representation of bell sounds). I also show a community mechanism, based on posting challenges to the community, which aim at animation of creators and often serve as an opportunity for experimenting with and expanding the commons. As I exemplify, all these actions intended to increase the quality of sound file and metadata activate the value of creations in the network established within the commons.

Chapter five outlines the approach of participants in commons-based production by placing content in a new context. As I show, the format of this artistic commoning is tied to the new idea of experimentation, based on endless building of new works that are based on other works. I argue that this practice is a new type of media-based collaboration, which raises the possibility of remixing existing work. I also show the perceived role of the content from the commons, which some artists treat like a unique source, allowing for production of unique products, much different from commercial components of production from stock sites or libraries. I also show how technical quality is of lesser importance than the unique properties of work, and how creators emphasise the role of processing and replacing in the context of artistic work.

Chapter six focuses on Creative Commons' mechanism of reciprocity: attribution. Attribution is a requirement of citing the author of the work that was modified to make another work. I focus on this convention and its relationship to internal commons-based reputation. I also show how some of the creators use attribution as a source of contacts and credibility and then outline their perception of attribution in commercial projects. I also address the problem of violation of attribution, showing actions and interpretations of this process by the creators, and outlining their laisser-faire approach to mitigating it. From the findings of this chapter, we see that Creative Commons works remain largely unprotected, because they lack intermediating institutions, such as labels and collecting societies in the music industry, and economic interest of the copyright holders. Lastly, I show how experienced producers resign from attribution, giving away all rights to their works to the public domain and adopting the most liberal of Creative Commons licenses.

Chapter seven studies the commodification of content. Despite the limitations in protection, this book has identified several mechanisms of commodification of the commons, typical to FreeSound. Commoning is very closely aligned with industry practices, with important symbolic connections between the content and mainstream, big-budget productions in the creative industries. These models at their heart rely on the network of participants and/or the network value of content. In the case of multiple-channels sales and freemium model, I show how creators upload their work to the commons, to reach the broadest audiences and maximise the use value of content, while demonstrating their products and offering a commercial product, either based on the extension of licenses or a bigger library of sound. The usage and reliance on network is also used by two other models, based on acquisition of talent and content to secure exclusive rights; and in the model of generation of services based on the commons. These models either extended the commons, contributed to their production, or improved their operations, by providing new, alternative ways of accessing and using the commons.

The chapters are followed by the conclusion in which I assess the relevance of commons-based production practice, assessing its meaning and importance for creative industries. I start by depicting the relationship between the framework of Creative Commons to creative industries, pointing at the potential of shaping new cross-sectional practices and identifying insights produced to the study of creative industries. I emphasise the role of networked value, describing its role in the commons, briefly describing its functions and properties specific to the sound industry. Then I address the relationship between artistic activity and commons-based production, advocating the new model of artistic activity, based on approaching creativity from the commons-based point of view. I also reconsider the role of the Creative Commons in the political economy, summing the main insights and identifying its key weaknesses, such as lack of protection or reliance on participants' free labour. Lastly, I indicate the ways in which this book can inform future research.

CHAPTER 1

Managing and Organizing Openness in the Digital Economy

Proliferation of digital technology has provoked new ways of collaboration. With the emergence of the internet, digital communities have paved new paths to solving technological problems, working on products, and spending time together. The pioneers of the internet shared a unique approach characterised by the spirit of technological liberty, independence, and often strong opposition to commercial actors and regulators. They also strongly believed in digital anonymity and valued the elitist character of their participation. They not only pioneered new technologies but also pushed work and organisation in a new direction, influencing thinking about the role of technology and its relationship to society and business. This has translated to today's reality.

Broad (and inexpensive) access to personal computers, and later smartphones, have placed technology among the most important elements of daily life. With time, intertwining of technology and social life has become tighter, exponentially expanding products and services depending on the digital sphere. This also has been reflected on the consumer side. These shifts required new ways of approaching business. New ventures proposed new business models in the digital sphere, with new types of metrics and analysis, often reliant on digital innovation. Old businesses were forced to evolve to fit into the new landscape, learning digital marketing, transforming their high street chains into e-commerce stores and accepting the changes in the web. Technology has penetrated labour markets, transforming the creative industries and manufacturing. This commercialisation of the digital economy has faced strong resistance from some of the early adopters of technology. Their approach was embedded in postulates of maintaining the spirit of liberty, anonymity and openness in order to protect the unique environment that the digital sphere provided.

Management and organisation studies have followed the technological changes, observing different changes in the digital sphere. A wide body of literature has generated findings on how the digital sphere has influenced the way we think and manage. The debate over how to organise and manage the digital sphere has responded to different actions and postulates of openness. This notion has been vital to explaining and understanding of digital communities, new products embedded in digital technology, ways of production, as well as other activities relevant to operating in the digital sphere. In these writings, openness is widely represented, often juxtaposed to differently interpreted or understood negative effects of closeness. The diversity of this literature differs not only in the spheres of application of openness, but also in the ways of how openness is theoretically understood, why it is applied and what role it plays in expressing an organisational philosophy opposed to the traditional, closed model.

Openness is also crucial to consider as it provides an alternative to the established ways of thinking about management and organising. Secrecy has always been an important element of conducting business. In the past, proprietary knowledge has been central to achieving competitive and political advantage. In the process of formation of modern capitalism, proprietary knowledge became a central element, secured with multiple legal mechanisms and institutions. Some of them were present in the functioning of state becoming political doctrines, such as military-led innovations, which were later adapted by industries, generated economic advancements. Their central element was the legal system of modern copyright, constructed around protection of access to knowledge, guarded by systems of patenting and copyright. Several layers of social system were created to protect the interest of owners of knowledge and information.

Historically, science was one of the first systems that was highly closed and went through the process of opening. At the beginnings of scientific systems, inventions were strictly guarded and fortified. The dominant ethos was all about secrecy in pursuit of nature's secrets (David, 2004; 2005). Scientists of the Middle Ages carefully protected their methods and research data, fearing the loss of their exclusivity and status as experts as well as often relying on the value of their inventions in political and commercial work. Their scientific contacts with others also occurred in highly exclusive and secretive ways, limiting the exchange of ideas and collaborations to the most trustworthy partners. The Enlightenment brought this change to this form of scientific work. A key change to the way in which scientists have collaborated was introduced by the invisible college. The concept of peers (and peer review) emerged from the principles of the precursor scientist group of the Royal Society of London for Improving Natural Knowledge, consisting of natural philosophers around Robert Boyle. In this organisation, a small group of scientists regularly met to exchange ideas and support each other in their work (Crane, 1972; de Solla Price and Beaver, 1966). This format ushered in in the new model of doing science: with regularly published journals and discussion occurring between scientists working within the same discipline. It slowly evolved towards democratisation of science bringing new advantages, which we today, as academics, we take for granted. For instance, it facilitated cumulative knowledge generation, based on expanding of what has already been published and written. Its central means of communication have been journal articles and books, which permitted the circulation of information among scholars in a structured way, with the mediation of universities and libraries. Science has become more open yet evolving in the proprietary model of publishing and circulation. Even from the early beginnings of its opening it was tied to competition, also among 'cooperative rivalries' (David, 2004). The process of changing the ethos has dramatically evolved, relying on new mechanisms of patronage, common agency and scientific reputation (David, 2008). The opening of science lay at the foundation of scientific revolution.

In the contemporary understanding of openness, despite a wide variety of definitions, openness represents an organisational philosophy. It cannot simply be translated to one notion or explanation but frequently its meaning is closely associated with reduced or no payment (for example open access usually means free access to scientific publications), freedom from perceived disadvantages of the "old" model (e.g., open finance) or dispersed, decentralised community-based way of organising (open production). In many more examples, openness symbolises a different, alternative approach to managing and organising. Openness is their guiding principle, one that provides an alternative and promise for change. While there exists a multiplicity of conceptualisations and applications of "openness" in management and organisation studies, the literature continuously points at the definitional disputes regarding qualifying criteria of what makes something "open" (Dahlander and Gann, 2010). A recent call for papers postulates openness as identified the dimensions of "accessibility of knowledge, technology and other resources; the transparency of action; the permeability of organisational structures; and the inclusiveness of participation" (Schlagwein et al., 2017, p. 297). The proposed approach intends for an extensive recognition of three domains, identifiable as open. Open resources, such as open scientific publications, means that they are accessible to anyone interested (without monetary payment). Open processes, such as open source coding, refers to an inclusive participation in processes, which are shared and which anyone can join. Lastly, this framework identifies the effects of opening in different fields experiencing democratisation and easier access, such as open innovation and strategy (Chesbrough, 2007), based on lower exclusivity and smaller role of proprietary ownership.

Another way of conceptualising and distinguishing types of openness falls along the lines of external and internal openness. Internal openness, usually understood in the context of organisations that are highly reliant on innovation, seeks it inside the organisation, allowing its members to cross-exchange ideas. Notably, this model has been adopted in the technology and entertainment industries, adopting mechanisms such as co-creation platforms, enterprise social software, inner source software, and depending on the flattening of organisational structures and encouragement of sharing ideas. Organisations like the game developer Valve have championed this process (van der Graaf, 2012), where high trust in innovations of highly skilled employees working within an open structure has had tremendous success (despite a significant number of unfinished or failed products). External openness is understood as opening processes to the outside in different domains, such as innovation (for instance innovation bids and competitions; open sourcing) or financing (crowdsourcing). Most notable instances are LEGO's innovation model (Schlagwein and Bjørn-Andersen 2014), Philips Healthcare (Ågerfalk and Fitzgerald 2008) and SAP (Leimeister et al. 2009).

This chapter reviews existing theorisations of the process of opening. In doing so, it considers the foundations of multiple approaches embedded in the idea of going beyond the traditional copyright regime and guided by an alternative model of collaboration, usually associated with a series of benefits. A systematic review of the literature permits observation of several discussions in the literature that centres on three fields. First of them, examining strategic and operational management of openness, considers different ways in which an alternative, open approach translates to new sources of competitive advantage. Within this domain, a central role has been played by the "open innovation" stream, which proposes opening the model of innovation, which traditionally has been associated with the highest level of secrecy in a company. While using this form of capturing and organising innovation, this body of literature emphasises the productive aspect of reaching out beyond organisational borders. This field considers business models that adopt the idea of openness, often relying on open innovations or through openness transforming different elements of the organisation for a competitive edge.

Secondly, the literature studies openness by considering a variety of participatory cultures that are built within several industries. Their openness is usually positioned in the context of breaking with traditional, established ways and the inclusion of new stakeholders. In this domain, the management and organisation literature examines dynamics in two fields. One field looks at the process of opening of capital where openness principle is applied to the domain of finance and banking. In this field, communities of users and clients are organised, supporting new models of business organisation, obtaining greater transparency and participating in knowledge sharing. The other field looks at communities involved in open production, which at its foundation has copyright. In this sense openness denotes an alternative model of protection, organisation and management of property, either generated or replicated by community. To the studied participatory cultures, this form of openness provides a significant contestation of the ways in which copyright has been understood. The transformative postulates in approaching copyright propose several ways of changing the old patterns, responding to the perceived issues in the way in which they had been organised.

Thirdly, openness is studied in the context of public policy. An important part of it deals with public management and examines openness in the sphere of citizenship, intersecting with political approaches to technology. This domain considers how technology might facilitate greater transparency and efficiency of national states and governmental bodies. Here openness in often interpreted as a necessary tool of ensuring citizen participation, fairness, transparency and independence. Their common argument is premised on the idea that openness reflects the democratic idea of equal access to information, reflecting, on the technological level, the importance of equal access to public goods and information. The second stream of this literature deals with open scholarship, mainly advocating easy access scientific publications and work, arguing against closing them and requiring substantial payments for them, disadvantaging free circulation of ideas, innovations and hampering debate. The debate on copyright drifts to the importance of open data, which similarly to open science, can ensure greater liberty of work in a variety of spheres, such as: digital code, application programming, creative work (e.g., collage) or geo-mapping. In all of these domains, openness allows for a very specific resource polling, that unities independent actors under the same public idea of shared good.

Below I characterise the main fields in which the literature considers reconstruction caused by the adoption of principles of openness, identifying the main problems and theoretical interpretations.

1 Openness in Business Strategy and Operations

1.1 *Open Innovation*

One of the key transformations regarding opening emerged with the idea that innovation might be generated outside of organisation. The term "open innovation", at the centre of many conceptualisations of opening businesses was coined by Henry Chesbrough who developed it in the opposition to closed, intra-firm, proprietary approach. Chesbrough's premise was simple: not all people who might be needed for innovation work in organisations' research and development (R&D) departments; and now, with the proliferation of technology, they are now inherently more accessible. The literature treats these two opposing concepts of open and proprietary, as a continuum with the two ideal types on its ends (Dahlander and Gann, 2010). Chesbrough defined Open Innovation in the following way:

> Open Innovation is a paradigm that assumes that firms can and should use external ideas as well as internal ideas, and internal and external paths to market, as the firms look to advance their technology.
> CHESBROUGH, 2003: XXIV

This definition of openness expresses the idea of going beyond managing research and development as reliant on internal capabilities and skills. Its main premise is that commercial knowledge diffuses beyond the firm, failing to be protected by existing models of intellectual property. Instead, it proposes both a modification of the way knowledge is protected and opening it to other actors who had not previously been part of the organisation. In this approach, innovation gravitates to experts, for instance conducting research in labs or based at universities; as well as turning to customers, whose expectations, feedback and experiences can be central to innovation. Further work has identified other parties to which an organisation can open to innovate, such as competitors as helpful source of innovation (Surowiecki, 2006). The open innovation approach also proposes work on reward systems to research and development from both within the firm and produced outside of it, depending on their commercial viability. While earlier work, has mentioned user-led innovations (Von Hippel, 1988), the growing amount of opening of corporate processes led to "democratising innovation", with diverse communities and organisations catering innovations for themselves, being highly reliant on information technology (Von Hippel, 2005). However open innovation is not limited to IT. Even though it initially emerged from the high-tech industries, open innovation literature identifies its elements in more traditional industries, seeking growth in revenue of many products (Chesbrough and Crowther, 2006), causing issues of measurability (Spithoven, et al., 2011), and integration of open innovation with management theories (West et al., 2014).

The open innovation literature also considers its extra-organisational outcomes. Stefan Lindengaard (2010: 4) describes Open Innovation as a "two-way process"; on the one hand it is a source of new developments and ideas from the outside, but on the other hand, it presents an opportunity to sell, license and share internally developed ideas and technologies. As some outcomes of a company's research and development do not have a potential to be commercialised within the existing business model, some innovations may find their place outside of the organisation (Chesbrough, 2006). Other work centring on the opening of business models, considers the effects of implementing open innovation and observes that it can improve its value creation and capture capabilities (Chesbrough, 2007). Significant portion of the open literature concerns small and medium enterprises, which increasingly adopt the model of Open Innovation when seeking strategy, networking and collaborations (Hossain and Kauranen, 2016); or public administration, benefitting from new business models, especially in the domain of generating value and delivering services (Feller et al., 2011).

Open innovation created a strong and vibrant stream in management, business and operation research disciplines, and strongly influenced other related domains (Hossain et al., 2016). Chesbourough (2007) expanded the ideas of his book arguing that "companies must develop more open business models if they are to make the most of the opportunities offered by Open Innovation" (p. 107). There were numerous proponents of several business models based on open innovations (e.g., Goldman and Gabriel, 2005; Saebi and Foss, 2015; Yun et al., 2016). Literature reviews have identified several outcomes of opening of innovation, as well as broad diversity of the scope of application (Elmquist et al., 2009; Dahlander and Gann, 2010; Giannopoulou et al., 2010; Su and Lee, 2012; West and Bogers, 2014). Durst and Pirjo's (2013) literature review argues that core insights of this body of literature identify the facilitators of open innovation, such as relational issues, people, governance, facilitators, resources, strategy and leadership, culture, and process of open innovation process. Other review work includes considerations of Open Innovation in Strategy ("Open Strategy"), with findings relevant to theoretical developments and core problems drifting around transparency and inclusion (Hautz et al., 2017) as well as the relevance of strategy-as-practice lens (Tavakoli et al., 2017).

Parallel to open innovation, the literature has witnessed the booming of the notion of co-creation, shifting organisational activities to customers. The concept was initially developed in relation to software markets with consumers identified as a new source of competence for organisation and useful, for instance for the purpose of testing and usability changes, substituting previous intra-firm work and development often producing better results in that domain. Ramaswamy and Gouillart define co-creation as "the practice of developing systems, products, or services through collaboration with customers, managers, employees, and other company stakeholders" (2010: 4). In the literature, co-creation has been represented by two major uses of stakeholders. The first use applies co-creation to improve production efficiency, with customers participating in co-production of specific activities (Prahalad and Ramaswamy 2000; Vargo and Lusch 2004; Von Hippel 2007). The second use utilizes co-creators to increase added value for company, participating by providing their inputs in product and service innovation (Prahalad and Ramaswamy 2000; Vargo and Lusch 2004). In both understandings of co-creation, the perception of activity of consumers occurs through the prism of creativity and out-of-the-box thinking brought in from customers/users to producers/service providers (Piller et al., 2010). In this literature, it is assumed that at the heart of co-creation lies the process of defining stakeholders' engagement in value creation (Vaisnore and Petraite, 2011: 66). As a result, some streams of the co-creation literature concentrate on research of organisations, their adaptation to co-creation and customer research (Galvagno and Dalli, 2014).

The idea of co-creation has been widely adopted in service industries. For instance, the tourism sector has adopted this model to involve customers in the design of new products and services (Santos-vijande et al., 2012) and in production, consumption and evaluation (Eraqi, 2011; Zouni and Kouremenos, 2008). In cases such as co-creation of tourist experiences, co-creation brings several benefits, including a sense of interactivity and individualised, custom experience (Cabiddu et al., 2013; Füller, Hutter, and Faullant, 2011). An important role in facilitating this form of engagement is played by technological means, such as platforms and ecosystems (Ramaswamy and Ozcan, 2014) but at the same time co-creation strongly accents organisational change for co-creation. For example, in the tourism industry a key role is played by frontline and marketing staff who are the main facilitators of user participation, requiring the staff to develop new competencies relevant to more open, adaptable mode of providing and designing services (Bharwani and Jauhari, 2013). Some conclusions even include observations that co-creation might be a central condition for competitive advantage in the industry, due to continuous pressure of new developments and innovations (Compos et al., 2015; Grissemann and Stokburger-Sauer 2012), linking co-creation to involvement (Andrades and Dimanche, 2014), mindfulness (Moscardo, 1996), and attention (Ooi, 2010).

Another form of distributed innovation is expressed by crowdsourcing, first mentioned in *The Wire* magazine in 2006 (Howe, 2008), referring to "the act of a company or institution taking a function once performed by employees and outsourcing it to an undefined (and generally large) network of people in the form of an open call" (Howe, 2006a). Howe used this definition to initially to describe platforms such as iStockphoto and InnoCentive, which require specific talent, but later also applied it to describe engagement in platforms such as Amazon's Mechanical Turk, on which "anyone possessing basic literacy can find something to do" (Howe, 2006b: 5). Crowdsourcing was thus used to delineate an engagement of an undefined, large group of employees into organisational activities. Crowdsourcing is often supplemented or interchangeably used with the concept of collective intelligence or the wisdom of the crowd. Other definitions of crowdsourcing emphasise the varying motivations of participants to respond to serving specific organisational goals, as well as its online nature (Brabham, 2013: XIX), and closely tied to specific architectures of information systems of innovating organisations (Majchrzak and Malhotra, 2013; Schlagwein and Bjørn-Andersen, 2014). The current work on crowdsourcing has concentrated on the identification of these processes as materialising in practice by connecting online dynamics with the outcomes produced by this work (Orlikowski and Scott, 2015)

Numerous sources place crowdsourcing among the key types of open innovation (Marjanovic et al., 2012; Remneland Wikhamn and Wikhamn, 2013) and argue that crowdsourcing is one of the most popular types of innovation in this field of the literature (Ebner et al., 2009). The notion of crowdsourcing has produced several streams in the management studies literature (Hossain and Kauranen, 2016). Firstly, this body addresses its outcomes for idea generation, replacing or supplementing traditional research techniques, for instance by replacing distant search with local search (Afuah and Tucci, 2012) or by opening calls for ideation (Poetz and Schreier, 2012). Surowiecki (2006) emphasises the role of the diverse voice of external stakeholders and stresses its higher usefulness when compared to a small group of experts. Secondly, the crowdsourcing literature considers microtasking, materialising in open competitions where users need to respond to a problem posed and finely formulated by organisation (Olsen and Carmel, 2013). The literature produces two major considerations, on the one hand giving field for highly specialised, technical work occurring through competitions, where users are activated by incentives and motivated by a possibility of participating in a promising, innovative project (Leimeister et al., 2009). Innovation competitions, such as IMB's Global Innovation Jam or Dell IdeaStorm, yield thousands of ideas but also raise questions of trust of information asymmetry (Ågerfalk and Fitzgerald, 2008) and pose challenges relevant to leveraging user innovation communities. On the other hand, crowdsourcing reduces the cost of labour through platforms such as Amazon's Mechanical Turk (Mason and Suri, 2012; Paolacci et al., 2010). Similar to traditional offshoring, the outcome of this form of opening produces controversies in the domain of ethics, for instance in regards to work standards (Bergvall-Kåreborn and Howcroft, 2014); type of services that can be crowdsourced (Swan, 2012); taxation and wage (Berinsky et al, 2012). Thirdly, crowdsourcing is often applied to the domain of public participation, such as planning projects (Brabham, 2009; Hilgers and Ihl, 2010) or design and discussion of new laws, enabling participation not for monetary interest but rather focused on the perceived public good (Heipke, 2010).

1.2 Open Business

A crucial step in integration of the idea of openness to the management literature has been Chesbrough's (2007) book on open business models, which proposed linking open innovation with the growing popularity of the business model (George and Bock, 2011; Morris, et al., 2005; Zott et al., 2011). Chesbrough (2007), the proponent of open business models, argues that "To get the most out of this new system of innovation, companies must open their business models by actively searching for and exploiting outside ideas and by allowing unused internal technologies to flow to the outside, where other firms can unlock their latent economic potential" (Chesbrough, 2007, p. 22). While some authors substitute the concept of open innovation with open business models, understanding them as the outcome of research and development (e.g., Chu and Chen, 2011; Gassmann et al., 2010), there is a stream of literature showing that open business models go beyond that domain. A key argument is embedded in a claim that the concept of the open business model should be mainly understood through the prism of collaboration explaining value creation and capturing of a focal firm (Weiblen et al., 2013). In a similar tone, Holm et al. (2013) argue that "openness to innovations and openness of business models needs to be adequately recognized, understood, and treated as separate phenomena" (p. 18). This collaboration is often conceptualised in organisational (Cheng, 2011) and technical terms (Vetter et al., 2008).

A central issue within the open business literature is the modular character of its organisation, central to the way in which it extracts value. Skarzynski and Gibson (2008), for instance, understand it as "a set of open integrated building blocks, all of which can be looked on as opportunities for open business model innovation and open advantage". In practice, open business model research studies the evolution of information technology architectures, which embrace the idea of openness by creating ecosystems, within which particular, often independent, components can facilitate the systems evolution. At the same time, the direction of this evolution depends on the emerging needs of participants in the ecosystems, in addition to choices made by system architects in regards to technology, goals or partners licensing of the ecosystem. An enabling factor within this process is embedded in the integration of proprietary and non-proprietary license frameworks and allowing for new, non-centralised ways of developing the system and its components. An open ecosystem thus relies on independent actions of component producers and consumers, integrated by the system architect, or integrator designing the system. Such an ecosystem relies on components, produced outside of integrator, which are linked together through "interfaces accommodating use of dynamic links, intra- or inter-application scripts, communication protocols, software buses, databases/repositories, plug-ins, libraries or software shims as necessary to achieve the desired result" (Schacci and Alspaugh, 2012, p. 2). In this case openness is driven by a collaborative and complex integration of processes within a uniform system, also contributing to its development and agility.

The main object of study of open business models are open platforms, which epitomise the idea of establishing relationships inside a complex, integration-ready environment available for both innovators and customers. Boudreau and Lakhani (2009) have extensively conceptualised open business models and considered the role of platforms, identifying three types: integrator, product and two-sided. The integrator platform is the model whose platform integrates external innovation to sell final products to customers. The product platform model uses the idea of allowing external innovators to use the platform to release products that are then sold to customers. On the two-sided platform, both external innovators and customers use the same platform. Boudreau and Lakhani (2009) observe that these models also impose different levels of control, from very tight control with platform acting as a mediator, to more autonomous model in the case of the two-sided platform. Boudreau and Lakhani (2009) also consider how these platforms operate in different realities: on the one hand competitive markets, for instance in the case of Apple's application store (integrator); cloud computing services (product) as well as Facebook's integration of widget developers and advertisers (two-sided). On the other, they show the usefulness of these models to foster collaboration within communities, for instance giving example of threadless.com, a site permitting custom design of t-shirts (integrator); video game modders and their collaboration with Valve (product platform); and insight clubs such as Big Idea Group (multisided platform). An emphasis on both markets and communities, allows for considerations of open platforms also in regards to their non-commercial applicability and character.

From the technological side, an important role in platforms is played by open application programming interfaces (APIs), which provide developers with programmatic access to a proprietary or open software application or web service. Open APIs allow software designed by independent developers to rely on product on service performed by the platform and added, according to the rules and functionalities of the access, add value relying on this communication channel. At the same time, several studies have considered the role of platform openness and variables linked to developers' continuous platform contributions (e.g., Benlian et al., 2015; Eisenmann et al., 2009).

2 Participatory Cultures

2.1 *Open Capital*

The idea of opening was also applied to the financial domain. Technological development permitted seeking and acquiring capital beyond organisation. Within the literature a new field of "open capital" has generated discussion about enterprises seeking financial contributions of users, stakeholders and fans who were willing to co-participate financially in investments or self-organise, intending to overcome politicisation of finance or seeking a safe haven. The opening of capital has been grounded in financial process, but its core was based on seeking partners beyond traditional financial institutions, such as banks. The emergence of new type of open organisations, often based on grassroots initiatives, has posed a significant challenge to the existing legal systems, taxation and business organisations. Financial regulators have often struggled and opposed the newly emerging, technology-embedded trends and ideas. Quite often they lacked instruments, or legal tool to monitor them and ensure their genuine intentions. A major influence within the realm of open capital has been played by two main forces: crowdfunding and cryptocurrencies, which has been reflected in the literature.

One of the first experiments with crowdfunding was brought in by portals such as ArtistShare (established in 2001), where supporters were given an opportunity to fund artistic activities of musicians and other artists. The process of opening of this form of financing has again been made possible thanks to technology that connected both sponsors and enterprises. The trade-off offered by this model was based on the fact that artists remain independent in the process of production and publishing and their supporters receive not only the record but also some extra material, not accessible elsewhere. This initiative grew in opposition to mainstream music industry, trying to financially back the freedom of artists. From such early stages, crowdsourcing was a way of supporting projects by seeding artists, creators and innovators with much-needed capital (Agrawal, Catalini, and Goldfarb, 2014). With time, new crowdfunding platforms emerged, going beyond creative arts.

Crowdfunding research has extensively examined intermediation models as the model was widely adopted by a large number of industries. Findings report a diverse range of platforms and their approaches to regulating the transaction, for instance in the way of setting and enforcing the rules, handling financial transactions and ensuring clarity of information to both sides of the transaction (Berger and Gleisner, 2009; Cumming et al., 2015). Even though strategies of financing differ, two main ways dominate. In the first, the campaigns are based on voluntary donations, with no threshold or minimum level of donation ("keep-it-all"). In the second, a majority of campaigns is based on the return rule ("all-or-nothing"), when project has a minimum threshold set, and if the threshold isn't met, the capital is returned to contributors (Cumming et al., 2015). Additionally, the role of "superstar projects" has been emphasised, pointing out the role of innovative, unique and highly visible campaigns and their importance in encouraging support of other, less recognised ventures (Doshi, 2015; Onnée and Renault, 2016).

An important theme in the literature of crowdfunding are studies of fundraisers and factors contributing to their success (Kaartemo, 2017). The literature identifies factors such as geographical proximity of capital providers (Agrawal, Catalini, and Goldfarb 2014), their activity on social media and interaction with potential lenders (Kromidha and Robson, 2016); as well quality and contents of campaign descriptions (Yuan et al., 2016). Research reports that non-profit or public good-oriented enterprises have a higher chance of receiving financing than do those of a more commercial nature (Belleflamme et al., 2013a; 2013b). Studies of Kickstarter, the largest crowdfunding portal, have shown at least several correlations to success in funding, including projects that are shorter in duration (Mollick, 2014); project leaders with large amounts of social capital and a widespread network, including social media presence (Saxton and Wang, 2013), reward type and quality of idea (Frydrych et al., 2014), as well as cultural proximity to potential funders (Cumming, Leboeuf, and Schwienbacher, 2015; Frydrych et al., 2014; Mollick, 2014).

Motivations of capital seekers identified in the research include promptness of financing, informality of the process, and raising capital with limited or no loss of ownership and control (Deschler, 2013; Macht and Weatherston, 2014). Non-financial gains include increasing value through a pilot test of products and services and increased visibility of the enterprise, extensive feedback and involvement of potential consumers and gaining publicity and public awareness and obtaining new exposition and contacts to the business (Macht and Weatherston, Moritz and Block, 2016; 2014; Surowiecki, 2004). Embedded in the culture of consumer investments, enterprises financed by crowd additionally receive an opportunity to rely on knowledge and commitment of capital providers, who by scaling the enterprise and providing funds for its functioning, legitimise the business idea and allow for consolidation of market potential (Mollick, 2014, Mollick and Kuppuswamy, 2014; Skirnevskiy et al., 2017).

Studies of capital givers in crowdfunding observe that they are most often not solely guided by financial motives but rather gain exposition, visibility and reputation as well as are guided by case-specific intrinsic motives (Allison et al., 2014; Kuppuswamy and Bayus, 2018). Ordanini et al. (2011) report that a common feature is shared interest in a company or highly specific product, often in a niche market. The literature also investigates the role of campaigning, studying the activity of entrepreneurs on social networks and their effects on campaigns, such as "herding" – the mass financing of projects by users from a single channel (Herzenstein, Dholakia, et al., 2011; Lee and Lee, 2012; Yum et al., 2012) and evolution of campaigns over time, manifesting in a U-shaped interest at the beginning and end of the campaign (Kuppuswamy and Bayus, 2018). Another important role has been played by entrepreneurs' network of friends, peers and family, who are central in the earliest stages of crowdsourcing (Kuppuswamy and Bayus, 2018).

While crowdfunding platforms are understood as non-profit and steeped in community spirit, other models are also reliant on independent capital providers in the for-profit model (Kirby and Worner, 2014, p. 9). With time the evolution of crowdfunding has produced a range of business models, which not only were embedded in financing using online platforms, but that also connected technology to earlier ideas of open capital. For example, the idea of social lending linked to community-driven financing and opposed to the mainstream liberal model of lending, has generated a p2p lending model (Hulme and Wright, 2006). Sites such as Zopa, Prosper, CircleLending or Vancity, propose an alternative model driven by ethical, altruistic and transparent principles and often associated with the idea of resistance (Hulme and Wright, 2006). Other studies of peer-to-peer-lending, show numerous examples of intermediary-free loan systems within specific groups and communities, such as small and medium enterprises (Green, 2014; Mach et al., 2013) or real estate (Shahrokhi and Parhizgari, 2019). A significant part of this literature also warns about potential risks (Freedman and Jin, 2017), stemming either from lack of transparency of the emerging models, or borrowers' lack of knowledge. The literature on crowdfunding centres on examining online platforms and their economics, leaders and supporters (Bouncken et al., 2015; Kaartemo, 2017). A key question was their compliance with local regulations and the cultural approach to crowdfunding (Ingram et al., 2014; Kunz et al., 2017). This research has extensively considered if and how crowdfunding should be regulated, and if so how, given the high risk of financial fraud and associated problems (Baucus, 2016; Cumming et al., 2020; Hazen, 2012).

An important role in this process has been played by crowd equity, usually occurring with smaller role played by the intermediaries and platforms. Crowd equity spinoffs from open, democratised offering of shares to non-professional small investors, are often being launched via crowdfunding platforms. With time, crowd equity attracted more professionalised investors, including business angels, limiting open access to capital (Wang et al., 2019). Equity Crowd Platforms have been recognised as a source of high-stake investment into early-stage ventures, offering a range of passive investments to investors. At the same time, governments adopt a variety of stances on this type of funding, for instance offering tax incentives in the United Kingdom (Vulkan et al., 2016; Nehme, 2017), or interpreting them as conflicting with existing regulations (Borg, 2007; CAMAC, 2014). Crowd equity brings in significant benefits, parallel to crowdfunding, such as product feedback and publicity, but research also shows that start-ups reliant on crowd equity have a better chance of survival and success (Di Pietro et al., 2018). However, crowd equity is now going beyond start-up enterprises, being increasingly used in financing innovations of larger firms, or rescuing indebted organisations such as football clubs.

Lastly, a significant part of the opening of capital occurs through the creation of digital, virtual coinage systems, allowing users to store value and make payment for goods and services without any authority. Cryptocurrencies rely on technology that encrypts information about legitimate, unique transactions, decentralising it from any hierarchy and establishing it within a peer-to-peer network. In a white paper, the anonymous creator of Bitcoin emphasised that the purpose of the cryptocurrency is to remove a "trusted central authority", typical to traditional currencies, and replace it with cryptographic proof, with benefits such as low transaction cost, anonymity and quick responsiveness (Nakamoto, 2008). Cryptocurrencies use a digital ledger where transactions in bitcoin are logged. The appeal of opening capital to be stored using independent (and secretive) means resulted in an explosion of cryptocurrencies, with over 550 available worldwide at the peak of their popularity in the mid-2010s (Farell, 2015). The research addresses cyptocurrencies' ability to offer easy and open access to capital, independent of regulation and political and geographic attachments (Liu and Tsyvinski, 2018). While cryptocurrencies have potential for speculation, they are also valuable in opening capital to users, free of steering and control.

The difficulty in controlling bitcoin resulted in its freedom from regulation, stemming from the fact that legal models may be unprepared to cope with its technological, dispersed nature and lack of intermediaries (Tu and Meredith, 2015; Parveen and Alajmi, 2019). Cryptocurrencies' use also raises concern, as its intangible character and anonymous structure is often used for payments for illegal substances or financing crime (Irwin and Milad, 2016; Paul, 2018). The proliferation of these financial products, usually with no regulatory backing, has provoked a strong regulatory action (Peters et al., 2014). This action, however, has not been unified. The government of Australia recognises cryptocurrency transactions as taxable income; the European Central Bank defines it as "a digital representation of value (…) which, in some circumstances, can be used as an alternative to money" (ECB, 2015, p. 4); and other governments are ignoring cryptocurrencies entirely.

Opening of capital has several effects, which include the reintermediation of financial transactions and redefinition of already established ways. Crowdfunding allows consumers, friends and supporters to participate I then financial dynamics of an organisation in a systematic and networked way. Crowd equity and peer-to-peer lending introduces a diverse range of potential investors for exchange of profit. All these open capital forms are still unregulated or remain categorised in different ways. Similarly, societies struggle to understand them. At the same time, researchers struggle to work with them. For instance, cryptocurrencies force researchers to "discover a new object of concern, a digital currency that untangles itself from our assumptions about what counts as money" (Kavanagh et al., 2019, p. 532).

2.2 *Open Production*

One of the key transformations guided by the idea of openness has occurred in the domain of production. Digital technology, since the emergence of the internet, has created a new communication channel, which as one of its effects, has contributed to the organisation of an independent, digital production model. Within it, user communities gathered around a shared interest, perceived social problem or expand their knowledge through practice. A key mechanism permitting the growth of open creation was reliance on non-exclusive legal permissions (open licensing). As an effect, open production model was adopted by a broad range of projects, which have been addressed mainly in the context of open source software, focusing on improving and generating computer programmes, and open design, working on solutions aimed at generation physical products and solutions. Both usually relied on legal frameworks which do not incur licensing or patenting costs. Chapter two concentrates on types of licensing, outlines their regulations and applications and drafts the main outcomes of their collaborative dynamics.

Studies of open source production have been broadly represented in all disciplines of management. Their high scope and all-encompassing impact was explained by Von Krogh and Spaeth (2007) who argued that studies of open source software is an important field that allows researchers to study phenomena characterised by:

(1) high impact, as they cause social reconstruction and are visible in numerous social spheres
(2) theoretical tension: confirming predictions and explanations of existing theory in different fields
(3) transparency: granting unprecedented access to data and practices

(4) communal reflexivity, for instance addressing issues such as community functioning and internal relations
(5) proximity to science, as many projects are derived from the academic research and scientific communities. Their reflection also applies to all spheres of open production, sharing joint characteristics with software.

A pillar of this research field has been the open source software movement, which emerged as a result of the work of highly skilled software developers and users who directed their efforts at production and maintenance of unpaid, open products and services (Lakhani and von Hippel, 2003). With time, millions of users on thousands of projects have produced a variety of products, from operational systems to highly specialised, advanced tools for operating machinery or graphic editing. Open source software has found broad application and in many domains it has proven more useful than traditional, closed operational systems. However, open source software has been the foundation of collaborative work, generating projects that have attracted millions of users and defended the way in which such software is created (Hauge et al., 2010; Wu and Lin, 2001). In short summary of the immense body of literature, I follow and update the division of key themes of von Krogh and von Hippel (2006), who categorised publications into three groups: (1) user and contributor motivations; (2) organisation of the process; and (3) competitive dynamics caused by these projects.

Studying motivations in open-source projects is an important theme. It might at first seem irrational to spend time and effort in order to enrich non-commercially circulated projects. However, the literature reports both intrinsic and extrinsic motivations relevant to the participation in open-source projects. One of the most important studies by Roberts et al. (2006), reports on status motivations and argues that they enhance intrinsic motivations; it additionally reports that paid participation results in above-average participation, which is boosted by user participation rankings. Inventive mechanisms are also an object of study in the context of motivation (Baldwin and Clark, 2006). An early study of Linux kernel developers (Hertel et al., 2003), reported that participation was closely tied to self-identification as a "Linux developer" but also for pragmatic reasons: developing their own software, and having plenty of time to commit to this project, as well as participating in teams offering support and motivation. Trivial reasons of needing particular solution by a user-developer, working on a tool that he misses and then sharing it to community, has been a recurring theme, also tied to the beginnings of the open-source software scene (Bitzer and Schröder, 2005; Feller and Fitzgerald, 2002).

The literature also reports that users are motivated by the idea of fun of play, or '*homo ludens* payoff' (Bitzer et al., 2007), based on social integration and participation. (Hars, 2002; Zeitlyn, 2003). These dynamics have also created a specific culture of participation, highly reliant on the rule of reciprocity and social norms regulating participants' behaviour (Bergquist and Ljungberg 2001; Zeitlyn, 2003). Extrinsic motives addressed by the literature include gathering experiences in leadership or networking (Chan et al., 2017; Feller et al., 2008), for instance treating it as milestone in career development as participation and experience evidenced by name visible in credits to these projects. Studies have also considered mechanisms of attraction of contributors to projects, taking under consideration the license choices of projects and resources available to participants (Santos, 2013).

Another pillar of open-source software research has concentrated on governance, organisation and innovation process, quite often intersecting with the open innovation literature. Open-source software has created a new dynamic, reaching the highest scope of application, with millions of users, networked within specific systems of unique architectures and problems, such as freeriding (Baldwin and Clark, 2006). The communities and their unique voluntary models of participation have played a central role in defining user roles, the way in which community-guided innovation might happen (Lee and Cole, 2003), specifying the model of knowledge sharing (Kuk, 2006). Faraj et al. (2011) identify an important mechanism occurring in these projects has also been played by continuous responses of community in relation to the dynamic and fluctuations of resources from and into the project, such as passion, time, identity, social disembodiment of ideas, socially ambiguous identities, and temporary convergence. In this interpretation, knowledge collaboration occurs through responses to these tensions, as a fundamental mechanism organising these projects. Furthermore, a significant body of research examines network effects, such as relationship among projects and developers and their outcomes on the success of open-source projects (Grewal et al., 2006); the role of earlier collaborations and ties (Hahn et al., 2008); or founders' social capital (Mallapragada, 2012). Further considerations on organisation include studies of sustaining user participation (Fang and Neufeld, 2009; West and O'Mahony, 2008) and formalisation of participants' roles (Stam, 2009).

Finally, this body of literature has outlined the effects related to new competitive dynamics caused by open-source projects. One the one hand these studies look at particular industry effects, such as the role of open source on software industry, pointing out that open source projects cause a fast evolution of the industries (Economides and Katsamakas, 2006), as well as observing propagation of innovations (Hicks and Pachamanova, 2007) or arguing that open source provides a field for radical innovation which would otherwise not be possible (Inauen and Schenker-Wicki, 2012). As a result of highly innovative outcomes of open-source movements, the way in which they organize, develop and create support has also been translated to corporate innovation and software development practices, being labelled as "innersource" (Stol et al., 2011; Stol and Fitzgerald, 2015) or adopted by large corporations such as IBM (Samuelson, 2006). Furthermore, the discussion of the outcomes of open source has also examined their effects on pricing (Casadesus-Masanell and Ghemawat, 2006; Economides and Katsamakas, 2006). A further part of this dynamic includes work on open code, stored in repositories such as GitHub, one of the major forums for code sharing and discussion. Creative content, such as sound, music and pictures is shared online and creators embrace the philosophy of open data for several reasons. Parts of chapter three of this book fully address the application of principles of open data to the context of creative industries, showing the importance of technological possibilities given by the digital economy, as well as adoption of some of the licenses by external, commercial companies in order to cater emerging user needs seeking for content that can be reused in their projects, from creative independent work to commercial, contractual labour. As I show in this book, a key role in this domain is played by the Creative Commons license.

The concept and mechanisms of open production have also spread to the other industries beyond software. The key impact and importance were embedded in the generation of knowledge. Jemielniak (2014) extensively describes the politics of knowledge in Wikipedia, the biggest human-created project. Thousands of users with a common interest in knowledge sharing have created wiki-pages for all types of ventures: from annotating maps with historical comments (e.g., wikimaps), exchanging fan information (e.g., fandom.com), to developing parodies of wiki-sites (uncyclopedia).

In this decade, open-source paradigm has expanded with three-dimensional (3D) printing technology, combining computer design and physical printing and creating the model of open design. The availability of this technology has enabled movements specialising in the production of 3D printers using open-source microcontrollers operated by systems created with open-source license (Pearce, 2012). Open design is already being implemented in a variety of projects with different organisational and institutional structures, and is growing in popularity (Raasch et al., 2009). A key development in this field has been played by Arduino Instruments, a hardware project of electronic prototyping, with openly distributed electronic component specifications, as well as the programming software, freely available for anyone to use or modify (Fisher and Gould, 2012). They are also available as ready-made products (according to these specifications) sold for a highly affordable price ($20-$30 per piece). Developments embedded in this platform enabled creation of not only at-home printers but also elaborate research and production tools (Raasch et al., 2009; Vallance et al., 2001). The key platform of open design Thinkverse, contains several projects that have proven useful not only for individual users but also for research purposes, such as portable cell analysis device for DNA extraction (thing:25080); open-source orbital shaker for cell and tissue cultures (thing:5045); as well as automated filter wheel (thing:26553), all of which are fraction of the cost of commercially available ones (Baden et al, 2015; Pearce, 2012). Moreover, some of the emerging needs provoke new initiatives, such as recently publicised initiative of an open-source life-support ventilator, VentilAid. The stated goal of this project has been to help overloaded health systems in less developed economies weather the health crises of COVID-19, and to offer a last-resort device, "applicable only when professional equipment is missing" (VentilAid.com).

Open design consists not only of ambitious electronic projects but also of alternative accessories for electronic gadgets, cars, or home appliances, with participants treating open design in a similar way to how DIY movements treat idea forums, supporting non-commercial production using DIY methods. Such groups rely on an open, patent-free construction files, blueprint designs and scripts allowing to produce or modify products otherwise not available to the public. A significant part of open design is the question of manufacturing, which unlike in the case of crowdfunding occurs in the user's or company's site. One of the key examples is RepRap, an open source low-cost 3D printer, many parts of which can be printed on another RepRap 3D printer. Similar dynamics, connecting users' at-home capabilities and outside "on-demand" printing in specialised "print stores" have been labelled as "Manufacturing as a Service" (MAAS) and attributed to the open design movement, with full flexibility of production (Howard et al., 2012). At the same time, the literature points out that a significant part of pushing these initiatives forward stems from their business models, despite their openness, aimed at selling finished, manufactured products (Arduino), selling services and consulting projects (RedHat), or accepting outsourced processes (e.g., experiments) (Pearce, 2017). Initiatives reliant on open-source code and proprietary software, such as Raspberry Pi, a small micro-computer initially created to facilitate teaching of coding, have been broadly adapted, mainly using open design.

3   Openness in Public Policy

Finally, one of the domains that was the most challenged by the processes of opening, was the field of public policy, where openness emerges as a desired direction of changes in civic society. The process of opening in this domain is guided by an alternative perception of the role of intellectual protection – shifting it from being held by one entity, to the more transparent and open distribution of its contents to all interested parties.

3.1 Open Data Movement

According to the Open Data Institute's mission statement: "People, economies and societies are not getting the best value from data" (ODI, 2020). Open data policy can be understood as a set of initiatives rooted in a shared perception that the abandonment of traditional copyright brings sole benefits of public good. The Open data movement connects a set of initiatives to promote open licensing of content and generate awareness of the benefits of open data sets. The idea of opening access also occurs through the release of all kinds of digital content with specified permissions in regards to usage and modification. The generation of new content, not only relevant to data sharing but also to user communities, discussions and dissemination of practices translates to many domains that had previously been either isolated or hidden from the public. Some of them, such as data based on biology (genomes, cells) is arguably open and non-proprietary. Some initiatives take a perspective of open data, postulating broad availability of data to anyone who wishes to reuse it without restrictions. The Open Data Institute posits that the open data movement includes geographical information and initiatives such as open maps, where independent users might be allowed for data generation and sharing. The guiding principle of these movements can be summarised in the three points:

1. Transparency

    In a well-functioning, democratic society citizens need to know what their government is doing. To do that, they must be able freely to access government data and information and to share that information with other citizens. Transparency isn't just about access, it is also about sharing and reuse – often, to understand material it needs to be analyzed and visualized and this requires that the material be open so that it can be freely used and reused.

2. Releasing social and commercial value

    In the digital age, data is a key resource for social and commercial activities. Everything from finding your local post office to building a search engine requires access to data, much of which is created or held by government. By opening up data, government can help drive the creation of innovative business and services that deliver social and commercial value.

3. Participation and engagement
   Participatory governance or for business and organizations engaging with your users and audience. Much of the time citizens are only able to engage with their own governance sporadically – maybe just at an election every 4 or 5 years. By opening up data, citizens are enabled to be much more directly informed and involved in decision-making. This is more than transparency: it's about making a full "read/write" society – not just about knowing what is happening in the process of governance, but being able to contribute to it
   German Open Knowledge Foundation, 2020

Similar initiatives operate worldwide and their activities actively promoting open data access through activities such as training and education to the public, consultation of projects and services and organisation of communities.

The scholarship gives accounts of the activities of these bodies and their role in influencing data politics. For instance, Baack (2015) identifies three modes in which open source politics occur: through postulating usage and sharing of raw data – opening it for independent interpretation; by connecting the open source model to political participation; and by including the intermediaries that are necessary for making data accessible to the public. Milan and Van der Velden (2016) observe the intertwining of datafication and civic society, resulting in the emergence of new epistemologies, equated with greater civic awareness and participation. Similar processes are observed in the realms of journalism (Appelgren, 2018; Baack, 2015; 2018) and healthcare (Chamakiotis et al., 2020; Ruckenstein and Schüll, 2017). Advocates of open data also emphasise the need of reforming the educational system to ensure data literacy (Frank et al., 2016; Gray, 2018).

3.2 Open Scholarship

The central steam that influences public policy is tied to open scholarship, a term expressing several postulates relevant to how knowledge is created, what are its outcomes and who has access to it. Postulates of open science have been by numerous stakeholders (Vicente-Saez and Martinez-Fuentes, 2018). They have been identified as central by supranational intergovermental organisations across the world such as the European Commission, the European Parliament, the European Council, the Organisation for Economic Cooperation and Development, the United Nations, and the World Bank, all of which recognise them as a solution to the challenges of public health, food production or environment in the 21st century. On the micro level, open science has made scholarship easier and more transparent. The possibility of digitalising and disseminating publications was an opportunity to accelerate and accumulate an immense set of data. Like invention of moveable type, information technology allowed a new pace of orchestration and inflow. Although it was possible to circulate endless amounts of data and information, open science still faces limitations. The limitation includes high cost of access to journal articles (imposed by an oligopoly of publishers), enforcing the centralisation of publishing and innovation in Anglo-Saxon and West European schools. Quite often, limited access to publications made it difficult for scholars from less affluent educational systems to have their work published (Rufai, et al., 2012). These changes have been resisted with the idea of open science, for instance based on immediately paying publishers for unlimited access to a published article (usually by the author's institution), or publishing it in an alternative, 'open access' journal, which might not be mainstream but is embedded in the alternative proprietary regime of creative commons.

In the literature, open scholarship has centred upon the principles of transparency, sharability and the full inclusion of all stakeholders (Mayer, 2015). This approach manifested in several discussions over the building of new scientific practices based on information technology infrastructures (e.g., Open Access, Open Research Data, Open Methods, Open Education, Open Evaluation, and Citizen Science), all aimed at distributed collaboration, accountability, and verification of scientific findings. The scope of application of these new practices has varied on the public policy level, being led by Western European states and the European Union. For instance, the Amsterdam Call for Action on Open Science (2016), issued during the Netherlands' presidency of the European Union proposed several recommendations for the European Commission and the European Union "to take a leading role to facilitate and accelerate the transition towards open science" (p. 2). The result of bringing open science into this political conversation has translated to several approaches to scientific public policy. Fecher and Friesike (2013) identified five schools of thought (see Table 1) within the open science movement, arguing that they differ in their aims, methods, and central assumptions (Table 1). Their main assumption is identification of a varying interests of (1) how societies can potentially democratise knowledge distribution (democratic model); (2) how to facilitate knowledge exchange (pragmatic model); (3) how to improve tools and applications of knowledge (infrastructural model); (4) how can science be more accessible (public model); (5) and how to measure scientific impact (measurement model). The overview of these problems leads to an understanding of

TABLE 1   Five open science schools of thought

School of thought	Central assumption	Involved groups	Central aim	Tools and methods
Democratic	The access to knowledge is unequally distributed.	Scientists, politicians, citizens	Making knowledge freely available for everyone.	Open Access, intellectual property rights, Open data, Open code
Pragmatic	Knowledge-creation could be more efficient if scientists worked together.	Scientists	Opening up the process of knowledge creation.	Wisdom of the crowds, network effects, Open Data, Open Code
Infrastructure	Efficient research depends on the available tools and applications.	Scientists and platform providers	Creating openly available platforms, tools and services for scientists.	Collaboration platforms and tools
Public	Science needs to be made accessible to the public.	Scientists and citizens	Making science accessible for citizens.	Citizen Science, Science PR, Science Blogging
Measurement	Scientific contributions today need alternative impact measurements.	Scientists and politicians	Developing an alternative metric system for scientific impact.	Altmetrics, peer review, citation, impact factors

SOURCE: FECHER AND FRIESIKE (2013)

the postulates of establishing of highly inclusive participation in science, with transparent research procedures, results, and outcomes.

One of the key elements of open science, are shared standards of openness, usually in open access journals and results and regulations regarding publishing and authorising open access of general public (Suber, 2016). The literature shows the outcomes in the form of greater exposure and dissemination of work of scholars publishing in open access (Phelps et al. 2012) as well as releasing their research through portals such as academia.edu (Niyazov, 2016). These arguments are supported by bibliometric studies of interdisciplinary open access publications which have a greater impact than those published using closed access (Antelmann, 2004). Additionally, the literature points out the inefficiency of the subscription-based system and argue that the cost of access has been inflated with popularisation of technology (Caroll, 2011). There are also strong arguments in favour of the openness of data as a commodity that can be stored and protected by the publishers and reused by other researchers (Vision, 2010).

Further efforts on opening science are guided by the goals of distribution and efficiency. The current model of digital web 2.0 and its inclusivity are central to these goals. The literature starts with the postulation of broad knowledge sharing (Haeussler, 2011) and argues for a new, networked model of scientific progress, rooted in technology but also requiring the adoption of a new model of science by institutions and scientists alike (Nielsen, 2012). The form of inclusion might go beyond academia, adopting modes of generating knowledge similar to crowdsourcing, embedded in participatory model and relying on tools such as wiki-pages (Arazy et al., 2006). Moreover, this distributed form of participation is reflected in the infrastructural model of open science (Fecher and Friesike, 2013), which uses technological solutions to enhance and facilitate the openness of science (Altunay, 2010). An important part of that model is the idea of distributed computing, which grants programmes access to computing power of devices owned by private users, for instance to run simulations or mathematical computations (Kshemkalyani and Singhal, 2011).

Another discussion of the inclusivity of science concerns metrics and the established forms of assessing publication quality. One of the major issues raised by the literature concerns peer-review, a format that is typically low-paid or voluntary, time-consuming, and arbitrary (Hardaway and Scamell, 2012; McVeigh 2004; Priem and Costello 2010). Further questions raised in the context of journals contest the role of impact factor measurements (McVeigh 2004) and the increasing role of alternative means of publications (blog entries, self-published documents) that are often frequently cited even though they neither follow peer-review nor are tied to a journal (Yeong and Abdullah).

Furthermore, some of the citation methodologies and assessments of scholarship do not translate well across disciplines, for instance, natural science metrics and ways of publishing are much different from highly context-specific publishing in the international social sciences.

Finally, an important stream in opening science is grassroots activity that offers free access to knowledge, mediated by the digital environment (Peters and Britez, 2008). One of its most successful formats is Massive Online Open Courses (MOOCs), based on "free to access, cutting-edge courses that could drive down the cost of university-level education and potentially disrupt the existing models of higher education" (Yuan and Powell, 2013: 5). This movement has led to the establishment of start-ups (Emanuel, 2013), and adoption of this model by institutions formerly specialising in distant learning, such as the United Kingdom's Open University (Futurelearn, 2013). Opening formerly closed, fee-based courses has greatly increased the number of enrollees. The results of this development are the establishment of platforms and new ventures in addition to the emergence of new business models in education (Belanger and Thornton, 2013). One of the most successful MOOCs is edX.org, supported by the Massachusetts Institute of Technology and Harvard University which contributed more than $60 million to support the project. These changes have provoked innovations in the field of higher education (Henderikx et al., 2017), and changes in policy and quality assurance (Stracke, 2017).

3.3 *Open Government*

The opening of data has been closely associated with claims that public sector data should be made public because of their public funding and functioning and their potential role in improving the understanding of how public administration works. Open government is basically a political idea aimed at the creation of platforms and repositories of open data (Robinson et al., 2009). Proponents of open government argue that by making government data public, citizens would have greater access to information and documents and thus will make more informed political and civic choices (Kijn et al., 2008). In that sense, open government enhances decision making and management. Meijer et al. (2012) argue that the literature on open government makes two main arguments: one regarding transparency and open access to information; and the other pertaining to participation (voice) in a variety of public sector decisions, both formal and informal.

Open government has been implemented globally since the early 2000s. It has become an important element of political campaigns, usually associated with the theme of digital transformations of the state into political programmes. One example is Barack Obama's Memorandum on Transparency and Open Government (Harrison et al., 2011). A large body of literature has studied these political interpretations of open government at the municipal (Clohessy et al., 2014; Moon, 2002; Norris, 2013; Kassen, 2013), national (Attard et al., 2015; McDermott, 2010) and supranational levels (Beyers, 2004). These studies have found that the introduction of open government policies had some potential for empowerment (Kassen, 2013). Tolbert and Mossberger (2006) cite three pillars of what they call "e-government": (1) accountability, achieved for instance through government websites and other means of digital communication (Bertot et al., 2010); (2) transparency (through open data), playing a significant role in democratisation (Peled, 2011; Zuiderwijk, 2014); and (3) participation (in the form of interactive electronic services). Based on these changes, new business models emerge, often based on the open innovation model, proposing new business models innovating public service delivery and value creation . The literature also observes that implementation of open government generates value beyond the public sector, for instance fostering improvements in or the generation of new private products and services (Magalhaes et al., 2014).

This idea has recently become an integral part of smart cities: data-driven concept of collecting and processing information relevant to management of urban zones (Gil-Garcia, 2015; Gonzalez-Zapata and Heeks, 2015). Access to public data is part of an ongoing analysis of elements such as traffic, utilities supply networks, waste, crime detection or public transportation. Data plays a central role and comes not only from live monitoring and sensors but also from the mapping of public spaces, space planning and considerations relevant to the monitoring of public space for more efficient public services (Pereira et al., 2017). In fact, literature on smart cities often concentrates on the role of open data (Hielkema and Hongisto, 2013; Kitchin, 2014; Komninos et al., 2019) and the ways in which it can produce local innovation or generate value (Khan et al., 2015; Mirri et al., 2014). This body of literature often predicts the intertwining of expanding open data sets, social innovation and new investments in technology, resulting in potential public benefits, as well as identifying barriers and risks supporting decision making in the management of urbanities (Janssen et al., 2012; Zuboff, 2015).

∵

It can therefore be concluded that technology has been instrumental in the organisation of economy and society. Technology mediates a desirable kind of openness one that supports not only production but also fairness, clarity and transparency of procedures, data and decisions. This chapter offers an initial review of streams of studying openness, outlining its role in changing social practices and its significance for the future. These streams permit observation of a profound social change in multiple domains mentioned in the literature. This book uses the literature on openness to study the opening of creative industries. So far, little attention has been given to the dynamics in creative industries, in which, similarly to academia, openness is based in the idea of creativity, which like business innovation, stands to benefit from the process of opening.

The contents of this book expand the field of openness by showing the collaborative dynamics within the domain of creative industries, a topic that so far has not extensively considered in the literature on management and organisation. By relying on findings from sound industry, I concentrate on numerous overlooked aspects of opening of creative industries. I focus on the Creative Commons (CC) framework, which despite broad application has not been extensively researched. Although there have been some smaller co-authored studies (e.g., Kostakis and Drechsler 2015), of CC-mediated projects, no publication to date has addressed a large community within a single industry, with thousands of users and millions of works open to access and distribution. In my work, I look at one of these communities, and examine the outcomes of opening, based on the creation of a platform for exchange of sound (FreeSound), reliant on Creative Commons licensing. I explore the outcomes of Creative Commons on the creative industry practice. Despite a large literature on Creative Commons' legal outcomes (for a detailed literature review see Chapter 2), my work looks at the artistic practice enabled by the Creative Commons and addresses aspects that emerge from this form of opening that are different from the traditional sound industry model. They include specific mechanisms guiding the organisation of production, content-mediated collaboration dynamics, mechanisms of attribution, and commodification practices that rely on the produced content.

The next chapter focuses on projects based in the tradition of digital commons. It summarises the cultural, legal and organisational foundations of digital commons, describes their common features, and explains the model of peer-to-peer-production and governance.

CHAPTER 2

Cultural, Legal and Organisational Foundations of Digital Commons and Peer-Production

Chapter one showed how the paradigm of openness has been applied to multiple domains and how the idea of crossing conceptual boundaries, old schemes and regulations causes actors and organisations to pursue new projects and enterprises, abandoning exclusivity and appropriation and opening themselves to new ways of sharing and distributing knowledge, processes, or participation. This chapter expands the research on openness by focusing on a commons-based model of peer production (Benkler and Nissenbaum, 2006), and describes three aspects of this model of peer production: cultural roots, legal framework, and organisational dynamics.

In the social sciences literature, 'commons' is a general designation for a shared resource, such as a language or a space. In academic language, a commons has two connotations. In 'common-pool resources', commons are economic goods that are independent of property rights and regimes. Like forests, they are subtractive, meaning that with high usage depletes the resource. In the second understanding, 'common property', commons refers to a legal regime, a jointly owned legal set of rights (Bromley 1992; Ciriacy-Wantrup and Bishop 1975). Commons theory studies the governance of shared resources. It resides in an observation that any shared resource raises several social dilemmas, such as competition for use, free riding, or over-harvesting. At its base, commons theory has focused on natural resources, the natural commons, such as forests, or rivers, under the care of local populations and communities (Healy, 2015). In the earliest theorisation of the commons, Hardin (1968), an ecologist concerned with overexploitation, described a "tragedy of commons", based on the issues with managing a natural common, observing that in an open pasture, herdsmen attempt to maximise economic return by keeping as much cattle as possible, contributing to the deterioration of the natural resource. So, in this standard theorisation, a commons dilemma touches on overexploitation and scarcity.

There were several responses to this problem of over-utilisation of the commons. Hardin (1968) argued for privatisation and restricted access to commons for ecological reasons. Ostrom (1990) revisited Hardin's tragedy of the commons and opted for its governance through the cooperation among users of the property and proposed a model based on self-governance, collaboration, and collective action. To her, the commons dilemma was more about the closure or commodification of the access to the commons. She suggested that these communities need to develop 'common pool resource institutions', including rules, self-monitoring, sanctions, low-cost conflict resolution, all in the interest of the protection and maintenance of the commons (Hess and Ostrom, 2007: 7). These milestones in the discussions of commons exemplify the discourse surrounding the commons and reflect the problem of openness versus closure.

With the proliferation of technology, we started to speak of "new" types of commons, associated with technological access and different from natural resources (Benkler, 2014). Benkler defines commons-based peer production as "radically decentralized, collaborative and nonpropietary: based on sharing resources and outputs among widely distributed, loosely connected individuals, who cooperate with each other without relying on either market signals or managerial commands" (2006, p. 60). Greater access to personal computers and online sharing allowed for the production and use of digital goods and services, and the emergence of a new 'digital commons' (Hamari et al., 2016). These commons contained shared knowledge, software, data and design, and they represent the generation of productive knowledge that might be applied to both physical and digital goods. The main difference from traditional, ecological commons is lack of overexploitation, since digital commons are characterised by an abundance of digitally stored information.

Like the traditional commons, digital commons are maintained by communities, such as 'digital technology commons' and 'information exchange commons' (Hess, 2000). The purpose of these communities is parallel production and consumption of digital resources, which is asynchronous and usually dominated by production and contribution, termed in the literature as "pooling commons resources" (Bollier and Helfrich 2015). Digital commoning is thus collective practice of production, usage and management of information and knowledge that is offered in an open and non-exclusive way (Cahir, 2004; De Angelis, 2010; Roggero, 2010). Commoning practice, like the traditional commons, is not subjected to any market activities or constraints stemming from for-profit orientation and seeking. Commons usually have a goal that is aimed at meeting a need or filling a gap that the community perceives. Commons production follows a unique logic that is intended to be outside of the bracket of capitalism, meaning that it is non-commodified and oriented to social needs. Its rationale is often based in a shared perception of a missing product, production components, or reinstating the power of control in a certain tool. Healy (2015: 345) calls this a 'postcapitalist corrective', meaning that commons establish an alternative circuit of production aimed at releasing specific tensions generated by capitalism.

In this chapter I address three fundamental aspects of the digital commons. The first is the culture of resistance characterising the earliest adopters of technology who often have also supported the development of the commons. To them, technology has created new, different and more egalitarian ways of participating in society. At the same time, those ways were colonised by the new entrants that started commercial activities that used that technology. In response, these participants generated alternative frames of circulation in the form of commons and other technological cultures that paralleled its emergence. The second are the legal frameworks that regulate the functioning of the commons. Within that domain, I characterise the regulation of the digital commons, showing how open licensing frameworks establish its functioning and use. Lastly, I describe the organisational foundations that grew on the commons enabled by the software license. I concentrate on showing the mechanisms that govern the use and function of the commons.

1 Culture of Resistance and the Roots of the Digital Commons

The idea of commonality and co-participation in production of content and ideas, something separated from capitalist realities and based on joint work by peers, stems from a technological culture that emerged in the early years of the popularisation of information technology. The philosophy of techno-libertarianism transgressed a paradigm of collaboration tied to the hacker ethic model (Benkler, 2006; Himannen, 2001), largely based on enthusiasm, joy, peer-equality and altruism rather than commercial production. A seminal publication on the formation and study of hacker ethics is Levy's *Hackers: Heroes of the Computer Revolution*. The book concentrates on the earliest phase of hacker movement from the 1950s to the modern digital era of the mid-1980s. Levy (1984) argues that hackers have exploited the revolutionary potential of the computer. He argues that hackers empowered by technology worked on opening multiple domains of social life. As he shows, despite their different backgrounds and motivations, they were visionaries, risk-takers, and artists, united under the same ethic and following similar principles, often based on collaborative production. The defining factors of hackers' approach to technology are quoted below.

> 1. Access to computers – and anything which might teach you something about the way the world works – should be unlimited and total. Always yield to the Hands-on Imperative!

2. All information should be free.
3. Mistrust authority – promote decentralisation.
4. Hackers should be judged by their hacking, not bogus criteria such as degrees, age, race or position.
5. You can create art and beauty on a computer.
6. Computers can change your life for the better.
LEVY, 1984, pp. 32–38

This manifesto is a utopian vision of organising society on the idea that information should be free. Hackers strive to learn about informatoin, manipulate it, and make it free. Levy remarks on unlimited access to means that can teach us about the world, emphasising hands-on practice to gain experience, and expressing a strong belief that direct involvement and active participation are more significant than theoretical or impractical, academic knowledge. For that purpose, Levy emphasises the need for the free and unlimited flow of information and for decentralisation. This approach also means that hackers should be judged by their achievements. Levy emphasises the new avenue that art and beauty can take through the usage of personal computer, which draws a new horizon for new types of creations and artistic boundaries, including the code being "a beauty of its own" (Levy, 1984, p. 36). Finally, this ethical manifesto talks about social change caused by programmes, which once created can last and be used whenever needed. Even though Levy's vision seems utopian and idealistic, it remains an important point of reference for understanding the process underlying the culture of peer-production and openness. The following excerpt explains how hackers emerged as a technological elite in the early days of the computer:

> Jedi-like in their computer skills and dedicated to optimizing and protecting the nascent computer system – were referred to in the community as "hackers". Systems were set up so that "hackers" could openly and freely make fixes and patches to the communal product. On the one hand, hackers often competed against each other, routinely breaking into each other's systems in a game to beat each other and to showcase their own skills. On the other hand, hackers also collaborated and freely shared code and knowledge, enabling each to learn from each other and to implement even more robust systems.
> YU, 2007, p.377

With time, this creative ferment catalysed into community-based organisations that specialised in software production. With their growth, new type of organisation proliferated, giving way to first attempts to organise the commons, also influencing their culture and legal frame.

While these legal frameworks emerged from highly technological circles of university researchers, the second generation of users, who were early adopters and technology enthusiasts, propelled the mass sourcing of ideas, following the initial elite of hackers, promoting equality and sympathising with the resistance to mainstream media and technology. The new users of the internet treated online life as a unique and distinct social space, often allowing for abolishment of many restrictions that had been present in non-digital realities. Early internet users engaged in different activities, from sharing files and developing software, to discussing video games, car repairs, dating or simply socialising. The increased interest brought millions of new users. It also attracted commercial enterprises hoping to profit from this expanding community. Their commercial profit-oriented products aimed at capturing value from the internet. Quite quickly this commodification resulted in the emergence of new products that were easier to use, user friendly, and serving for-profit needs. They often contradicted less appealing and more challenging tools used by the early adopters of the technology. For instance, while earlier adopters used peer-to-peer Internet Relay Chat (IRC), the truly mass scope of technology was achieved by AOL, the biggest internet company. Shifts caused by the entry of commercial actors raised concerns about privacy, security and produced resistance. One of the responses was the demand for open-source software, the first open source projects, and early attempts at open innovation.

The internet has always rested on a unique social dynamic of secrecy and elitism. Commercialisation has changed this dynamic. In his autobiography, Snowden remarks on the shifts that took place in the 1990s which he sees as instrumental in his critical stance on privacy violations. In the first few chapters of the book, Snowden recalls his formative experiences with IRC, BBS, technology and hacking. He then describes his moment of transformation:

> In the 1990s, the Internet had yet to fall victim to the greatest iniquity in digital history: the move by both government and businesses to link, as intimately as possible, users' online personas to their offline legal identity. Kids used to be able to go online and say the dumbest things one day without having to be held accountable for them the next. This might not strike you as the healthiest environment in which to grow up, and yet it is precisely the only environment in which you can grow up – by which I mean that the early Internet's dissociative opportunities actually encouraged me and those of my generation to change our most deeply held opinions, instead of just digging in and defending them when challenged. This ability to reinvent ourselves meant that we never had to close our minds by picking sides, or close ranks out of fear of doing irreparable

harm to our reputations. Mistakes that were swiftly punished but swiftly rectified allowed both the community and the "offender" to move on. To me, and to many, this felt like freedom.
SNOWDEN, 2019, p. 47

This spirit of honesty and rebellion reflects the hacker ethos and the culture of openness. Snowden mentions the real-life dissociation of online personas, which fostered his growth based on democracy, merit and the process of testing and dismissing ideas. His vision of freedom yet fell into the trap of business and regulation. Since the 1990s, the perception of shrinking freedom has surfaced in several literary and academic works and influenced political agendas. Their shared view was that legal regulation of the internet is solely shaped by economic interests.

The perceived shift in approaching the Internet and resistance to commercialization of technology has also emerged in popular culture. The blockbuster film *The Matrix* (1999) was about a hacker who became a prophet by disconnecting from the system and exploring a reality unknown to the masses. In this film, oppressive technology was used to surveille and isolate people. At the same time, the protagonist's hacking skills liberated him from that technology, making his capable of transcending the limitations of the lived world, giving him superpowers, and allowing him to create a better world. This narrative played an important role in the interpretation of changes in societies undergoing technological transformation.

At the same time, popular media glorified hackers. The mid-1990s were Kevin Mitnick's moment of fame. Mitnick was notorious for using his technical and social skills for his own benefit. He was a technological outlaw who made international headlines. These, and many other, pop-cultural examples have associated reliance on technology and digital skills with resistance against powers of commodifying the digital sphere. This ethic and aesthetic is still practiced in some platforms, where perceptions of technology and community constitute an alternative environment for consumption and production.

Hacking has now been normalised. Instead of denoting illegal activity, it now signifies activity based on interest in technology and computing. 'Hacker spaces' have proliferated worldwide (Kostakis et al., 2015), creating the possibility of sharing equipment, technology and knowledge and building a network of support and collaboration. These spaces have followed the initial idea of sharing and alternative environment, but also been tied to the generation of new start-ups and followed the trend of open innovation. In this sense, hacking focuses on inclusivity, and the use of technology for social and economic growth and advancement.

The academic literature on hacker culture has observed that early technology had a strong ideological dimension, based on the perception of an oppressive commercial or governmental body aiming at taking away online liberties and freedom. One of the main bones of contention in this struggle has been the discussion of copyright. While computer piracy was an unsoluble problem in the 1990s, the proliferation of new actors and business models has significantly decreased this issue. Yet, the hacker ethos of sharing, remixing and disseminating has become an inherent part of the culture and ethos. Local hacker scenes that became hubs for creators, innovators, and pirates in Western European states have received a strong support from the voters.

2 Open Licensing: The Legal Foundations of Digital Commoning

A program is free software if the program's users have the four essential freedoms:

> The freedom to run the program as you wish, for any purpose (freedom 0).
> The freedom to study how the program works and change it so it does your computing as you wish (freedom 1). Access to the source code is a precondition for this.
> The freedom to redistribute copies so you can help others (freedom 2).
> The freedom to distribute copies of your modified versions to others (freedom 3). By doing this you can give the whole community a chance to benefit from your changes. Access to the source code is a precondition for this.
> A program is free software if it gives users adequately all of these freedoms. Otherwise, it is nonfree. While we can distinguish various nonfree distribution schemes in terms of how far they fall short of being free, we consider them all equally unethical.
> GNU, 2019

The approach to freedom shortly drafted above, has quickly translated to attempts at codifying new ideas of copyright. The digital commons originated in the proliferation of free/open software frameworks in the 1960s. Their emergence is associated with the opposition to proprietary rights, especially the orientation of law to the individual, protection of private property and enabling of market exchanges (de Rosnay and Musiani, 2016; Soderberg, 2002). Simply put, any of the national regulations were suitable for protection of information-based digital commons, being unable to recognise their model of authorship and regulating the derivatives of this work. As a result of these inadequacies, in parallel to the cultural changes, the early commoners have been working on alternative frameworks of copyright protection. The legal work is often attributed to the later leaders of the free/open software movement who were working on the Unix operating system in the 1970s and 1980s. The four freedoms of open licensing permit users to run, study, modify, and redistribute content. The language of the commons makes a semantic distinction in the meaning of "free".

Stallman (2020) emphasises that "free" has a significance beyond "gratis", "for zero price". Instead, free software "gives the user certain freedoms" (Stallman, 2020). In its first meaning, free/gratis is the mode of distribution based on no monetary compensation on the user side, and it might refer to both open and closed source projects, proprietary software, as well as public domain content. This distribution mode is often known as free/gratis ("free as free beer"). In the second meaning, the understanding of "free" centres on the freedom of access and distribution, hence often termed as free/libre ("free as free speech"). This understanding parallels the four freedoms, specific to the open-source nature of content, for example, software distributed with open code, providing liberty of use, modification and redistribution to users, as permitted by the specific license. Both distributive modes are typical of the legal regulations of the digital commons.

While the distributive mode remains invariable, since all open content requires no payment, the terms of usage of content can be located along a broad spectrum of restrictiveness. On the one side of this spectrum is a model of protection, known as "copyleft". Copyleft is the opposite of "copyright", indicating the open character of the content, ensuring its openness to any further modifications, and the transparency of the license. The term "copyleft" expresses the opposite of both frameworks: the removal of protection and exclusivity of access and usage and the intention to broaden access and transparency of authorship. Copyleft is defined as "a general method for making a program (or other work) free (in the sense of free/libre) and requiring all modified and extended versions of the program to be free as well" (gnu.org, 2020). A model situation of application of copyleft could be a program written by a creator who: (1) states that the program is copyrighted (e.g., by giving his name); (2) adds distribution terms, understood as 'the rights to use, modify, and redistribute the program's code, *or any program derived from it,* but only if the distribution terms are unchanged' (gnu.org, 2020); (3) and stipulates both the program's and the distribution code's inseparability (so the program needs to be distributed with license). This example shows that copyleft follows a pattern: embedding content in the specification of copyright, granting users permissions and rights, while ensuring further usage of the same framework based on the same license.

In the terminology of open licensing, the stream of copyleft reflects a license permitting usage of content following specific restrictions under the license. It usually means that the user can distribute derivative works, including all linked programmes and documents, using the same license and providing the full source code. GNU General Public License (GPL) v2, written by the Free Software Foundation is a a copyleft license. It permits copying, distribution and modification of software only if all changes and dates of the changes in source files are tracked. Any modifications to the GPL-licensed code must be made available using the GPLv2 license. The files containing the modified programme must refer to the GPLv2 framework in the text format, provide the source code, make reference to the disclaimer of warranty, and be distributed with the original software code along with build and install instructions. All these requirements oblige users and recreators to perpetuate the generation of shared content and ensure that the new works are within the same framework, prohibiting sub-licensing.

However, responding to the strict and long set of regulations by copyleft, the proponents of these frameworks have distinguished a stream of "weak copyleft", which contains fewer restrictions, allows easier usage of files, with no requirements such as reliance on the same framework of derivative work or lack of permission to modify it. In 2015, Github.com, the largest open-source development platform published a short report showing that the largest number of Github's users had chosen weak copyleft licenses: MIT license (44.69%), Apache (11.19%), BSD 3-clause (4.53%), and BSD 2-clause (1.70%) (Github.com, 2020), accounting for in 62,82 per cent of all content. There are several reasons for the popularity of these frameworks, but the MIT license remains especially attractive because of its simple structure and ease of communicating the conditions of users. In other words, "you don't need a law degree to understand it, and implementation is simple." (opensource.com, 2020). The MIT license exemplifies the idea behind weak copyleft: full permission to use the work, as long as the original license extends to all further copies and derivatives of work. Distribution of the work with or with modifications is allowed. MIT license is concise and suitable for all types of distribution. Its full contents are as follows.

> Copyright <YEAR> <COPYRIGHT HOLDER>
>
> Permission is hereby granted, free of charge, to any person obtaining a copy of this software and associated documentation files (the "Software"), to deal in the Software without restriction, including without limitation

the rights to use, copy, modify, merge, publish, distribute, sublicense, and/or sell copies of the Software, and to permit persons to whom the Software is furnished to do so, subject to the following conditions:

The above copyright notice and this permission notice shall be included in all copies or substantial portions of the Software.

THE SOFTWARE IS PROVIDED "AS IS", WITHOUT WARRANTY OF ANY KIND, EXPRESS OR IMPLIED, INCLUDING BUT NOT LIMITED TO THE WARRANTIES OF MERCHANTABILITY, FITNESS FOR A PARTICULAR PURPOSE AND NONINFRINGEMENT. IN NO EVENT SHALL THE AUTHORS OR COPYRIGHT HOLDERS BE LIABLE FOR ANY CLAIM, DAMAGES OR OTHER LIABILITY, WHETHER IN AN ACTION OF CONTRACT, TORT OR OTHERWISE, ARISING FROM, OUT OF OR IN CONNECTION WITH THE SOFTWARE OR THE USE OR OTHER DEALINGS IN THE SOFTWARE.

MIT licenses which permit copying and linking code with other software; however static linking (placing original code in a single, executable file) requires permission. Redistribution of works under these licenses, both in the form of code and binary forms are permitted and distribution is generally allowed with and without modifications. A similar construction of the license is followed by the BSD licenses: "two-clause BSD", offering almost unlimited freedom of usage, as long as the BSD copyright notice is included; as well as "three-clause", additionally prohibiting usage of the names of the original copyright holders and contributors to endorse or promote derived products (unless permitted in writing).

The last way of sharing content is a release to the "public domain". Public domain is a legal concept that expresses a status of work that is not subject to intellectual property protection and is therefore publicly available (Guibault, 2006; Guibault and Angelopoulos, 2011; Moore, 2005). Under traditional copyright law, public domain is a legal means of regulating the status of works in situations affecting the expiration of copyright. For example, in most legal instances a creative work's intellectual property protection lasts for 50 to 70 years, after which it enters the public domain, meaning that the content is no longer copyrighted. This is the case of public archives, books or musical compositions. In light of changing copyright protections there was a need for public-domain-equivalent license, responding to a need of creators to provide full access to works that they produce. In the commoning context, the public domain license, in its varieties (CC-0 Public Domain, WTFPL, the Unlicense, Zero Clause BSD), allows creators to surrender their copyright, allowing for full access and usage of content with no restrictions. Public domain is not considered part of the free/open-source licensing movement because from the functional perspective the public domain is not explicitly connected to the programme of changing how intellectual property works. Yet, as shown in Chapter three, it plays an important role in commons-based production in the creative industries.

The legal terminology in free/open-source software production has formed the understanding and needs of alternative licensing, separate from the copyright's role in protection of the economic value of source code and media. In cases such as software or data, copyright builds a framework around their protection and – most importantly – in the protection of value exploitation. Under the law, alternative licenses have permitted the creation of an alternative circulation, embedded in commonality of production and recognition of these frameworks. In simpler terms, these licenses are a simple way of sharing productions by other users, who, by understanding the license, were capable of recognising the basic permissions such as modification, copyright, distribution or commercial usage. Chapter three shows, how, parallel to these developments and adopting similar principles to the frameworks intended to regulate the usage and production of free/open-source software were transplanted to the creative industries by the Creative Commons license.

3   Principles of Digital Peer Production

Production of Digital Commons rests on the rules of peer-to-peer production. Bauwens (2009) explains peer production as reliant on distributed networks, composed of a structure allowing participants to take independent action and maintain relationships 'on their own' (p. 97) as well as 'self-aggregation', understood as ability to create the commons, immaterial value in the form of cumulated work. Digital commons provide an environment of production that responds to individual and collective interests, usually ignoring market pressures, or being adjunct to them (Bauwens, 2009; Powell, 2012). Benkler (2017) writes that peer production emphasises 'cooperative continuity', which can be understood as a combination of 'motivational diversity', so catering and combining diverse motivations of participants; with specific 'social integrity' – a shared understanding that fosters long-term involvement and creates patterns of reputation building and recognition. The organisation of production of digital commons depends on organisational patterns established by the communities producing open software, embedded in cultural dynamics influenced by hacker ethics, and using free/open licensing frameworks. The production mode that is generated by these communities goes far beyond software, at its heart having generation and maintenance of the commons, as well as catering community needs, such as solving disputes, supporting users and promoting the ongoing projects.

The organisation of peer-production, due to its technological roots, adopts a decentralised, democratic model, based on broad integration of users willing to contribute and following the rules of the specific commons. Peer production relies on flat structures, based on a model of dispersed production, with access to production components enabled by technology (Barley and Kunda, 2001; Benkler, 2002). Even though governance and management structures of commons are flat, users have a significant role in administering the commons. This power is, however, separated from property and contract, being oriented towards productivity and continuity of the commons (Benkler, 2017). Kostakis and Bauwens (2020) calls the organisation of commons a 'heterarchy', referring to the organisational model of peer production, expressing both the importance of networks and denoting the crucial role of editors, moderators and leaders. While the networks of users provide the production power and generate outputs, it is community leadership and moderation that maintains the quality and direction of production. The scope and depth of this moderation depends on the type of commons, from being absent (Sound Commons), to being central (open source software production).

Software production projects use mechanisms aimed at maintaining productivity and momentum, sometimes called "consensus decision making" (for instance, apache.org, 2020b). These procedures prevent an impasse, when a community faces a conflict over the direction of a project, and there is a need for a definitive decision. The mechanism in place can be a voting procedure or an arbitrary coordination of production, intended to accelerate the pace of production. Software communities at such turning points also often use a "benevolent dictatorship" (Raymond, 1998, 1999), a function typically reserved to the creators or developers of the digital commons, who retain a final say in disputes, arguments over the commons, often being retired from their participation in the commons. These mechanisms all foster production and prolong the existence of commons but often also cause situations in which some users are displeased with the decision and ally with other unhappy users and move to another project.

Peer production is also characterised by the openness of communication, which rests on asynchronous collaboration, usually based on tracking the production, atomisation of the work process, and full access to this data by all participants in the commons. This might depend on sharing the code in repositories or platforms. Raymond, who studied software projects coined the metaphor of "cathedral and bazaar" to express these forms of collaboration, reflecting their transparency and access to code (Jemielniak, 2014; Raymond, 1999). The cathedral model reflects an organisation rooted in releasing source code with each software release, with constant development between releases. In this model, users do not see the code until the final product has been developed. In the bazaar, all production takes place in public view, often with no clear centre or direction of production. In this model, more typical of peer-production outside of the software domain, the community around a project has full access to the information, often tracking its progress and monitoring the entire cooperative system. All communication has a requirement of transparency and needs to be public for other participants. In some communities, such as Wikipedia, this transparency is organised by sets of bureaucratic procedures, which due to scale of project allows for enhanced productivity (Jemielniak, 2014).

Voluntary work is the non-profit gifting of time and labour. There are, however, different motivations tied to the involvement of the users. And while users can seek for-profit motivation, for instance by building their portfolio or improving their coding skills, digital commons offer no formal profit, other than the possibility of participation. Research shows that participants' motivation ranges from professional goals typical of free/open-source software to more community-specific recognition, ideological and emotional value (De Filippi, 2015), and individual satisfaction and goals. At the same time, commons-based production offers a productive activity separate from property relations and the managerial hierarchy (Benkler, 2002; Lakhani and Wolf, 2003; Von Hippel and von Krogh, 2006). The literature on commons speaks to motivation within the commons as largely driven by non-monetary intentions, both of intrinsic factors and extrinsic social status, with a strong emphasis on the latter. Some communities explicitly propose an ethos of humble meritocracy, rather than ego-driven actions to promote the contributor (Jemielniak, 2014). In some communities or commons, there is an emphasis on public good. For instance, the Apache Software Foundation (ASF), supports content permissiveness and ensures free circulation and reuse. ASF's mission is "to provide software for the public good. We do this by providing services and support for many like-minded software project communities consisting of individuals who choose to participate in ASF activities" (apache.org, 2020a). Apache also fosters collaboration through community engagement and development. The organisation's philosophy of "The Apache Way" espouses principles of diversity, awareness, and self-help. For instance, ASF uses the concept of limited amount of structure and wide permissiveness.

Digital commons are based neither on gifting nor on reciprocity (Bauwens and Kostakis, 2020). The coordination of giving and taking inside the commons is not regulated so there is no individual requirement for reciprocity. Moreover, there is no exclusive proprietary control over the products of collaborative or individual contributions. Instead, production takes place within the commons, relying on a specific legal framework that ensures non-exclusivity of access, at the maximum of restrictiveness requiring either using the same legal framework for derivatives (copyleft) or attributing the original creator. There are also no limits to participation. A hallmark of the digital commons is voluntary participation that stems from a willingness to contribute skills or products. The scope and quality of this contribution depends on the type of commons, but in general all participants donate their work and content to the commons. Commons often do not use any form of pre-selection of contributors and any user can join and enrich project as they wish. The literature calls it "anti-credentialism" or "equpotentiality" (Bauwens, 2005). Establishment of reputation depends on building credentials, often completely separate from participants' real-life backgrounds. Zeitlyn (2003) understands these newly emerging relationships as being based on the anthropological 'axiom of kinship amity', where like the extended family, direct economic calculation does not work. Instead, there is a process of process of internal trust and reputation building, which replaces the formal way of accounting for work and its effects. As noted in studies of commons, the establishment and maintenance of these relationships occurs through online interactions, allowing users to be out of the axes of discrimination such as, appearance, social class or gender (Jemielniak, 2014). Some of the software projects value merit, for example treating it as a publicly earned authority, based on the contribution to the project. Merit remains only relevant based on the contribution of the user, independent of background, employment or country of origin. Yet, this does not mean that the participants remain equal, and with work done inside the commons, key participants may become an elite, with "important contributors are few and ascend to the 'core group status' "(Lerner and Tirole, 2002, p. 206). Even though the formation of such elite is more typical of software projects, key users are important outside of the production, for instance on the commons' forum or other communication channels.

The organisation of commons also offers a different positionality in a market economy. Peer-to-peer production offers a symbolic separation of commons from both commercial actors and the state (Bollier and Helfrich, 2012), manifested in low interest in generation of for-profit value of content and a rather strong orientation to community needs (Bauwens 2005, Bauwens and Kostakis, 2021). Bauwens (2009) argues that this model of production is both immanent to capitalism, especially in its digital forms, and to transcendent – fostering capitalist alternatives and increasing autonomy of producing communities.

Commons-based peer production captures a dynamic of collective production, management and consumption of value (Benkler and Nissenbaum, 2006), which can be captured and valorised towards profit maximalisation (Bauwens and Pantazis, 2018). Almost all instances of commons contain examples of marketisation, for example in commercial products offering a better customer experience (Red Hat as opposed to GNU community). At the same time, organisation of peer production often requires financing of current affairs, generating an urge for market activity in the form of fundraising or commercial for-profit associations, separate from the initial communities.

Commons-based production offers an alternative model of production that relies on digital technology, dependent on alternative copyright frameworks. This chapter has shown the fundaments of digital commons and the three dimensions central to their functioning: cultural and ideological component, legal framework, and internal rules of the community of contributors and users. In the next part I concentrate on the specificity of creative industries to show the political economy of the digital commons in the creative industries.

CHAPTER 3

Creative Commons

Political Economy of Creative Peer-to-Peer Production

> Get a license or do not sample.
> *Bridgeport Music, Inc. v. Dimension Films*, 410 F.3d, 792, 801, 6th Cir., 2005

∴

The previous chapter described the mechanisms at the heart of newly emerging models of commons-based peer-to-peer production. This chapter focuses on the Creative Commons, the framework that enabled this model of production in the creative industries. In this section I show the framework in the context of the global creative industries. I begin by showing the basic copyright protection mechanisms that apply to the creative industries and exploring the role of copyright in the distribution of power in these industries, privileging powerful media corporations and collecting societies, acting as intermediaries. I then show the crisis that this model faced with emergence of digital technology and global access to media. I reflect on the changes in the most affected industry – music – and the challenges posed by bootlegging and digital sampling. Lastly, I propose the rules of Creative Commons as a response to these practices in global creative industries.

The Creative Commons license, compared to frameworks in the production of software has a shorter history and is designed for the creative industries. The focus on regulating the usage and distribution of creative works, not pieces of code, differs in the way in which portions of content are approached. Both contain elements for production, but in the case of creative content, the possible scope of usage of shared elements is significantly higher than the usage of lines of code. Contents of sound files are saved as digital portrait of signal, which can later undergo transformation, becoming a completely different object. For example, a footstep can be easily turned into a drumbeat just by trimming and looping. Sound designers often transform and merge sounds; their work is often based on their ability to apply different techniques to generate sound effects that fit their artistic sense of how "things sound".

While traditional copyright law creates the default rule of "All Rights Reserved", making permission necessary for every use of a work, Creative Commons facilitates an environment where "Some Rights Reserved" or "No Rights Reserved" are the norm. In other words, it seeks to "use copyright to authorize (rather than inhibit) copying, distribution, modification and reuse of software and other copyrighted works" (Dusollier, 2006: 274). In nearly all cases, the content remains owned by the creator who can charge for additional permissions, like commercial application of the material; the CC license allows only non-commercial usage. Creative Commons follows the idea of Free/Libre Open-Source Software, which aimed at promoting the open exchange of information in user-led development of computer programs, allowing for greater participation among users, stimulating a collaborative spirit of creation, and increasing the supply and stock of knowledge. Numerous works identify the goal of Creative Commons as ending imbalances in spheres that rely on restrictive use of intellectual property, such as the cultural industries (Berry, 2008; Shemtov and Walden, 2013).

This chapter argues that Creative Commons is an alternative to traditional copyright practices, consistent with the digital model of music distribution, also responding to previously neglected distribution and production practices, such as sample-based production techniques, by providing a set of simple licensing tools based on "building 'a layer of reasonable copyright' on top of existing law" (Goss, 2007: 977). In the creative industries, the Creative Commons (CC) initiative has achieved truly global scope and recognition. So far, the studies of Creative Commons have been most extensively done from the perspective of legal studies, and they concentrate on analyses of licenses, legal risks, and legal contexts of copyright and CC (Elkin-Koren, 2005; Goss, 2007). By depicting the actual practices of creators and describing Creative Commons' role in the organisation of both commoning and professional activities, this study complements the partial perspectives on this process, for instance depicting the significance of open access to cultural goods (Garcelon, 2009) or studying joint authorship mediated by CC (Kostakis and Drechsler, 2013).

Below I expand upon the relationship among the creative industries, copyright, and value of Creative Commons content by presenting the theory of content valuation.

1   The Basic Framework of Copyright in Creative Industries

It is necessary to begin with the relationship between two frameworks of legal protection to show the distinctiveness of Creative Commons' legal specificity (based on design for creative industries), in fostering work and collaboration. In short, copyright is an exclusive right that exists in creative works that have enough originality (individual character) to warrant such a right. Copyright gives its holder an exclusive right to copy, reproduce, distribute, adapt, perform, or display a work of creative expression. Its function is to protect and reward a work's creativity, uniqueness and specificity of. In the first instance, copyright gives the artist "the right to control copying", securing the artist's exclusive right to copy, reproduce, share and broadcast his or her creative work. This right can be transferred to any other party, such as a distributor, publisher or music label. Copyright protects literary and academic works and works in artistic domains. The type of expression makes no difference in terms of protection, and the right is given automatically to the creator of the original work. For instance, an unpublished song recorded on a home computer can receive similar copyright protection to a song by a world-famous recording artist, as long as it is original. The only conditions are originality and that the work is recorded or saved to a medium, such as a computer, paper, or tape.

Some exceptions in copyright permit the copying of a work by some parties which intend to engage in its "fair use". Fair use refers to acceptable ways of using copyrighted works to provide commentary, criticism, news reporting, research, teaching, library archiving and scholarship (Aufderheide and Jaszi, 2011; Gasaway, 2013). To determine fair use, courts consider four factors: whether the use is commercial; whether creative rather than factual elements of the existing copyrighted work were used; how much of the existing work was used; and whether the market for that work has been harmed (Westbrook, 2009). Artistic activities, such as sampling for composition or mixing are not considered fair use and requires permission for "transformation".

Today, copyright protection crosses national borders, alongside economic and political integration. Most countries have their own national laws and regulations, but several documents had laid the foundation of international copyright protection. Their goal is not only to regulate cross-national use but also to address issues such as translation or adaptation of works to different cultural contexts. The past decades created a need for the application of local copyright regulations to the digital environment.

The Berne Convention (1979) laid the groundwork for global copyright. The Berne Convention for the Protection of Literary and Artistic Works drafted an international treaty for signatories in 1886 that enshrined several elements of modern copyright law. The convention created a union, composed of signatory countries, whose members are obliged to recognise and respect copyright. It is the first international act to recognise copyright protection in the moment of creation of a work (as opposed its registration). It has also defined principles such as fair use, country of origin or specified artists' right to authorise translations, reproductions, adaptations, performances, broadcasts or other communication of their work. There are several recognised issues regarding the Berne Convention's application to digital creations, such as recognition of country of origin. Currently 171 signatories of the Berne Convention (UN members plus the Vatican), have adopted the convention to suit their needs.

Furthermore, the mass popularisation of copy technology and booming film and music industry in mid-20th century has posed challenges for copyright law. The emergence of copying technology stimulated the need for regulation. The key response in the domain of copyright emerged in the Rome Convention (WIPO, 2020). The Rome Convention was signed in 1961 by the members of United International Bureaux for the Protection of Intellectual Property. It was the basis for provisions on the rights of performers, producers of phonograms, and broadcasting organisations, acknowledging limitations and exceptions, such as private use, use of short excerpts and use for teaching and education. This act extends copyright protection from the author of works to creators and holders of particular physical manifestations of intellectual property (at that time, tapes or vinyl records).

In 1996, the Rome Convention was replaced by the WIPO Performances and Phonograms Treaty (WPPT). The WPPT (1996) extended and clarified issues raised in the Rome Convention by expanding to the rights of two kinds of beneficiaries in the digital environment: performers, and producers of phonograms (persons or legal entities that take the initiative and responsibility for the fixation of sounds). The treaty stipulated that the performers obtain economic rights to their performances fixed in phonograms in several forms: reproduction, distribution, rental and making available (authorising access). At the same time, it regulated the rights of unfixed (live) performances as well as specified exceptions.

In parallel, digital technology and issues stemming from low barriers in distribution led to new developments. The 1996 WIPO Copyright Treaty (WCT, 1996) extends the regulations to issues surrounding the dissemination of copyrighted material in the digital world. For instance, it recognises copyright protection of computer programmes and databases ("compilations of data") and addresses online rental and distribution. Moreover, local regulations emerged, largely influencing the Western world's circulation of works:

– EU Directive 2001/29/EC (EU, 2001): The European Union has strongly influenced integration of copyright protection between European nation states. Directive 2001/29/EC (InfoSoc Directive), implements WCT in the European

Union countries as well as brings together various elements of copyright law in Europe. InfoSoc Directive also responds to technological development and attempts to harmonize European Union's internal market.
- DMCA in the United States: The Digital Millennium Copyright Act (DMCA, 1998) is a United States adoption of WCT and WPPT, but it also regulates a number of issues related to management and enforcement of copyrights online. DMCA provides a mechanism for copyright holders to protect their content online, for instance by ensuring the ease of infringement-related removal of content and protecting internet service providers from liability of such infringement (Clark, 2015).
- The UK Digital Economy Act (2010): The Digital Economy Act provides legal tools of enforcing copyrights by limiting, suspending, or terminating Internet service to copyright infringers. It also requires service providers to notify copyright owners of potential infringement.

Copyright law emerged as a social construct created to secure rights to creative works and the economic regulation of their reproduction in a capitalist society. Its primary effect was the definition of borders, in the form of actions done on copyrighted material, to protect actors with an economic interest in commodifying works.

Copyright law was intended to protect creators, to prevent their exploitation by commercial distributors, and to stop plagiarism. However, its creation coincided with industrialisation, which influenced the creative industries with revolutionary inventions such as the machine press and phonograph. For instance, music, or more broadly sound, was decontextualised and made into "an immutable mobile" (Latour, 1986) when it was disconnected for the first time from local environments and oral cultures, thus becoming a fictitious commodity on the global market. This market for copyright produced adverse effects, as it is driving the commodification of art, while constraining creative production and limiting the scope of material that artists could legally borrow.

Members of the Frankfurt School showed the deterministic and threatening influence of the market on the creative industries (Adorno and Horkheimer, 1979), and their findings have resonated in studies on copyright. The commodification of art has always been controversial, and copyright provided a frame for the trade in cultural works (Boldrin and Levine, 2002; 2008). The sociological debate produced a range of arguments on the outcomes of art commodification, for example showing how the market influences the type and quality of artistic goods (Griswold, 1981). A major result of these enquiries has been the assertion of the deterministic nature of law and regulations shaping cultural expressions. For instance, Dowd's (2003) study takes on a small number of works that demonstrate the socioeconomic functions of copyright by showing how the expiry of sound recording technology patents brought the new genre of soul music.

Today's creative industries are dominated by powerful actors that solidified their activity through copyright. Their development is tied to the commodification of intellectual property, which led to shifts in legal regulations of global copyright law and furthered the amount of power held by copyright holders at the cost of creators (Boyle, 2004; Graber and Nenova, 2008). This development favoured powerful intermediaries, whose business models relied on marketisation and speculation of copyright (Fredriksson, 2014; McLeod and DiCola, 2011; Scherzinger, 2014). Since the early 20th century, major corporations have controlled the global music market (Negus, 1998; Rayna and Struikova, 2009) and generated profits through the slow industrialisation of popular music and the standardisation of music products (Firth 2001; Hirsch, 1972). As a result, the creative industry has become globalised and more homogenous than ever, and major music labels became key actors by influencing the kind of cultural goods produced and shaping intellectual protection policy. These processes were theorised as a part of the process of capitalist accumulation (Coriat and Weinstein, 2012; Fligstein, 1990) and regulated by market logic (Griswold, 1981). As a result, significant efforts have contributed to either loosening copyright or adopting new strategies (e.g., Maier, 2002).

2   Creative Industries' Crisis in the Digital Era

The academic literature has placed increasing emphasis on the discrepancy between regulations and the directions of cultural production. Several arguments underscored the legal system's inability to prevent unauthorised use and reuse of cultural products (Marshall, 2005; McLeod and DiCola, 2011). At their heart is the popularisation of home recording equipment, which since the late 1960s, has transformed the ways in which music is consumed and produced (Lopes, 1992). Collage-like production techniques became available to anyone with a recording system. This development raised problematic applications of copyright, for example with home bootlegging and copying music (Marshall, 2004; 2005). Consequently, creators have changed their ways of production, adopting new remixed techniques that relied on other works protected by copyright (Rodgers, 2003), bringing out sample-based musical genres such as dip-hop or drum and bass. As this usage needed to be authorised for commercial circulation, composition has been accompanied with legal negotiations, which constrained artistic production (McLeod and DiCola, 2011).

This resulted in a growing resistance. The underground music scene emerged and practices such as bootlegging have been identified as movements against powerful copyright holders and driven by "people locating their experiences and their selves against the commodification of popular music" (Neumann and Simpson 1997, p. 323). As Marshall shows, even though these underground practices clearly conflicted with copyright, they were not necessarily harmful to the music industry (Marshall, 2004). The resistance was met with strong counteractions from music labels and royalty collecting societies, preventing copying without authorisation, for instance by developing DRM technologies to control the use, modification, and distribution of copyrighted works (Sinha, Machando and Sellman, 2010).

These tensions have only grown with digitalisation, as new digital formats and sharing platforms burst onto the scene (Berry, 2008; Juris, 2005; Tkacz, 2014). Changes occurred in the way music is stored and consumed with the development of easily transferable digital formats such as MP3 (Haring, 2000) and digital distribution channels (Hardy, 2012), such as iTunes or Spotify. With broadband internet, copying and sharing music became even simpler (Kretschmer et al., 2001). The creation of peer-to-peer sharing technology has also challenged copyright protection (Alexander, 2002; Cooper and Harrison, 2001; Jones and Lenhart, 2004; Ku, 2002). The literature on this intersection of technology and copyright has concentrated on the implications of digital distribution on industry practices, including copyright management (McCourt and Burkart, 2003, Styven, 2007), changing consumption habits (Molteni and Ordanini, 2003), or emerging business models (Fox, 2004, Vaccaro and Cohn, 2004). Studies have emphasised both the extensive success and power of major labels in the industry (Kretschmer et al., 2001; Young and Collins, 2010) and the increasing power of small music labels (Furgason, 2009). Research has also theorised on digital commodities (Poster, 2004) or explained the influence of digitalisation on the generation of economic value (Oberholzer-Gee and Strumpf, 2007). In many ways, studies of internet piracy understand it as a political movement aimed at challenging the existing copyright institutions and restoring more democratic ways of private consumption of music (Hann, 2007).

Sampled music has played a central role in depicting the paradoxes of creative industry and copyright. The literature considers sampled music a key example of tensions arising from proprietary rights regimes and the tensions caused by the dynamic in creative industries. Sampling is a widely used technique of music production based on taking a portion of sound recording (or 'sample') and reusing it as an element of a new composition. Sampling occurs either by using analogue methods, such as cutting magnetic tape or combining music played from vinyl records; or using digital technology and tools, such as audio workstations or drum machines. Since the 1970s, sampling has changed the way music has been created, when DJs transformed the record player from a technology of musical consumption to one of musical production. Later, technology supported the development of digital samplers that permitted compiling tens of samples into a single music track (McLeod and DiCola, 2011). The literature usually refers to sampled music to show the widening discrepancy between regulations and the direction of cultural production. Several theories underscore the legal system's inability to prevent unauthorised use and reuse of cultural products in connection with the increasing mobility of sound and recording technology (Marshall, 2005; McLeod and DiCola, 2011). In fact, all works relying on samples need to be authorised for the purpose of commercial circulation. This process of 'sample-clearing' is usually based on complicated and time-consuming legal negotiations between music labels.

Sampling conflicts with a model of distribution established by actors within the traditional copyright regime. For instance, in American law, the precedent for interpreting sampling was set by *Bridgeport Music, Inc. v. Dimension Films*, in which the court ruled that any form of sampling of a sound recording constituted an infringement (Lloyd, 2014; Webber, 2007). At the centre of music distribution is a global market for a variety of cultural commodities, which includes sales of physical records, music in digital format, performance rights or usage of music in the entertainment industries. The main actors of this market, the major record labels, operate as complex publishing companies that coordinate the production, distribution, marketing, promotion, and enforcement of copyright for recordings and music videos. It is estimated that three major record labels – Universal Music Group, Sony Music and Warner Music Group – hold 60 per cent of the world music market, thereby exerting significant control over the recording, distribution, and promotion of music albums and possessing the financial resources to gain access to a large customer base (Wintel, 2017). At the same time, thousands of minor labels concentrate in niche segments or collaborate with major labels to distribute commodities. These smaller labels are limited by the lack of resources to reach mass audiences (Bhattacharjee et al., 2007; Spellman 2006). All music labels are intermediaries between music producers and the market. They both market commodities and work with manufacturers, distributors and retailers of physical copies. Additionally, as part of the distribution, most music markets have national institutions known as collecting societies, which represent copyright holders to license copyrighted works, sanction usage, and collect royalties as part of compulsory licensing or individual licences negotiated on behalf of its members.

As of 2017, digital music accounts for 50 per cent of global recorded music revenues, while physical copies add up to only 34 per cent (IFPI, 2017). This gives significant power to digital music distributors and their models of sharing revenue with labels. The new systems of digital music distribution, such as streaming services and music platforms, have been identified as responses of the industry, which increase music mobility (Marshall, 2015). They came in the shadow of a major crisis in physical music distribution, which started in the late 1990s when digital sales were coupled with the development of easily transferable digital formats such as MP3 (Haring, 2000). At that time, due to the availability of broadband internet and peer-to-peer sharing technology, copying and sharing music became simple and accessible, thereby pushing consumer preferences in the direction of digital formats, but not yet giving them the tools to buy music legally (Alexander, 2002; Cooper and Harrison, 2001; Jones and Lenhart, 2004; Ku, 2002; Molteni and Ordanini, 2003). Digital distribution and streaming services offer a valuable alternative, and the growing digital mobility of music has shaped industry practices, including copyright management (McCourt and Burkart, 2003; Styven, 2007), audiences' consumption habits (Molteni and Ordanini, 2003), power shifts in the industry and the emergence of new business models (Fox, 2004; Vaccaro and Cohn, 2004), as well as digital distribution platforms, such as Spotify (Marshall, 2015). As a result, monopolised markets have undergone power shifts permitting the entry of new distributors and a stronger presence of independent music labels and self-publishing authors.

The popularisation of sampling-based music techniques, followed by easy access to production technology and equipment, and the digitalisation of music have combined to create a drive for new ways of coping with the production of sampled music that depends on access to sound and music available for reuse. In short, creators of music found that their re-mixes are unpublishable, because they depended on the music of others and were copyright-protected. Using any sample requires legal clearance, which has traditionally required prior permission from the copyright owners (McLeod and DiCola, 2011). A sample used in any composition infringes copyright in the music recording if it is a 'substantial part' of the original and is used without the necessary permissions. The sample is considered 'substantial' in terms of quality, not length. If it is recognisable as coming from the original piece of music or recording, then it should be regarded as 'substantial' and the necessary permissions should be obtained.

Sometimes artists coped with these problems by publishing "illegal", "underground" records. Examples are hip-hop mixtapes produced and circulated informally. The underground music scene has been an important part of the resistance to limitations. Creators pursued their activities without an interest in commercial distribution, focusing solely on the artistic shape of the final product (Marshall, 2004; Neumann and Simpson 1997). Later changes, brought on by the digital mobility of music, increased access to music and samples, but did not facilitate the process of sample clearing. Similar situations, most pronounced in the music markets, show that both producers and consumers facing traditional copyright have encountered difficulties publishing their work and authorising its sampling.

3   Opening Creative Industries: Creative Commons as a Remedy to Restrictiveness of Copyright

A significant response to the tensions in the domain of copyright has been the Creative Commons licensing framework by Creative Commons, an American non-profit founded by Lawrence Lessig, Hal Abelson, and Eric Eldred and in collaboration with the Center for the Public Domain. The organisation continues the work of the Open Content Project. Since 2001, Creative Commons has had the mission of facilitating free use, reuse and modification, of creative works. The set of licenses, issued by the organisation at no charge to the public, is intended to provide a simple, standardised way to maintain copyright while allowing certain uses specified in the chosen license. Creative Commons framework similarly to other open licenses is an add-on to copyright, not a replacement for it.

The Creative Commons framework has gained wide recognition and popularity and now serves multiple functions, not only stimulating freedom of exchange and re-usage of digital content but also facilitating the adoption and maintenance of digital art over time, for instance preventing the disappearance of content from the internet. While copyright law creates the default rule of "All Rights Reserved", making permission necessary for each use of a work, Creative Commons facilitates an environment in which "Some Rights Reserved" or even "No Rights Reserved" become the norm. Creative Commons has been built on similar principles to open-source software projects, such as the General Public License (GPL) initiative. They both "use copyright to authorize, rather than inhibit, copying, distribution, modification and reuse of software and other copyrighted works" (Dusollier, 2006: 274). All such projects share copyright's goal of increasing the supply and stock of knowledge and culture. These movements also serve a similar political function: to reshape the way in which works are licensed, created, modified, and distributed. In contrast to to the number of arguments that might emerge in discussions of the movements, they neither aim to abolish copyright or encourage the authors to relinquish their rights.

The idea behind the Creative Commons is to facilitate the licensing of creative works through simple licensing tools and based on "building 'a layer of reasonable copyright' on top of existing law" (Goss, 2007: 977). Replacing complicated permission procedures, frameworks such as Creative Commons would create an easy way for authors of copyrighted work to authorise its use. Instead of the classical, passive ways of one-way consumption of commercialised culture, Creative Commons gives a way of promoting access, collaboration and re-usage of work. The literature identifies several reasons why copyright owners release content using the Creative Commons license. Their scope is very broad and starts from institutional purposes (such as a public library granting access to historical manuscripts); social motivations such as altruism; ideology (for instance against policy of major music labels); but also could be based on a purely commercial strategy, such as promoting one's own work to launch a project or gain recognition (Elkin-Koren, 2006; Goss, 2007).

The CC framework contains six license types and two public domain tools. Once a license is applied to the content shared, the permissions granted to the content are irrevocable. However, in nearly all cases, the content made available by the author remains owned by the author, and the platform gains the rights to host it via the CC license (or via a separate license in the terms of service). Creative Commons underwent a significant evolution, now operating under the 4.0 licensing framework.

From the technical side, all Creative Commons licenses are based on three layers that contain the copyright, communicating it to several parties (Creative Commons, 2015). Firstly, the human-readable language (the Commons Deed), sets out the key aspects of the license in language that is universally intelligible, visible on each work's page and signalled through CC logotypes. Secondly, the legal language (the Legal Code), as developed by the lawyers from Creative Commons, is accessible through links redirecting to licensing pages of CC. Thirdly, machine-readable language (the Digital Code or metadata), which enables search engines to identify the licensed work, will be used by plug-ins and that integrated with a transactional protocol for machine-to-machine transactions.

The main idea behind the license set is that a user sharing the work has no claim to remuneration in the form of royalties, so the work cannot be published using a music label, or sales of work as the CC framework in its basic version does not provide any kind of remuneration. The licenses also exclude exclusive deals as Creative Commons licenses are non-exclusive, thus permitting public users to freely exploit copyrighted work upon compliance with the licensing terms. This rule applies to two situations. Once a work has been exclusively licensed to a third party, such as a conventional publisher or a collective licensing society, the author can no longer place that work under a non-exclusive Creative Commons license. Once a work has been placed under a non-exclusive Creative Commons license, the author can no longer grant an exclusive license to anybody else. According to the license, users will not receive any support from Creative Commons if the rights they retained are violated. Creative Commons does not provide any means to vindicate the author's rights if the user of a work placed under a Creative Commons license violates any of the rights retained by the author, such as the right of name attribution and/or of commercial exploitation.

Moreover, once a Creative Commons license has been granted by the author, it cannot be revoked. The effect of the license will not expire until the end of the copyright term of protection. The copyright holder cannot stop the continuous use and exploitation of his/her work, as long as the use and exploitation does not violate the terms of the license. Hua (2014) specifies additional aspects of irrevocability:

> The copyright holder also cannot remove the licensed work from circulation, regardless of the type which can be either a copy of the individual or in a collection, or a copy of the derivative work created based on the original work. The choice of the copyright holder to place the same work under other non-conflicting Creative Commons licenses will not influence the effect of the current license in use.
>
> As CC-license content disseminates quickly, once Creative Commons licensed copies are made available, they will generate more licensed copies, and it will not be possible to call them back.

The framework provides a simple and fast way of publishing under standardised terms. The intended result of this standardisation is simplicity of selection of which rights to grant and which to retain, with regard to an individual work allows control of copyrights granted to work that is to be shared over the internet.

The CC framework also gives opportunity for specifying permissions relevant to audience usage. Publishing work under CC creates an instant authorisation of the permitted uses to any member of the public accessing the licensed work, which means that any user interested in the work will understand the license and be able to use it right away without seeking permission or contacting the author. Finally, the premise of Creative Commons is to generate an increased potential for broad distribution of the work: because of the ease of location of

Creative Commons, licensed works might reach a broader audience through certain search engines and platforms, allowing new types of co-operations or increasing an author's recognition.

Creative Commons, outlines the characteristics of six license types and one public domain dedications, that users can apply:

– Attribution CC BY

This first license allows others to distribute, remix, tweak, and build upon an artist's work, even commercially, as long as they credit the artist for the original creation. This is the most accommodating of licenses, besides the public domain tool (CC-0). It is recommended for the maximum dissemination and use of licensed materials.

– Attribution-ShareAlike CC BY-SA

This license lets others remix, tweak, and build upon work even for commercial purposes, as long as they credit an artist and license their new creations under identical terms. This license is often compared to "copyleft" free and open source software licenses. All new works based on an artist's work will carry the same license, so any derivatives will also allow commercial use. This license is used by Wikipedia.

– Attribution-NoDerivs CC BY-ND

This license allows for redistribution, commercial and non-commercial, as long as it is passed along unchanged and in whole, with credit to the author.

– Attribution-NonCommercial CC BY-NC

This license lets others remix, tweak, and build upon a work non-commercially, and although their new works must also acknowledge the author and be non-commercial, they do not have to license their derivative works on the same terms.

– Attribution-NonCommercial-ShareAlike CC BY-NC-SA

This license lets others remix, tweak, and build upon a work non-commercially, as long as they credit the author and license their new creations under identical terms.

– Attribution-NonCommercial-NoDerivs CC BY-NC-ND

This license is the most restrictive of Creative Commons' six main licenses, only allowing others to download an author's works and share them with others as long as they credit the author, but they cannot change them in any way or use them commercially.

Creative Commons framework distinguishes the commercial from the non-commercial use of work. The three last-listed licenses are limited to non-commercial reuse. These types contain the clause in the contract (Section 2b-3):

– To the extent possible, the Licensor waives any right to collect royalties from You for the exercise of the Licensed Rights, whether directly or through a collecting society under any voluntary or waivable statutory or compulsory licensing scheme. In all other cases the Licensor expressly reserves any right to collect such royalties, including when the Licensed Material is used other than for NonCommercial purposes.

Even though the licenses do not give permission for commercial reuse, they do not exclude it, leaving a space of negotiation to the copyright holder. It means that obtaining a permit for commercial reuse is possible, however only upon agreement (and not through the CC license). In this case, negotiations, bargaining and settling an agreement are on a case-by-case basis.

None of the six licenses require securing any type of permission for non-commercial activities, meaning that a person wishing to reuse the content does not need to seek permission and therefore does not need assistance of intermediaries (Russi, 2011). This function produces an often-emphasised argument that Creative Commons has the power of counterbalancing emerging distribution mechanisms in the audio industry, including illegal distribution in the digital economy through channels such as P2P file sharing and facilitating new ways of producing music, such as sampling (Troutt, 2009). All Creative Commons licenses permit non-commercial reuse, defined in the Creative Commons legal code as:
– Not primarily intended for or directed towards commercial advantage or monetary compensation. For purposes of this Public License, the exchange of the Licensed Material for other material subject to Copyright and Similar Rights by digital file-sharing or similar means is NonCommercial provided there is no payment of monetary compensation in connection with the exchange.

This clause (and lack of specifying clauses for commercial reuse) signifies that a user needs to understand that commercial reuse excluded in this clause includes situations such as sharing a song on YouTube.com with YouTube's advertising campaign; mixing a song with video and using it in a commercial television campaign; or using it as a background music in a shop.

The licensing can be characterised by three main actions that the licensing regulates, and that are sanctioned by traditional copyright. At the heart of the CC framework is attribution. All CC licenses mention this condition. A user is required to attribute audio works either by mentioning them in a recording, or by displaying the information on the page where a piece is shared. Some platforms establish their conventions of attribution, where mentioning the author of a work is facilitated by the functionality of the platform. Besides human-readable attributions, there are several ways of making machine-readable attributions for the web. For audio files, such as MP3 or OGG, XMP-embedded metadata is often used. If, for instance, a user ingests a new remix of sounds, it would be highly desired if the attribution was automatised and the authors could be informed of re-usage and be given the possibility of accepting and/or changing license permissions after a request. The automatisation of this process could take place on multiple levels, from integrating attribution with the user's account to automatising attribution in plug-ins.

Another part that is of utmost importance in this form of licensing is the way in which users reuse content. CC distinguishes redistribution from the creation of derivative works. Redistribution is in other words copying the work without any modification. Two CC licenses: Attribution-NonCommercial-NoDerivs (CC BY-NC-ND) and Attribution-NoDerivs (CC BY-ND) permit only redistribution of copyrighted material (with proper attribution), with no possibility of distribution of remixed or transformed material. This means that users are not allowed to do significant modification or altering. Creating derivative works, which might be new sounds that include, modify or remix other sounds is permitted by the four other licenses that permit creation of derivative works: CC BY, CC BY-SA, CC BY-NC, CC BY-NC-SA. A derivative work is any new work based on an existing creation, such as a soundtrack created from using drum and piano samples and applying reverb and pitch processing. US law (17 U.S.C. § 106 (2)) defines a derivative work as:

> A work based upon one or more preexisting works, such as a translation, musical arrangement, dramatization, fictionalization, motion picture version, sound recording, ... or any other form in which a work may be recast, transformed, or adapted. A work consisting of editorial revisions, annotations, elaborations, or other modifications, which as a whole, represent an original work of authorship.

Stated simply, a derivative work uses content from existing copyrighted material to create a new and distinguishable finished product. The broad language of this exemplary statute gives the judicial system the flexibility to determine on a case-by-case basis whether or not a work should be categorised as derivative. In this subsection we concentrate on creation of commercial derivatives and the reuse of unmodified content for commercial purposes. Additionally, uploading a derivative work requires choices regarding licensing of work. Even though the matter might be simple with pieces that involve only a few samples, this situation might become complicated

in musical pieces that use an extensive number of sound effects. This situation requires verification of all sound samples and the search for pieces that might be under licenses prohibiting derivative works or commercial use.
– CC0 1.0 Universal (CC0 1.0) Public Domain Dedication

Additionally, users can waive all their copyright and related rights in their works to the fullest extent allowed by law, by using the "CC0" license that releases the work to the public with no restrictions or limitations. While copyright law creates the default rule of "All Rights Reserved", making permission necessary for each and every use of a work, Creative Commons facilitates an environment in which "Some Rights Reserved" or Public Domain relies on the rule of "No Rights Reserved".

4 Creative Commons: Alternative Production and Distribution in Sound Industry

In some legal contexts, CC activity is excluded from the mainstream market, imposing limitations on the creators. This was most visible in Europe, where royalty-collecting societies and powerful copyright intermediaries, such as major record labels, often have a monopoly on representing signed artists and limiting their decision-making on their work, such as extending control over future creations and activity and preventing them from leaving that group of artists (Rochelandet, 2013). Since sharing works using CC might undermine that control, collecting societies openly opposed the use of Creative Commons by the signed artists (Communia Association, 2021). In Europe, there have been efforts to normalise the use of Creative Commons, including formal EU-level obligation of collecting societies to allow their members to decide with what licence to release their works (EU Directive 2014/26/EU). The result of this legislation has been opening of societies to CC, but to the creators interviewed here, the approach of collecting societies remains incompatible with CC.

Even despite the tensions between traditional institutions and intermediaries, the Creative Commons framework has been remarkably successful. As a result, many industries chose CC as their dominating license, for instance academic works, with increasing pressure for open access publishing, have witnessed exponential growth of reliance on the Creative Commons license. In the Creative Industries, CC has led to the creation of platforms allowing for sharing CC-licensed content and placed pressure on traditional providers to open themselves to this licensing. Many of the providers were large platforms, catering to users who wanted to share their work in a domain such as photography, music, text and sound. The idea of these platforms was based on allowing users to upload third-party content, and if so, based on which Creative Commons licenses. This model has been quite successful, usually adopting a set of CC-licenses and generating a dynamic in which users gained awareness of the different licenses. The result has been a large growth of content which became readily accessible, including through mainstream search engines, like Yahoo!, which permitted searching content using a filter of Creative Commons license. As a result, the broad adoption provoked greater availability of content and exposition of the authors. Content hosting pages, such as Flickr hosting photography, at the same time became repositories of creative production components, providing an alternative to commercial stock libraries and other sources. Similarly, the biggest video hosting platform YouTube, provides a possibility of sharing and searching for CC content. This process has provoked a change, facilitating access to content and generating a new type of market following a structure different from that of the traditional creative industries.

Similarly, sound and music industries have adopted creative commons licensing. The platforms that were created contained sound pieces separated from traditional intermediaries and labels. A table with summary of websites, content types and license selections is provided below (Table 2). Even though some of these websites have either changed their business model or adopted alternative strategies, the table lists licensing associated with activity of the site when it was operated on the Creative Commons License. Some of these websites no longer exist.

These platforms have received extensive recognition and specialised in different types of content. Bandcamp is a home for independent publishing of records by music bands; CC-mixter allows for collaboration in music composition, Europeana Sound contains archival sound of public institutions, FreeSound contains sound effects and Musical Sound, and SoundCloud contains musical and non-musical sound. Some of these pages, as their business model evolved, have abandoned CC in their move to own or proprietary licensing (Soundcloud or Jamendo).

This book concentrates on FreeSound which as of 2021 comprises 483,213 sounds (FreeSound, 2021a). There have been more than 171 million downloads from the site. In 2020 alone, its users published 46,441 sounds corresponding to 772 hours of audio recording, and wrote 22 thousand messages, 1.1 thousand forum posts and made 65 thousand sound comments (FreeSound, 2021a). The portal opened on April 5, 2005 and was established by the Music Technology Group at Universitat Pompeu Fabra. The site has academic roots, and in its early stages it was intended to allow sound sharing by users, and to encourage the academic study of sound processing. The site initially addressed a diverse community of sound designers, recordists and musicians, who shared

TABLE 2 Creative commons license application on major sound and music platforms

Platform	Content type	CC-licenses
Bandcamp	Music	CC-BY, CC-ND, CC-BY-NC-SA, CC-BY-NC-ND
CC-Mixter	Music	All 6 CC variants + CC0
European Sound	Archival sound	All 6 CC variants + CC0 + non-CC licenses
Free Music Archive	Music	All 6 CC variants + CC0
Freesound	Music samples, sound effects, field-recordings	CC0, CC-BY, CC-BY-NC
Internet Archive	Music, auditions, concerts	All CC variants + CC0 + non-CC licenses
Jamendo	Music	All CC variants + non-CC0 (changed to closed licensing)
Magnatune	Music samples	CC-BY-NC-SA
Soundcloud	Music, music samples, audiobooks	All CC variants + non-CC licenses (changed to closed licensing)

and circulate their content. The site has a significant role for different communities, and engages in different cultural practices, such as field recordings (Stanisz, 2018). The site is still run by an academic team, funded through donations and academic funding. The site is non-profit and had never sold advertising. The Music Technology Group uses the site for multiple academic projects. FreeSound was a central party in the Horizon 2020 project (Audiocommons.org) and provided a platform for discussion and experimentation for a generation of students working on plug-ins and interesting programmes.

The next pages will examine the adoption the Creative Commons and the use of peer-to-peer production in the sound industry. The literature has discussed the political economy of peer production, observing that this mode of production does not play a central role in the capitalist economy. It means that participants in this production cannot use peer production to support their social reproduction, instead, using it as a source of meaning and value (Kostakis and Bauwens, 2021). There are scenarios in which peer production can outcompete its capitalist alternative, such as a proprietary, commercial platform, but the role of commons-based peer production is rather different and steeped in the spirit of digital value and commoning. Some findings assert that peer production leads to the generation of digital commons, which by providing "mutual aid, care, trust conviviality and the common-wealth" (Birkbine, 2021, p. 41) counterbalances the hyperaccumulation by powerful digital companies (Huws, 2014). The movement aimed at the generation of digital commons has been tied to the idea of alternative circulation and valuation.

In the next chapters, I reflect on the significance and procedures of the model of peer-production in the sound industry. The findings will reveal how cc's legal structure supports a distinctive organisation of labour, based on commoning performed through sharing and sourcing of sound pieces. Even though exchange value and content markets are identified as crucial elements of this process, its function is tied to the undiscovered use-value, which might be unveiled and valorised by other users in the process of commoning. In the growing debate on digital labour, my interpretation of commoning labour process helps to highlight labour relations, production processes, products and their relationships to capital accumulation. In each of the chapters I rate the relevance of my empirical findings by situating them in the literature on openness.

CHAPTER 4

Creative Commons

Peer-Production and the Quest for Networked Value

> I am doing this because I can't see any value in the content that I share. And I know that it has good quality, and can be useful for someone. But simply, I will never use it and I am really hoping that it will be useful for somebody else.
>
> a user of FreeSound

∴

What is the model of production? What is the approach to distribution of the creative commons? How is it different from the traditional proprietary model? How do creators perceive the content that they release?

In this chapter I consider the model of peer production and the key mechanisms guiding commoning in the sound industry: search for value for content and activation of value. I call this "networked value". I show how finding a use for content attracts users to release their content using Creative Commons licensing. In the next pages, I concentrate on the ways in which creators approach maximising the use value, arguing that the key aspect of this process has three mechanisms: building works' (and creators') identity by relying on self-categorisation of their creations; usage of FreeSound's social dynamics, such as participating in scenes specialising in specific types of sound; and responding to requests or challenges posted on the platform's forum. At the same time the key process enhancing the quest for networked value is sound annotation, based on assigning descriptions and categories to sound and presumably, making the content easy to find through online search mechanisms. I argue that the search for use value is closely tied to annotation and to specific models of understanding sound, enhanced by social activities of users.

Sound shared on FreeSound does not have a universal origin and represents an enormous variety of productions. Even though there is little commonality in the type of content and in the way in which content is produced, creators share a vision of participation in the site: the possibility of exposing and discovering the use value of their content. This manifests on several levels, usually

© MIŁOSZ MISZCZYŃSKI, 2022 | DOI:10.1163/9789004504240_006

in connection to strong identity and beliefs in their content and the FreeSound audience. The search for use value is manifested in attempts to make a digital object usable or valuable for another user, as well as for the commons. In the interviews, the most experienced users explained how their approach to production underwent an evolution towards maximising the use value of content. One of the most popular users on the platform commented on how his production changed from processing and editing sound to making it available for other users to process as needed. Experienced users discuss the learning process involved in sound production, from making sound very crisp, to leaving it raw, for other users to clean up and process. FreeSound's user survey reported that sample processing takes longer than looking for and making samples. The following passage exemplifies the evolution of users in connection to sample production.

> At the very beginning I recorded a lot and then filtered. Right now, after several years of experience, I basically publish everything I record, because I filter before recording. You know? I then mix on the fly. Basically I do field recordings. And I know my equipment, I know what is going to come out of the recording. So right now I don't have a lot of you know, editing or trimming or whatever. And there is a little thing that maybe, well, is a bit obsessive of me, but at the very beginning I used to upload samples no matter how long or short they were. Right now I don't upload anything that is shorter than 30, 60 seconds. I need some time, some length in the sample to allow the content to explain itself, because a too short sample is not enough. I'm not too, very fond of extremely long samples, 10 minutes or 30 minutes. I respect people doing this kind of work, but it's not my style. I am mostly on 1 minute, 5 minutes. On occasions, if I find a particularly pristine or pure environment, I record as much as I can because it's unique. But unfortunately, this doesn't happen very often. You know, there are cars and maybe a plane passing and a lot of disturbances. But if I find a very, very pristine environment, I try to record a very, very long sample. (R1)[1]

Rather than processing content, their productions acquire distinctive qualities by being recorded in unique locations and through reliance on high-quality recording equipment and the skills of the owners.

---

1 R1 refers to respondent comments (see FreeSound, 2019). Hereafter, references imply respondent numbers (e.g., "23" is R23, etc.).

The data shows that creators rely on a variety of production techniques, from field recording through remix and synthetic sound. After their work is created and saved on a local drive the creators make the decision to share it. The content often emerges from projects that are salaried and unrelated to commoning, for instance during commercial recording sessions and homemade (e.g., for the purpose of testing equipment settings). In the earlier instance, content is made during music and sound production, which requires a significant portion of material that is experimental and rarely shared by the creator. This production process generates a surplus of content on creators' hard drives, which normally gets erased or backed up and never sees daylight. Quite often this content is technically quite advanced; some of it is ready for use but its creators often struggle with project cancellations, changes in client preferences or simply decide that their product is unsuitable for the work that they are editing. This continuous surplus generated in the process of creative work is only occasionally distributed. However, to some creators this surplus is an important source of new work and creative activity – the production and sharing of samples that are intended for other users to use in other contexts over which the original creators have no control. The second instance is homemade content, which is often made using top-quality equipment; this group of users is more inclined to produce with the clear intention of uploading it to FreeSound but also while engaging in hobby projects, such as field recordings or experimenting at home.

The process of sharing tends to follow the sequence displayed in Figure 1. Following the production of work, creators evaluate their sound piece and focus on sound annotation. Uploading is the final step, preceded by a set of decisions relevant to the ways in which creators produce content and work with sound.

This chapter describes the key mechanisms that guide peer-production, based on creators' attempts to expose content to use value extraction. User interaction on FreeSound is generally mediated only by content. Creators and users of content have few opportunities to engage with each other and rarely interact outside of posting comments on the content (unless seeking permissions for commercial use). The result of this limited encounter is a strong emphasis on exposing the content through description, which is treated as a pillar of commoning activity, next to licensing and production. In addition,

FIGURE 1   Steps prior to sound upload on FreeSound

production places emphasis on making content easy to use and transform, and usually is not intended to generate a finished, heterogenous product for a specific audience or client, as often happens in the music industry. The next section presents the role of metadata and the basic mechanisms of platform functionality for extraction of use value.

1 Metadata and Content Annotation

Sound production does not end when the sound file is saved. A critical element of the process of creating sound is annotation, based on generating a description in the form of tags. In computer science, annotation is usually regarded as part of the ontology of media, containing a human- and computer- readable description of any digital object, known as metadata. There are different standards for the generation of technological ontologies, depending on the type of media, industry, and user base. The outcome of creating and adopting ontologies on the platform side, and annotating sound by uploaders, is to allow other users to find content to be categorised, but also found by users using keywords. A key skill in annotation is knowledge of the convention, for example an awareness of categories that describe sound; or knowledge of sound-related language expressions typical of particular sound groups, often represented by specific scenes. Simply put, users have different strategies of annotation, and they see it as a search-facilitating mechanism that links their work to the user. There is a strong connection between well-annotated sound and the popularity of users' content. More experienced users have emphasised the importance of metadata in making their content visible to search engines.

> I was always a big believer in providing rich meta data and always try to tag as richly as possible. And I don't know what changes there have been to the uploaders' sense, but I know when I did, I believe I was allowed to like have, I think it was like copying tags between all sounds. So I don't feel there was ever a point where I was lazy about that. So my method was kind of just you know, go through location tags, describe the fidelity of the sound, that sort of thing. But I think rich meta data is very important (4).

> Usually I try to think about the fact that if I had to find a sound, what would I have typed it in a search engine to find it. And it seems to me to be the best method to enter metadata. And of course I am not a fan of making 80 tags to one sound, because it really fades away after that. Well, I don't know the priorities of such search engines. It is different in

> every stock and also different in Free Sound. Well, sometimes it takes into account the description of the sound, which is also searchable, the title of the sound, and sometimes just tags somewhere. So that's what hit it would be. (23)

Like these users, creators with professional expertise in sound design have shown more determination in annotation. Somme creators save lists of tags in a separate file and when uploading they copy-paste it, adapting it to a specific sound. This process reflects the behind-the-scenes operation and the contents of these files often contain descriptors of the scene.

In one interview, a creator compared tagging to working with clients. According to him, in both processes he translates different expectations of sound into specific wording. For that reason, exposure to numerous tagging systems and clients creates a better awareness of annotation mechanisms.

> The part of my job with clients is trying to decide for what they are asking for versus what I'm trying to create. And sometimes it's a total mismatch. You know, sometimes you've got clients that you know, their vocabulary is just completely different than what I'm used to. So I think with FreeSound there is a bit of that. Probably more so than the commercial libraries just because people are coming from such different backgrounds and don't have the same vocabulary as the professionals. But I mean, I have fun just kind of browsing and happening upon you know, accidents, which I think that's where a lot of creativity can come from. So that doesn't really bother me but I don't expect the meta data to be as precise as it is with one of the commercial libraries. (7)

He also emphasises that commercial libraries tend to be more thoroughly annotated and to adhere to certain standards of ontology. On the other hand, FreeSound users often tag using their intuition, changing their tagging strategies over time or tagging in their own way. Although tagging can be frustrating, users generally understand the logic behind it, without being being fully aware of the rules and dynamics of search engines.

> I went through phase of egregiously overtagging things. And several people complained. And so I kind of cut back after that. But the tagging is ... How do you tag the sound? It's like, do you tag the origin? Do you tag the technical details? Do you tag the qualities of sound? It's a bit of a grey area. And I was doing all these ridiculous tags and it's a bit stupid of me, really. So I think, I would say that I'm trying to keep it mostly

> to the descriptions of the sound rather than anything else. Like I don't know, I can't really think of an example. But you tag a drum kit differently than you do a forest ambience, right? (...) My initial thought was to make things easier to find, but I soon realized that I was actually making it more vague for searching. So I think tags need to be specific, more than fewer better tags is definitely the way to go. More vague tags, that's what I was getting wrong. (5)

The task of generating a description in such a format is often considered highly uncreative. Especially less experienced or more content-focused users who were interviewed cited several problems with tagging content. One of the key issues that they mentioned is translating sound into words and making this distinction clear to other users. As one of the creators explained:

> So for example, here I'm looking at some other ones I've uploaded. What's 'chirp' versus what's a 'chime'. And I would try to be consistent about it. Or the other one that I used a lot, here's another one: 'flatter'. I thought 'hey, what ... Flatter, should it always be one kind of sound?' versus 'rustle'. Rustle versus flattering versus other things like I would tend to try to be consistent about it. And I was pretty satisfied with it. (49)

This user was particularly concerned with distinguishing the categories of sound and using them consistently. While his use of particular descriptors would have been consistent, the consistency across the page was limited, because all of them were user-generated and did not seem to be any form of standardisation. In addition, some specific phrases and language conventions, might overlap across scenes or not be easy to understand by users from other cultural contexts or who have a limited knowledge of English. A user reflects on this problem.

> I didn't plan on tagging my sounds well to make them popular because I didn't know how it [FreeSound's sound engine] works. Well, now I do it more or less like I do in stocks. And it is possible that there are some who achieve good results, such that their sound always pops up somewhere above, and it certainly is, but I think that I cannot learn it without living in an English-speaking country. Although it is also known that it is not only English-speaking countries that download these sounds, so you can follow the trail of thinking that if an Indian will look for sound in English and what he will write. Well, I don't think he'll write some complicated words that he doesn't know, but rather the simplest. Well, looking

at commercial stocks, which countries the customers come from, 2/3 are the United States, after all, because it is popular there, and in European countries, downloading sounds from stocks is less popular. (23)

This user links annotation to the main group of customers on other pages. While FreeSound has a good representation of speakers who do not have English as their primary language, English is the common platform, and in many cases specific phrasing is familiar to them, even if, as one of the users put it, "their English is far from fluent" (66).

Annotation is linked to the convention of peer-production in commons. Wrong annotation or the failure to accurately annotate a sound are indicative of a lack of belonging to the community. Such content cannot be found, and sends warning signals. Since most producers are also consumers, when looking for content, they might have difficulties with some of the annotations.

> Some people just have zero idea on how to tag content or describe it properly. This is how it never gets found (...). There are some attempts to describe stuff better but this is a lot of community work, we would have to be very rigid about it. I probably would move to banning users, but that contradicts the whole idea of commonality
>
> dance music producer, USA 3

Among these problems is the cataloguing data, which might not be properly described. All of the creators interviewed for this project agreed that finding the right material is one of the biggest challenges. In response to this difficulty, platforms include descriptions of the sound files and develop technologies that filter sound and include CC-licensed media in popular search engines. For sound files, objects not only represent sound, but also include a description created by the authors. Filtering scripts creates tags that help to catalogue the objects and the community has a significant part in this cataloguing. Lack of moderation also signifies problems with the standardisation of content. Some communities on platforms sharing CC content support better descriptions of the sound.

One of the most highly regarded ways annotation, inscribed in the architecture of FreeSound, is the geotagging of sound. FreeSound offers the unique possibility of connecting the geographic location (geotag) with an uploaded sound. Unlike a written format, sound is expressed through a description by geographical coordinates, which contains more objective information about the sound than the verbal description does. This feature allows the identification of sounds specific to different geographies, even displaying the location on a map on the sound's page. In this way a user can find sound that emanates from a specific place; a geotag usually carries the promise of being representative of that place.

> For example, I recorded a brilliant crowd ambience at the place downtown here, called Bud's On Broadway. And there was a band playing there. We were asked to record the feed of the mixer. So we did. So between takes, I got this crowd ambience. So I geotagged it, brilliant, great fun. And there have been a few other ones that I've done, I don't really remember but yes, that's awesome. Like if you're doing a forest ambience, show where it is. Why not? That's great. A waterfall or a fountain or I don't know, volcanos, they make a lot of sound. Why not? This is a great idea. It's like your photographs, just you can geotag your photographs. I used to love Panoramio before Google shut it down. That was a great service.

This tag also makes it possible to search the map, for instance to find sounds recorded in specific places of interest, geographies or natural environments.

Despite a consensus that metadata is of key importance to access sound, many users reported that they had trouble maintaining the motivation to generate descriptions, often postponing or abandoning the idea of uploading. Many users share sound as a result of their creative activity and for them annotation is an unnecessary duty. One user shared his experience.

> There was definitely a point where I had uploaded I think like 150 sounds and just let them sit in the like, you know, pre, like the unsubmitted form for like maybe 3 or 4 years. It was like 'alright, I never did that. I should go back and do that'. And I think I did that in 2018, the sounds that I had uploaded I think in 2015 and just never got around to writing descriptions for. [laugh] But like, yes, you know, I think like you know, that process is as smooth as it could be, but like you know, I don't know how it would necessarily be refined. (50)

Another user volunteered to upload sound in his sound design class.

> We made foley, every single sound. I mean, we had to run really good mics and so like, at the whole end of the project, the club, the teachers were like 'well, that's just for practice, I'm going to delete this, all the stuff' and I said 'wait, hang on, like these are really high quality, really good sounds. Does everyone is OK to put it on Freesound?'. (...) So I copied all the files and I like edited them, but I think it took me like a year or two, to actually

upload them, because it was, let me look at this pack. (...) It's 128 sounds. For the most part, I think the descriptions are all the same but I did go through and tag everything, based on the type of sound and I gave it a descriptive name which it did not have originally. (...) I think it probably took me at least a year to prepare all this meta data. Like not actually, like the entire time I was like working on it, but I was, I would put out this pack, put the meta data on. And I'm glad that I eventually got to it because actually yes, people have seem to like this, although it's, this is one of those things, I feel like this pack has like a lot better sounds than like some of the other things, but like most of them maybe have like around 100 to 400 downloads, whereas that crashes like 30 000 downloads (47)

The production did not take as long as annotating and uploading the sound. Even though he admits that this task was not difficult, finding the motivation and time to process the description was a deterrent.

The relationship between tagging and described scenes is crucial. Specific niches produce the terminology and semantic conventions that drive specific ontologies. However, metadata also plays an important role.

2 Sound Scenes and Their Cross-Fertilisation

Even though sound on FreeSound is not divided or categorised by the platform; there is a strict division of sound based on content and of users based on activity. This dynamic is similar to the organisation of musical scenes. Users informally think about their participation in FreeSound in terms of their own imaginaries of independent "scenes": communities sharing an aesthetic, modes of production or types of instruments used for musical activity. Scenes on FreeSound contain a range of non-musical sound types. What might at first seem a disorganised collection of sound, often has a certain logic, even though the usual way of accessing and browsing is only through the search bar. The interviews with creators have shown that most creators have a strong sense of belonging to scenes, understood by them as smaller communities of anonymous users, sharing similar ways of production and an understanding of sound quality and standards.

The user activity within scenes is understood as containing content that shares similar characteristics, often reflected in the form of metadata, and uploading content of similar qualities and descriptions. Naturally, members of different scenes use similar keywords that connect the works. But over time, users who represent specific scenes, for instance nature sounds, become aware of other users' activity as they explore content that follows their interest. While the construction of the platform presents many opportunities for relationship building (users communicate through comments on works' page), the content-centred orientation integrates creators and separates them from content that might not be of interest to them. FreeSound's construction is much different from the typical dynamic of thematic forum pages, where users interact and build long-standing relationships through posts. Interactions most valued by users do not stem from verbal communication but are mediated by content that is continuously downloaded, re-created and uploaded. The dynamics of scenes help users to understand, predict and find content suitable for certain projects. The descriptions of activity of interviewed core users have outlined some of the scenes; however, given the multitude of content, it is by no means extensive.

A significant difference with sound forums and FreeSound is that there are no strict rules or expectations of what type of sound should be uploaded on the platform. The highest volume of sound is taken up by sound effects. This general field however hosts several scenes: nature sounds (birds, animals, weather), location sounds, containing sound recorded in particular geographies, machine and mechanical sounds and effects suitable for multimedia (film, cartoons and anime), components for music production (loops, samples, instruments), soundscapes. These scenes attract individual users who have different ideas about content production and usage but also share standards, equipment and modes of production. Users often remark on the importance of a scene in their development. Scene experiences motivate them to upgrade equipment, change the microphone setup or learning recording techniques or simply acting as a source of inspiration, given the variety and quality of other users' sounds. Many of the interviewed core users have been remarkably successful in their FreeSound niches, often having the largest number of uploads in their niche. The high popularity of their sound sometimes translates to their reputation, to the degree that some of my respondents defined FreeSound's niches using nicknames of users who specialize in specific types of sound. For example, an author of nature sounds has more than 40 thousand uploaded sounds and his nickname is often synonymous with nature sound effects.

Like music scenes, these groupings are not strictly defined, and some users do not share the same understanding of the scenes or a clear sense of belonging. This, however, allows for the population and mixing of content from different niches, which might originate in field recordings but be processed into loops that will eventually become the basis for a musical production. A user opines on the cross-fertilization of niches on FreeSound.

> I would say on the surface we can talk about general sound categories, as we have nature and you can now distinguish nature in the forest, water

or whatever. It just works. And the same with instruments. You have the instrumental, you have the electronic way that you have a lot of electronic descriptions, what kind of synthesisers and so on. And you have stylistic descriptions of a certain style, of ambient or whatever you will find. So the surface and the day-to-day use of sound description, I think it works well. (…) But it is not very precise in sound. You can have someone working in a workshop as a hammer, making beats and then you have a kind of drum, which comes from an instrument. And then you have some electronic hammering of sounds, which would create a kind of class, category of sound with strong beats, right? Technically you could make an analysis and you could find some sounds together. The question is who would look for is and what is the reason that you look for it. And then it becomes even more interesting. Let me take as a composer, which is looking for this, I would like to have this kind of repetition but in acceleration or in going up and down in the rhythm. (…) I'm looking for the sounds that really match my imagination, it's better when I do it by myself. So you know, this is probably a conflict how to open it up completely, categorisation of sounds.

The interviewee mentions three important elements. Firstly, sound is difficult to describe, given its scope and the number of possibilities in recreating and processing it. As the respondent shows, the sound of a hammer might be transformed into the sound of a drum. This means that sound might be processed in ways that are different from the initially planned applications. Secondly, sound is hard to categorise. While creators might know the conventions of placing tagging a sound, or making it appealing to particular scenes, it does not exclude sound to be useful (and popular) among the other scenes. For instance, certain noises (e.g., clock mechanism), might be useful as a musical loop. Thirdly, this is reflected in the ways in which users work with metadata and choose different tags for their sound, where a seemingly unrelated sound (for instance, an industrial hammer), can become an instrument useful for musical composition.

3 Growing Commons: Providing Representation for Underrepresented Sound

Working within scenes is only one way of participating in FreeSound. For several users, enriching the platform with underrepresented sound matters more than participation in scenes. These users often see FreeSound as a commoning project, treating it as a public good, and trying to contribute to its quality and diversity of content. A similar perception of projects is typical of large operating systems and has been extensively reported on in the literature. But for Freesound, expansion is not based on adding lines of code, but on identifying niches of content. For users, this is a creative challenge and an opportunity. The following passage illustrates that strategy.

> In terms of the logic behind uploading what I uploaded, I felt that there was a lot of percussion hits already available on FreeSound and that I couldn't possibly add any more. There is a lot of bass kicks, a lot of snare drums, rimshots, whatever. So I focused my efforts more on things that would not be rarely found. So it would be like a little piano piece or a little intro piece to a video or some vocal whatever. So something that I didn't think was already done, is how I decided to go about it. (30)

Among interviewed creators, few admitted that their main strategy of uploading content is based on intentionally and actively seeking niches to fill in missing content. During the interviews, creators who worked exclusively in this way mentioned the extensive research done to identify these gaps on the platform. They argued that the resulting content has translated to popular uploads, unlike earlier content that was uploaded with no prior research. Other creators worked on niche identification when failing to find sound for their projects. In both instances the niche is leading to a creative concept of sound. A motivation of filling in that niche often precedes the upload and production of sound.

> I think I was targeting it a little bit because I noticed that nowadays, you know, sound editing seems to be a lot more prevalent and everything like that. So I've noticed some more obscure anime sound effects come to life but back in 2008 there was nothing on the Internet. No Wilhelm scream, no really important sounds. So for me it's part of like preservation, part of it, of like representing a niche. So yes, there was definitely a noticing like 'hey, there is some sounds here that are missing'. And I noticed how early content on Freesound remains popular because it captures niches. And that's why I felt like I wanted to upload content like that because, again, it filled a niche. But anyway, I noticed that there wasn't that many useful sounds for media that I was working on. So that's why I wanted there were screams and punches and anime sounds and sci-fi sounds because what I find fun to do them and love it, but yet again there was that void needed to be filled. (39)

This awareness of niches allows content to stand out. In contrast to underrepresented sound, there are specific types of sound, for example weather sounds, that number in the thousands. While there exists such wealth, niches have the potential to make the sound library of FreeSound more comprehensive. The approach to content generation based on capturing niches is closely tied to the role of use value in commoning. While users look for potential gaps (that can be of interest to other users), they adopt a careful strategy of maximizing the use value of their content.

Niche identification is also supported by the architecture of the platform. One of the most active sections of the forum is "Requests". It is an important facilitator of sourcing niches and engaging the community. In this section users ask for a recording, for instance describing what they need and how they plan to use it. The requests bring them to the attention of the community, potentially expanding the range of content on the site. A request is often responded to with numerous examples of a sound that meets the criteria in the description. In this way a niche not only gets populated with a single sound but also with numerous instances of the different variations on the same theme. Requests' public presence and visibility also promote uploaded sound as both sound and the creators are visible to the readers of the thread.

> A lot of my work came because of the sample request. So in a sense, some of it from my projects, some of it, because I just wanted to make something on FreeSound and some of it because people on FreeSound wanted me to make it or at least, you know, make something so that they could see if they wanted it or not. (30)

> So I've never considered myself a contributor for recorded sounds. And since I think that recorded sound should be the priority for FreeSound, because synthesised sounds can be synthesised by anyone with the same equipment I have, so I always saw that as sort of diluting, cluttering the FreeSound database with things that are not strictly needed as a unique recorded sound, maybe. But since there have been many requests for synthetic sounds over the forums, in that case I've tried to fulfil the requests by these users, plus I contributed sounds also for some of the dares, which were in two steps, where we were supposed to first contribute some sounds and then make compositions with those sounds and these drove parts of my contribution on the sound part of FreeSound. (11)

As these passages show, responses to requests use the work of creators who see an expressed interest in particular types of sound and then share their work or fulfil the request. Responses to requests are treated either as an exercise of creativity and a production challenge or an opportunity to upload a work. The interviewees who regularly make and fill in these requests insist that responding to requests and working on sounds for other users satisfies their creative impulse:

> I would occasionally go to the request forum, [and participate] if a user specifically requested some sound and nobody had done it yet. I would sometimes try to do something I could do, like sometimes it's easy, like I just saw examples like 'I need a sound of the slinky like being played with'. And I was like 'I have a slinky here in my room. I can just record that for you and post it, so I did that'. And I had a little list of requests that I wanted to do. I think for the most part, I wasn't seeking out and make a bunch of sounds just for FreeSound. I would more kind of be making sounds for some other project and then I would just put them up as a by-product and see on FreeSound. There is no like plan to making stuff. It was kind of incidental. (42)

This creator describes how his creative process has responded to niches while he produced sound samples in his professional life. Another creator, who was active in responding to requests shows how his content increased in popularity because he responded to the niches: "the requests forum gave me an impulse to work on sound that I uploaded there. And to my surprise some of these sounds became the most popular. Like really popular, way more than my regular sound". This creator compares the sound that he made without observing the niches and mentions that sound generated in response to requests was more popular than his other sound. The mechanics of requests and niche filling authors has enhanced the availability of sound available on FreeSound.

> So, two of my most downloaded pieces, one was the hunting sequence in G-sharp or A-flat or something like that. That was actually a sample request and that was the one that got downloaded about I don't know, 4000, 5000, 6000 times or something (...) I'm assuming that people found them useful if they downloaded it. (...) So I would say that other people have benefited also other people's requests. (...) It's so cool, now I think of it. Nobody uploaded it in the past and that's why they requested it when they needed it. So we uploaded it. And it is like a signal that everybody wants it. (30)

This user describes the mechanism of enriching the library: identification through niche description often exposes sound searched for by other users.

While the requests section is initiated by individual users who need a certain sound, there is another forum for sourcing sound and engaging community. The "Dares" section is an alternative way of seeking use value. The forum follows a simple principle: in different cycles it provides users with a task or a challenge that requires production and uploading of a particular sound. As the key animator of Dares, user AlienXXX offers the following description:

> What are dares? A Dare is a little friendly competition. Once a month I post a dare with a new theme. The theme and the rules change, so each dare is different, but essentially I ask people to create a composition using sounds from Freesound and following certain rules. Musical compositions or 'sound-scenes' are acceptable as entries for the dare. After submissions close, there is a voting period and then the winners are announced. At the moment there are no prizes, it is just for the fun of participating.
> Forum, https://freesound.org/forum/dare-the-community/32186/, accessed 15.01.2021

AlienXXX provides reasons for participating in dares, and the benefits of participation, including improvement of skills in audio production and opportunities for interaction.

> Why should I join? Because it's fun! It is also a chance to improve your music skills by trying some challenges and the chance to get organized by working with restrictions and a deadline. Also you will get feedback from others about your music, which is a great way to improve. Because you have to vote, you will also be listening to the pieces submitted by others and doing some 'critical listening', which is another great way to improve your music making skills. Even better, if you like what you hear on someone else's piece you can ask questions and often they will tell you exactly how they did it – learning from others is another great way to improve your music skills. Finally ... it is a chance to meet and interact with other people who mostly share similar interests to you.
> Forum, https://freesound.org/forum/dare-the-community/32186/, accessed 15.01.2021

The dares were usually very unconventional, and their main idea was to encourage the community to experiment with new forms of production and samples. Some tasks required reliance on FreeSound's database, for example a specific sample or a pack of sounds. Selected tasks posted in the dares section included: making a song from a sample, recording 10 beatbox samples, composing a retro song, processing existing samples (cut and trim), creating a soundtrack for sleeping or uploading sound recorded on tapes. Unlike the requests forum, dares follow more formalised rules, and new dares were posted only by users who were in charge of them. The rules of dares are as follows.

1. The dare is open to any FreeSounder. Limited to one entry per participant.
2. In all dares you are required to:
   2.1. use sounds from FreeSound (the details of what sounds you can and can't use will be specific to each dare)
   2.2. Post in the DARE thread with a brief description of your work, a link to the submission file (mp3 or ogg) list of attributions (i.e., list all sounds you have used from FreeSound).
   2.3. Unless specifically stated in the THEME rules, you cannot use your own FreeSound samples.
   2.4. Collaboration entries are accepted, but you still can only enter one piece.
3. If there are enough entrants, a voting will take place at the end of the DARE. The voting will be open for 1 week.
   3.1. All entrants to the dare must vote or will be disqualified.
   3.2. You are not allowed to vote for yourself. This means your own single entry or a collaboration entry that you are part of.
   3.3. FreeSounders who have not submitted an entry are allowed to vote IF they have been FreeSound members for longer than 3 months and have either uploaded 10 sounds to the FreeSound database OR have 10 posts in the forums.
   3.4. If there are enough entrants for this dare I will post the voting rules on the voting thread

   Source: https://freesound.org/forum/dare-the-community/17259/ (accessed 10.09.2020)

The construction of dares concentrates on the dynamic of creative competition, including audience voting.

In descriptions of dares, interviewees described their forms of participation. They identified dares as an interesting and well-regarded element of the platform. One of the earliest and most memorable dares was a request from a mother whose two children had been diagnosed with autism. She asked the administrator for a short piece illustrating how her children experienced sound so that she could bring it to a meeting with their teachers. She said, "[the child] hears all sounds on the same sound level, so the buzzing of a fly, a zipper, a clicking pen, streetworkers outside the school, teacher in the next class, scribbling of a pen, (...) and the teachers voice all sound equally loud and all compete for the first prize, so to say" (https://freesound.org/forum/dare-the-community/1133/, accessed 15.01.2021). The dare was to compose a piece using the library of FreeSound. The users took the task very seriously: "we really worked on that and that was a joint effort to make that recording. And that was wonderful, really" (57). The users who participated on that piece commented on the powerful message of this dare and saw it as valuable work for a good cause.

Stories of dares returned in the interviews and users have explained how dares made them look for unconventional solutions or experiment with recording. For example, "I remember the one where we had to record the sound of shower in the shower, something like that. And I made my roommate a bit surprised at what I was doing there [laugh], but it was great. Those were great challenges" (57). Dares are a good example of community animation, involving both participants and the audience, observing and discussing entries in the competition. Dares have attracted several users who are regular participants. However, interviews with core users have shown some interest in following dares and even though many of the interviewees have never responded to one, they were familiar with some of the tasks and enjoyed following the work of users. While participation in dares has not been very high, the community is aware of them. One user identified dares as the element of the platform that kept him engaged:

> And here is what made me stick around FreeSound. (...) I would regularly participate [in dares] and a lot of those would evolve around, you know, using the sounds that were available on FreeSound. And that just got me looking at the different sounds and there came a certain point when I was like 'oh, I think I can contribute also'. So I started either recording raw sounds or making little tiny piano pieces than uploading them. And one of the moist popular pieces on there is the hunting sequence which I uploaded. That's been like 10 years. And then, so that's how I got involved. (30)

For this user, who had been a passive use of the platform, seeing the potential use value of the content, even if discussed or used only in dares, proved so valuable that he began uploading regularly. Another user credits dares with integrating into the community.

> I did a couple [of dares]. And then I was kind of embarrassed by the quality of stuff that I would put together compared to some of the things,

so I didn't do it very long time. And I think last year I kind of got back into that. (...) There was a challenge, there was a user who had been on the site for a long time (...), who uploaded quality sound samples, weird stuff, drum samples and that sort of thing. And there was a challenge to produce you know, just a song based on those samples. I really enjoyed that. (59)

The valuable part of dares was the use of collaboration and new techniques. The last passage, from AlienXXX, the animator of dares, describes the automated conversion of digital pictures into digital sound.

People were using image processing software to process sounds and then uploading those sounds back into FreeSound. Most of them sounded pretty horrible but it was just the fun of it. (...) There is a lot of people doing crazy stuff and they were interested in that and that kept going for a while and it kept going several times and people posted links to software, some of which I still have, which allowed to convert images. That was actually software designed to do that. So you had an image and it would convert the intensity of the pixel, it would convert into intensity of sounds. And depending on where that pixel was on the vertical scale, it would give it a frequency. (18)

This description provides valuable information into innovation and discovery. Dares are a fundamental illustration of the maker dynamic: a synchronised, organised process of recreation and increasing site's content. Their experiences showed that dares generated extensive interest in how content is processed and how it occurs. They found the remixing process as well as observation of how content finds unconventional applications as a very interesting and important demonstration of how and where the works can end up.

4   Sharing Building Blocks: On a Search for Use Value of Content

These strategies stimulated creators to share and participate in the platform based on group dynamics of scenes, responses to requests or competition within dares, where use value emerges as a response to predicted and interpreted needs. The last form of this involvement is embedded in lack of aspiration to reveal the use value prior to the upload. This form of sharing, based on the assumption that use value remains to be discovered by the mediation of the platform persists through the platform and its strength values, depending on the approach of the creator, the experience, and the type of sound.

Core users have argued that they often share their work in progress. There is no single reason but often it could be content that creators abandoned in their creative work; perhaps they rejected it, or did not find it useful for their closed projects. For example, creators professionally working in sound design often take a practical approach, knowing that their content is of professional quality but won't be used by them because their projects have commenced. One user shared his experience working as a composer in the indie game sector. His projects were often cancelled, leaving him with large quantities of high-quality sound that someone else might find useful.

> I think there will be people there that will spend three weeks composing the perfect drum loop and then they will upload that. There are people there that will write it themselves and say 'oh, I've got these leftovers from a musical project or musical project that never came to be'. Sometimes they even say 'oh, I was making some music for a game project, whatever, that what cancelled, all these loops and samples'. Here you go. Maybe it's of use for someone. So I think some people will obsess about it and upload the perfect drown and the perfect drum loop and something like that. Other people will have things that they've spent time on and in the end they didn't use for whatever reason and they will say 'if somebody want to use this, here you go, it's free to use'. Some people will be rehearsing, playing their guitar and they will upload that with mistakes and everything. (...) As I have done the same thing, I've sometimes created a very nice loop and I upload that and I have uploaded half-way through a project and making the music for some, it could be for a competition, it could be just for my own use. And I'm 2 or 3 weeks into it, and I haven't finished but I have made some good parts and I will upload that and I will say 'ok, if somebody wants to use this bass loop, here you go, you can use it'. So you get all kinds of things.

This user also outlines different ways in which creators upload their work to FreeSound. In his description, there is a variety of ways in which sound is produced and ends up on FreeSound. In the final part of the passage, he mentions that his unfinished sound has "some good parts" and sees its potential usefulness for others. This description provides a good instance of the ongoing process of matching sound that otherwise would not be used with new, unknown future projects. This idea, along with the concept of making the content public, resonates among all users.

The release of content is sometimes explained in terms of heritage. Some interviewees hoped that their sound will be carried into the future and emphasised the role that they attributed to FreeSound: an online sound archive accessible to the public. One of the most prominent creators' comments on the perception of his activity on FreeSound.

> Well, that's part of my ... Well, you know, I'm getting old and I have no kids. And somehow I decided that I have something to give to future people. (...) You know, there is sort of a collective knowledge. I have seen very rare plants in Spain and I have seen animals. I listened to very peculiar sounds and somehow it's my memory and I want to share it. That's why. (...) I have rejected money, always. I have had some offers but I always said 'please, donate some bucks to FreeSound. I don't want'. Not because I think that money is something dirty or whatever, but because I don't want to mix things. It's something I want to be pure. You know, because, for the sake of humankind somehow, not my personal interest. (1)

This creator sees his activity as a way of preserving his broad experience of nature and hopes that the content will be useful for future generations. He notes that his interest has never been guided by commercial desires. Instead, he propagates the platform and records and uploads new sound.

Similar treatment of content in terms of heritage takes place among users who for different reasons stopped working professionally in sound design. For the interviewed creators, retirement was cited as the main reason. One of the users had severe health problems that forced his retirement. Because of high volume of sound that he accumulated over the years, he decided to share it on FreeSound so that it "can be used in other projects by people who never met me" (13). A respondent who changed industries said, "I'm kind of turning the page in my life right now. So I guess that I uploaded like a whole tonne of stuff a year or two ago because I was down with it. I was like 'OK, well this is the best what I have', you know, what I have I guess the right to, whatever, you know, that isn't someone else's stuff and just kind of, to give it because I wanted to help" (34). This interviewee associates uploading with helping other users. Knowing the unique qualities of their sound, this group of creators stresses the fact that the usage of content by other people gives them the satisfaction of seeing their content carried over to other projects. The fact that new contexts can emerge from their work is meaningful to them, even if they never know where the content ends up.

Another strong commitment to opening archives emerged from less professionalised users who shared their entire sound archive on the site. One interviewee stated that all of his content was exclusive to FreeSound. He did not store this content on his computer's hard drive, and insisted that FreeSound is a better platform for browsing and using content. Another user's hobby was feeding FreeSound with sound that he created and making it useful for others. He said, "[The sounds] were created especially for FreeSound. Everything I posted, was created especially and in most of the cases, uniquely for FreeSound. I don't use those sounds anywhere else. But on the few exceptions, but it's very minimal. Everything which I posted was created especially for FreeSound. 99,9%, let's say." (71). This form of participation aimed at making content usable for as broad an audience as possible.

In one interview, a creator compared his sample sharing to recycling sounds from other users. He mentions how he tries to help potential reusers to apply his content to their creative projects by making the sample loop and making it available for use by users who are less familiar with sound editing.

> Yes, sure, because it's quite, there is so much. I think that's a bit of everything. I'm possibly guilty of, I've got few tracks that I didn't do anything with but you know? I'll share them because they might be useful for someone else. I would say more in the positive way of like recycling, not maybe dumping, not in the negative way, but I think there is a bit of that going on. It's like 'well, I didn't use that, I didn't work out, I put it out there'. But also sometimes it's like 'Oh, this is really cool, I like this. This might be really useful'. So I will definitely put just this and then I'll even strip it down and I'll get the different versions to give someone else the ability and I'll loop it correctly and I'll even shake the file and clip it and I'll make it so easy for even a beginner to put it to a door, to start looping and learning themselves, giving kind of more creative flexibility. Sometimes it might be an element of a sound, of a loop that you want, but they don't the high-end, they just want it to be or something like that for example. So not all the time, but sometimes I would strip them out. When you find stuff like that, you know that people actually participated and they are actually helpful and they want ...

This users' engagement in making the content suitable for the audience is not rare. Quite often users mention that the content that they share often meets the requirements that they have for sound that they look for. For example, one of the users shared a preference to unedited, uncleared sample because this is his preference: [I don't need any edits, I prefer to clean the sound myself than somebody do it for me. With editing I am particular, so I try to make it of good quality but not edited].

Lastly, another kind of building block is by users with only casual involvement in the platform. For instance, users might have a bit of free time or be attracted to the platform for a short time, such as a weekend uploading specific types of sound. Sometimes these users do irregular sound drops, for instance after a couple of years. A characteristic of this form of sharing is users uploading a huge number of sounds in a short time. For example:

> When I was at the peak of my uploading behaviour, I was uploading what I found relevant and what I felt was lacking in quality that was on the platform. So yes, uploading things in a very quiet studio for instance, it was like anechoic chamber even, screaming there to have only the purest screams. This is going like to a crazy extent in some cases, not all of them, not by far all of them. (45)

This user uploaded sounds only after completing his experiments. One of the best examples is content uploaded by the user acdbicycle whose content to date remains highly used and rated. This creator created all of the uploaded sounds on his account in one day. He spent another day tagging and uploading them. After this one-time upload he never added anything, yet his one-day session and the choice of sounds that he recorded has given his account high ratings. He is among the creators of most popular sounds. Years later his content is still downloaded and used. In the interview he commented that for he had forgotten all about his commoning episode and was surprised to learn that his content and profile have remained so popular.

∴

These findings are an instance of how creators engage in authorship that is oriented to the future extraction of use value. It introduces the mechanisms of commoning in the sound industry, by describing the activity of uploaders and identifying the mechanism of sharing as part of the processes of value of activation. This approach to production gives a perspective on an alternative model of creative activity, based on engaging in peer-production that makes production components for other users. It relies both on the accessibility of production components and the increasing proximity between creators with the same ideal of collaboration. Creative production has traditionally involved interaction and collaboration, both among creators (e.g., McAndrew and Everett, 2015), and between creators and their audiences (Toynbee, 2016). With adoption of the commons-based model of production, there has been a significant change in the way in which collaboration occurs. Direct contacts have been replaced with content-mediated relations based on uploading data and usage of the content. Creators' attention has moved to enhancing the quality of the content, for instance ensuring their technical properties, as well as contents' metadata – the digital description of the file that allows for finding it by other users. While computer technology provides the means of labour, playing a key role in the composition process and permitting content exchange, it is an open license that establishes a legal framework for this type of connectedness, sanctioning the use, development and consumption of content. Unlike platforms that host content, open licensing is a new type of networked creative production as material is not tied to any webpage and can be legally distributed across platforms (as long as the original source and author are displayed). I have also discussed community efforts, aimed at work inside the commons, such as niche identification and filling, as well as operating inside small fractions of the commons, which I describe as following the similar mechanisms to the musical scenes. I also show a community mechanism, based on posting challenges to the community, which often serve as an opportunity to experiment with and expand the commons. All these actions that improve the quality of sound file and metadata aim at activating the value of creations, which is itself activated in the network established within the commons.

The next chapter will examine the content user side, studying the dynamics behind creative production that activate the use value of content deposited to FreeSound.

CHAPTER 5

The Art of Commoning and Content in Context

What happens to sounds after they are shared? How is sound function freed from traditional intermediation using the Creative Commons license? Knowing license properties, how do users breathe new life into works? In this chapter I show how copyleft licensing mediates openness and fosters an alternative route of artistic innovation. Sharing work using Creative Commons license assigns unique qualities to content, which places the works into a new context. This occurs through processing procedures, such as remixing, which are directed at transformation of objects. This transformation, as I show, often relies on specificity and uniqueness of existing works that obtain new qualities while being processed. This form of use value activation, even though usually occurring without direct, personal communication is an alternative form of collaboration, mediated by content. In this aspect of creative activity, Creative Commons provides a legal framework and sanctions the rules between the creator and the user of content. On the following pages, I summarise the approach of creators who rely on the CC-license to achieve their professional or artistic goals.

> My track is never finished; it is an ongoing process. I love to see how my sound gets people involved and let them work on the material however they wish. The possibility of sharing content opens new possibilities, and the horizon is endless. I make [drum] loops and this is really good stuff for people to use. Most upload it back, which is great, or even make full tracks. I think this is where music should be heading, that kind of openness I feel and this is where my work belongs.
>
>   music producer and DJ, Israel

Protecting cultural objects with CC connects works under the same license and opens them up to new types of reconfigurations and modifications. The next pages explore how open licensing generates a unique property in objects of creative production. Creative Commons make "networked objects": not only shared and used based on the license, but also often understood by users as a combination of original content placed in relation to other objects from the network. The networking of objects is mediated by license, allowing for deposition of value that other users can activate.

Recent literature notes the vital role of collaboration in artistic production. For instance, working with other artists is an important determinant of artistic success (McAndrew and Everett, 2015) and an intrinsic element in the process of music production (Thompson et al., 2016; Umney and Krestos, 2014). This chapter enriches the arguments brought by this literature by exemplifying the ways in which creative production relies on collaborative relations enabled by cc's legal framework. Unlike other online forms of sound composition, such as remote online improvisation, cc-licensed, networked objects are a distinct (and not widely addressed) form of collaboration, as the actions of the collaborators are not synchronised and there are no limits on the number and type of collaborating artists. Networked objects are elements of proprietary interrelations based on the disconnection of creative works from a single artist that are inserted into sharing platforms, therefore becoming a potential element of a future work for other authors. In that domain the co-creation occurs in a democratic and autonomous manner giving the potentially involved parties time, freedom and autonomy, solely through the object. Objects thus are a medium of collaboration, decontextualised, positioned against and combined with other objects as well as opened to unregulated, asynchronous collaboration. Users often forget about their uploads, or even their FreeSound accounts, making the content available but abandoned by and disconnected from the creator. The next sections show how the open licensing model affects the sharing and collaboration by extending collaborative relationships beyond interpersonal ones.

Yet, understanding object as a mediator of collaborative relationship needs to be explained in the social context of production, similarly to other collaborative mechanisms of creative production. Easy access to objects might transform the form and nature of the creative process and the way an author perceives his/her own position, both in relations to other authors and the whole network. Set permissions allow to specify how the work might be used without an author's confirmation. This process of distribution propels the development of objects that are at the disposal of every author by requiring that all new works using open material be shared under an open license. This is why this chapter accents the process of placing work in the context, to get a full picture of the process of use value activation typical to sound production. A respondent explains his relationship to Creative Commons.

> It is about the actual commitment to music. (…) not only is there so much data to be reused and within reach [under cc license – mm] but also, in particular, all that data has an address that you can use [for instance to contact the original author]. Most owners of that data are open to

collaboration, open to making new arrangements, adjustments, and look forward to new projects. But even if they don't respond, their data is there to be used. This is what makes it worth it all. (...) Before [the CC] it was all impossible. All sound needed to be cleared or produced from scratch.

Sound engineer, UK

The respondent compares his involvement with Creative Commons to the use of content protected by traditional copyright. He cites several benefits of openness, such as the ability to contact the original creator and the possibility of going beyond the object. In his interpretation, sound is "data", technology-driven production rather than an intimate creative activity typical of the creative work. A key aspect to explore in this chapter it to understand object operations and property relations.

At the same time, the quote indicates the model of production, aligned more with the distribution model within Creative Commons framework than with traditional copyright. This model is aligned with "maker movements" based on an individual's ability to be a creator, or in other words "a maker" (Dougherty and Conrad, 2016). The term "maker movement" was coined in 2005 and is tied to a variety of creations and hobbies, usually amateur and semi-professional. However, maker movements have recently become linked to innovation and technologies of production, such as 3d printing, microcontroller-based robotics or computer building (Georgiev et al., 2017; Papavlasopoulou et al., 2017). Developments of the maker movement also include physical venues, often co-sponsored by local governments, known as Makerspaces, Fab-labs (fabrication labs) or Hackerspaces, where makers can physically share tools, observe each other's work, have face-to-face discussions of their products, and find collaborators (Kafai et al., 2014). Makers apply the idea of openness to projects that vary in professionalisation (with domination of amateur makers), with a specific model of distribution, often non-commercial or based on gifting the final projects, and collaboration, based on seeking experience and production components (Dougherty and Conrad, 2016). At its heart is often the DIY, customised approach, often posed as resistance to manufacturing by commercial actors (Lindtner, 2015; Stangler and Maxwell, 2012). This model is parallel in the way FreeSound is organised and approaches creative production, allowing creators a pool of resources for their own projects and tools. This dynamic follows the principles of openness as digital content acts as a source for production components and often is a basis for new reconfigurations.

Objects mediate relationships between creators by constant repositioning. An important aspect of understanding collaboration is examining relations among objects. The literature has recognised that any type of remix work and collaboration is based on the establishment of relations between objects that are changed and repositioned. Participating in Creative Commons is an agreement with a specific form of reciprocity because the framework establishes a recognition pattern based on chipping the object with not only a classical property ownership license but also a machine-readable digital license. This signifies that objects with a CC license and their owners are easier to trace, also acquiring new qualities in the form of metadata. Applying any CC license to sound inputs a work into the system with the requirement that any resulting copies or adaptations are bound by the same licensing framework. This "viral" mechanism of reciprocity makes cultural creations undergo Luhmannian autopoiesis, based on continuous reproduction and progressive growth on the basis of existing material (Luhmann, 1990). New objects are either new or recreated. At the same time, citing authors is enforced and objects naturally become items of networked authorship, forming pyramidal property relations. This changes the positionality of the object from what it is under traditional copyright (Carruthers and Ariovich, 2004). The monitoring of relationships between authors establishes a re-usage pattern and learning how patterns co-exist. In the next paragraph, I depict the way that remix groups are established.

Content generates relationships among objects and the way they are reconfigured. Theorising this knowledge will make an important argument that the open licensing model has the power to transform the traditional linear value chain of media. Instead, the license establishes basis for a fully interconnected industry model that supports communication among stakeholders. This interconnectivity reflects how the original copyright owners are connected to both CC framework, their own work, and the network potential re-creators and all other types of industry actors thanks to the objects. The license thus not only asserts copyright properties of the object, but also uniquely communicates the creator's openness and readiness for virtual collaboration. In the classic copyright framework, artistic practice and license obligations play an oppositional role. Instead of creating barriers, open licensing is an integrating force.

This chapter considers the role of commoning practices in the generation of use value. The underlying assumption is that the network of objects is an important way of releasing undiscovered use value. In practice, it means that creative components, such as sound effects, are combined in new, unexpected contexts and projects. This chapter addresses this function of commoning within the three dimensions that intersect with this process that guides the search for use value. The first is the role of quality. While quality might be tied to the properties of equipment used in the production of sound and the experience of the creator, the interviews show that notions of quality remain highly subjective and reliant on the users' projects. As a result, objectively understood quality is secondary, giving way to highly subjective perception of content matching the project's context. The second, the decision to work on Creative Commons content is often tied to the philosophy of creative production. Like the maker movement, it rests on the principle of openness and assumes that diversity of content stimulates artistic experimentation. The diversity of sound types enables creators to come up with new solutions, styles and designs, often reflecting a range of production techniques, creator backgrounds, their industries and personal intentions tied to the final effect. The third, the open licensing of creative works normalises the relationship between building blocks and the creator who uses them. Traditional copyright has often regarded remix as a form of piracy, because production components, such as bits of songs or sounds sampled from movies, had to be authorised by the copyright owners, usually at a high price and through complicated legal procedures. By equipping objects with unique permissions, and tying them to the original creator, Creative Commons added important functions to content that was missing while disabled by traditional copyright. These three elements contribute to greater understanding of how content is placed into the context.

1   Technical Quality and Context

FreeSound is a platform of sound exchange. An important theme in interviews but also present in forums and in expert interviews is the technical quality of sound. Users and experts tend to understand quality as a set of variables relevant to recording parameters, low compression or lack of background noises. Naturally, a continuous discussion on quality poses a question of space for more amateur productions and their usefulness for sharing. A recurring theme in interviews with producers relying on sound from FreeSound was the argument against the techno-centric approach to sound; instead of a greater focus on content rather than the form of the sound to be reused. The following respondent, a professional sound designer, explains the role of quality.

> Yes, I've spent a lot of my professional life trying to demystify that quality myth a bit actually, because if you've got the unique sound that no one else has got it, it doesn't matter what you recorded or what microphone you've used. You know, there is a kind of saying 'the wrong microphone in the right place is better than the right microphone in the wrong place'. It's like, if you are the only person there returning, you know, recording the heist going down, that's the sound so it's going to get used, you know? So yes, I don't buy into all that tacky stuff. I've got a lot of very tacky stuff

but you know, if you've only got this when you, you know, when you're recording. And the real thing is happening in front of you, that's what you are going to record on rather than have nothing, but I would be saying that I wouldn't put anything up there myself that I didn't think was of usable quality for somebody else. And I did kind of, I think initially with FreeSound, sort of use it as a bit of a like storage space for myself. You know, when I'd organised my sounds and thought I might want that again, I need to know what that is, if I put it on FreeSound, then it's there (52).

She describes the importance of sound's uniqueness. She comments on the technical aspects of recorded and its potential value, arguing that equipment does not necessarily play a central role in production. She adds that high quality equipment and the way recording is realised should lead to better technical quality on FreeSound. Indeed, FreeSound's focal topics include discussions of recording technology, processing software and its different uses. Many posts offer advice on hardware purchases, pop filters and windscreens in addition to techniques of recording and the positioning this equipment. However, as this respondent shows, there is opposition to extensive attention to these matters.

Indeed, quality is often treated as an entry barrier. While the interviewed core users often have a professional or semi-professional background and are highly knowledgeable of technology, less experienced and newer users often seek their advice and help, trying to match the quality of sound that is popular. The respondent is not the only interviewee who diminishes the role of quality. Some interviewees reflected that interaction with FreeSound has helped them to learn and develop, and that quality does not equal popularity:

I guess that was one part of being the part of the FreeSound community was it motivated me to upgrade my equipment. So people tend to describe their recording chain which I often look at and so there is some events that I have gone to, that happen once a year that I like to record. And so, one of them was coming up, so I thought 'maybe that is the time to get some better recording equipment'. So that kind of motivated me to do that. And I upgraded it a couple of times. But as far as being able to say why things are highly rated or popular, I have given up trying to predict that. Because often something that I think should be popular and I'm pretty proud and it doesn't get hardly any attention. And other things that I don't think are worth listening to at all are very popular. So I think there is kind of different aspects of what make something go popular. (8)

This user describes how FreeSound helped him to learn more about other users' workflow and to develop better recording skills. This user reflects on his equipment upgrades but says that his predictions about the popularity of content and its relationship to quality have often been incorrect. Interviewees often remarked that even though they have libraries of high-quality sound, the most popular pieces are often recorded on the fly with a portable recorder. For example, "my most popular content is a howl of a wolf. It is just me pretending to do it. It became so popular at some point that it even became a ringtone on mobile phones. And I made it to test the mic; it is not even good quality" (71).

The assessment of quality varies by several dimensions, user backgrounds, needs and experience in sound editing.

> I tend to think of it as the upper echelon of what's being put up on the Internet, as far as sound recordings go. I mean, because it's not moderated in terms of quality, you know, there is a little quality control, but I think the users are savvy. I think most of the users that are on there, at least that I've encountered are well interested in some way in sound and have a genuine interest in it. And I think when you have a group of people that have that combined interest in one thing, in this case sound library comes out really good. (04)

This opinion states that FreeSound contains top-quality sound available for free. This user understands the problems with quality, mostly in terms of moderation. FreeSound has content moderators whose goal is not to screen sound for quality but to ensure that uploaded sound fits the requirements of content on the page. Other forms of moderation, such as the elimination of sound recorded with basic equipment (e.g., old mobile phone), do not take place.

The open and inclusive sound policy translates to a variety of content that requires filtering and abilities to comprehend the content. One interviewee had realised that some of the content is not acceptable. At the same time, he stressed that he values creativity and an unorthodox approach to sound production.

> I think that users create a higher bar and the sounds on FreeSound, I mean you come across occasional sounds that you are like: 'oh, come on, like really, that's not decent enough!'. But most of the time it's really impressive to see what sort of creativity comes out of people. They put a lot of work into their sounds. It makes you want to lift to your bar too. Again, it's not to say that there is not crap, but for the most part in my experience, I experienced really high levels of content of material there. I really do.

> It's one of the reasons I keep coming back to be honest because it's like a real, you know, that's a professional place to me. (53)

This user's knowledge of sound editing was growing with his involvement in FreeSound and how it translated into better and more specified content. The claim that the platform is "a professional place" is also interesting because this user often uses content from FreeSound in his work as a sound designer.

A similar view is shared by the next two respondents who work as professional sound designers and who have also used and contributed to commercial sound repositories.

> I've kind of learnt as I've gotten wiser as far as the film industry at large, and there are lots of different industries: film, YouTube, radio or podcast even. It's that I think there's a lot of sources for input. Like you look at big budget movies and you assume that Disney v-effects on a film are going to be perfect. Well, there is always little imperfections. Nothing is ever perfect. So I feel like it's not an issue with FreeSound's quality. I mean, obviously, you've got to pick and choose and some sounds are going to stand out more than others, but I don't think there is anything that stops, that holds, FreeSound back from being able to supply for those projects, those types of projects (4).

> For me, the most important idea behind any sound [refers to content on FreeSound] is that it should be useful. It may even be a sound of worse quality, or it may seem totally ugly and bad, but it needs to be useful. I was very surprised with some of the uses of my sounds [available] on FreeSound, because people sometimes wrote to me to tell what they used them for. There were funny stories. For example, once I got an invitation to the theatre in Berlin. They used my child's cry in a theatre play's soundtrack and invited me. And I was offered a ticket, but unfortunately I'm quite far and had no time. (23)

Both users emphasise that quality is less important than the potential usefulness of the sound. Interestingly, respondents found the new context of their content exciting. It is impossible to project the application of sound at the moment of upload. FreeSound's ability to match content with new context also encourages contributions.

However, FreeSound is not only a source of content. It is a source of transformation that supplements production based on in-house recording or reliance on sound packs and stock libraries. Instead, it allows the operation of content that often is not pristine in terms of quality but due to its diversity has a great potential to become a unique product. For example, the user below explains his development as a creator on FreeSound:

> You know, like what I'm willing to put out as a final product for me, has changed over my career, based on the amount of experience I have. Like things that I do now, I think would be much harder to do when I was younger and less experienced just because I didn't really know a) what was expected and b) what was possible. And you know, throughout my career I've tried to kind of push boundaries of quality and possibility. So I hope that the stuff I'm putting on now is of better quality than it was when I was less experienced. So I'm willing to tolerate, you know, some kind of rough edges. If like the underlying structure of the recording is useful. (7)

Interestingly, in his description this creator stresses his tolerance of sound with "rough edges". What is meant here is that the process of creative work in the sound domain based on FreeSound's content is usually quite far from being ready for use in a project. This means that the sound downloaded from the platform requires work to become suitable for the project that it will be used in. A similar understanding is shared in this passage:

> Some of my sounds may turn out like crap, but also I know, like I don't just release … so I've released bad-sounding sounds. But I also know how to go back and fix those sounds or improve for the future. And I would say the majority of the community is fine to work on the content. (…) I edit or change content to suit my needs or suit to what I think sounds good. It's not to say that it originally was bad, more it was not to my liking; it's just I have in the back of my head a little, I feel like there's a little more potential or a little insight sound, if that makes any sense, where nobody knows it's there and then once I play with it and mix it, mash it and stretch it out and then I'm just like 'oh, wow, that sounds really good and nobody would have known that was even there unless I actually did it'. So everything is very professional. It's just I like the thing that the sounds I make through editing and mixing is a little of a form. It takes practice, a lot of practice. (16)

This respondent can spot sounds that have the potential for use in his projects. The description of his creative process is based on revealing the hidden quality, activating the sound in the context. The other respondent expands upon this reasoning:

> Free content is good as long as you have skills to make it suit you. (...) I think there are two elements that make it [CC content] not for everyone: you have to know how to search and you have to spend some hours processing it to suit you. (...) Both are similar to using sound that's copyrighted, like from vinyl records, but with CC you have a much different situation. You don't go to music stores but rely on an online search and probably less than 20 per cent of sound is equivalent to professional sound library and ready to use.
>
> game music producer, UK (1)

Even though the creators are sometimes frustrated with the properties of sound at their disposal, they argue that no other source offers such a volume of sound that meets the requirements of their production. The interviewees seem to have an implicit belief in the potential use-value of their content and require a significant level of post-production for their composition needs. The respondent assumes that production based on sampling requires similar handling procedures to sampling from traditional works, but acquisition and selection depend on online access and the lack of professionally recorded content. Another aspect of the adaptation of content depends on professional software and production tools. Both the software and the terminology depend on the same principles as the traditional music industry. Several factors influence it; the creators often work in commercial studios and projects where they have access to the most advanced (and expensive) commercial software and equipment. Only two respondents who had no access to this software is unavailable because of its costs have commented on its technical functions but never mentioned making a conscious choice to abandon it.

Many creators therefore rely on FreeSound, instead of capturing their own sounds. Their decision is often incorporated into their workflow – they either don't have the time or the equipment to capture the sound. At the same time, they are reluctant to use commercial stock libraries, perhaps because of budget constraints. According to a British sound designer: "doing it yourself means that you have to fulfil another role and become a foley (...). But this is not the way to go about it, I prefer to make songs (...) but can't buy everything either" (music producer, UK 2). Other creators emphasise acquiring commercial content for production: "it is really hard if you want to go beyond mixtapes [refers to selling music] (hip-hop producer, USA 2)"; "it is not worth it to pay for stuff unless you have some certainty that you will get it back" (experimental music producer, Israel). As these opinions show, FreeSound fills an important niche, allowing creators to support the legal publication of their work, as opposed to publishing it unofficially and using unauthorised distribution methods.

The last aspect of FreeSound relevant to quality is its rating system. The FreeSound platform has a rating system, where users can assign stars to rank the quality of the content (1 star =bad, 5 stars=very good). Interviews with creators revealed that this system is often ignored or treated as a marginal source of information about content. Interviewed users have stated that this rating system is controversial because users' needs are different; for example, some users give few stars to the content that is good but is incorrectly annotated:

> They find something and they think from the title of from the description 'this is going to be exactly what I need', but then they listen to it and they realise 'this is crap, I can't use this'. Well, it may not be crap. It actually is useful for what it is. It's just not what they need at that time. So if they give it a low rating, then is that really a fair representation of how useful that sound is? Probably not. I don't know how to get round that. I mean, we've got to figure out a way to review or rate or critic sounds and to encourage that kind of community input to the existing database of sounds. Otherwise I just don't know. And I'm sure we'll never even get the majority of things to have like kind of review, but if at least people go looking for something and then they have to read it down, if they could take all of the things that they discard and I don't know, what would you do that would be fast, because that's not writing your review (26).

One result of these discrepancies is that core users do not often rely on the ranking, arguing that it neither reflects the quality of content, nor are there enough reviews of all sounds to make the review credible. Because needs differ and the content plays a different role in each project, the rating system is not central in general usage of the platform.

2 Openness and Artistic Experimentation

With digital technology, composition and music making depend on the integration of digital sources. Previously, the music production process had been changed by the broad popularisation of digital audio workstations (DAWs), a type of software that allows for processing and composition, control and storage, integrating digital sound samples stored on local hard drives into production. With time, users of DAWs have come to rely on digital sources that they have either purchased or downloaded. The result of the shifts allowed for the incorporation of new types of sounds and through popularisation and de-professionalisation of DAWs, making production of sound more accessible and transforming ideas on how music is made. As a result, composition was more frequently done on personal computers that depended on online libraries.

This process might be illustrated by one instance of applying sound from FreeSound for composition of music and sound effects for a game. The co-creator of *Minecraft* has always relied on content from FreeSound and for creative reasons has sustained it. Interestingly, the approach taken by the composer of the *Minecraft* soundtrack emphasises the creative approach that places content in context through experimentation. As C418 (real name Daniel Rosenfeld), emphasises on his home page:

> Here's my personal opinion on how to make music. Get all the free things you can find, just smash them into each other and have fun! All this stuff that costs money ultimately really doesn't matter if you're still learning the ropes of making music. It's WAY MORE IMPORTANT [emphasis original] that you know your stuff rather than how big your library is. There is NO point collecting a big database of stuff. Rather, learn with what you have already. And again, don't force yourself. Have fun making music! Ignore what everyone says!
>
> Source: https://c418.org/2017/01/26/what-does-daniel-use-to-make-music/ [accessed 08.08.2020]

This passage shows that context and artistic vision outweigh other elements, such as equipment, software or paid access to databases. While FreeSound policy does not permit musical sound, there is a high representation of instrument recordings, drum loops, riffs and jingles, making FreeSound an important resource for soundtrack composers and some of the core users specialise in music. At this point it is worthwhile to ask whether or not the use of sound on FreeSound is related to financial constraints that C418 and the team might have faced. Perhaps this was the case in the early stages of Minecraft's development, but given the game's commercial success, with sales topping $ 200 million, 125 million users playing the game each month, and Microsoft's purchase of Mojang, the maker of the game, for $2.5 billion in 2014, the composer clearly has great possibilities for both acquiring sound and using the libraries. However, the game not only still relies on the sound from freesound.org, but some of that sound is in public domain. On the game's official site, there is a list of attributions to the sound, and as of August 2020, there are an estimated 200 references to FreeSound's resources.

The pursuit of the use value of sounds provides a unique opportunity for observing how creators find and use content on FreeSound. Like other industries, licensed opening of sound carves new paths of delivering and working on compositions. Below two opinions emphasise the shaping of creative process by seeking appropriate sound and experimentation, with attention to why the author chose an alternative path of creation.

> I compare working with open content to dumpster diving. You need to look carefully and have a logic in looking; most of the stuff is bad, but you might find treasures, or you might just find stuff [refers to content] that might be sufficient for trying [refers to musical experimentation]. For some [creators] this is enough to start with.
> music producer, Belgium

> To me making music depends on luck and a good feeling. Sometimes the most unexpected sample might turn out really amazing. (...) This is why I like to work with open [CC] content, there is so much of it that it allows for discoveries; I am fed up with [the custom of other producers of] taking samples from classical music or jazz bands. I look for trippy vibes, like unconventional; I recently got some amazing historic sounds recorded decades ago from some museum site [obtained with CC license], and I cut them into a really good set (...) After cutting I had it exported as part of my catalogue and have it on DAW [refers to part of library of sounds used for composition].
> music producer, Germany (1)

The first respondent, a producer of electronic music and a studio engineer, compares browsing to dumpster diving. The metaphor emphasises the fact that hosting platforms contain a hodgepodge of type and quality, which makes it difficult to find pieces appropriate for music production. At the same time, he calls his creative process "trying", a form of prototyping of his compositions. The sound on FreeSound supports and stimulates his creative process. The second respondent, a member of a rap collective specialising in the creation of drum loops, emphasises the breadth of CC content and the matter of luck not only in looking for appropriate pieces but also in sample-based composition itself. He also contrasts standard sources of samples, taken from jazz or classical music, with the unconventional sources, such as historical recordings available via public domain CC license. He then describes how this material is processed and put in his library of sounds that he later uses for composition. Both quotes identify the potential contexts of re-usage of CC content, mentioning musical experiments and discoveries. To both respondents, digital commoning is an alternative way to meet production needs.

Among the users of FreeSound a common idea of participating in the platform often comes from the site's diversity of sound, much different from any commercial sound pack or online stock library. As one of the respondents stated: "it does not have profit to make so it represents all types of sound" (71), referring to non-existing pressure on the type of content, typical to stock libraries, which the respondent interpreted as beneficial for creators. Other respondents concurred, valuing less standardised content that offers a different creative experience. One of the respondents remarked:

> I don't actually have many of those, you know, CDs with sound effects on, but I can remember, probably at the time I was coming to FreeSound, there was like a kind of famous set of CDs that the BBC did. And it got to the point where you could recognise when people had used those because you know, there was this joke about the BBC seagull, you know, everyone used the same thing whereas when you go on FreeSound, you've got stuff from all over the world. That's unique, you know? It's not coming from those few sources. And I would be looking for, I'm not sure whether I found it on FreeSound in the end, I might have got someone to record it for me but someone was looking for, like a call to prayer from a mosque and they wanted one that sounded like it was in an Arabic country, not in Britain. And that is kind of quite difficult to get if you're like sitting in your office in Bristol. But you know, so that kind of thing, you're more likely to find on FreeSound than on those CDs probably. (53)

This respondent emphasises how useful it is to have access to non-standardised, more diverse type of sound for her projects. In addition to a variety of content, my interviewees address further advantages provided by the access to content via CC. For instance: "no hassle with clearing makes me more eager to browse for stuff that might be useful. After previous trouble [refers to acquiring permissions], it just saves time to have samples that are open" (electronic music producer, USA (1)). This quote points at the benefits of the absence of clearing procedures, which for most of the studied creators is the main motivation to use CC content. Both accessibility and lack of complicated legal procedures enhance the sample-searching process and thus facilitate production.

However, CC also has significant limitations. As content distribution is not moderated, CC brings in cultural objects that were otherwise excluded or available only to select audiences. This includes the digitalised material of public institutions with archival sound, such as the "Europeana Sound" collection of historical recordings from museum repositories and works that might not be useful: unfinished, recorded on inferior equipment or created by unskilled authors. Among the respondents of my study, creators point at similar aspects, sharing a common belief about poor quality of CC sound, using expressions such as: "the majority of [CC] content is regarded as crap, and, in fact, it is crap" (music producer, Brazil). It was also not uncommon to hear: "one third of it [CC sound resources] is people making fart sounds or failing to make music" (music producer, Italy (1)). Facing the multitude of content, problems of creators using CC-licensed material, shift into another dimension: navigating and finding suitable objects under the protection of a suitable license.

3 Sound Commoning and a Sense of Community

The literature has recognised that remix is a particular type of collaboration based on establishing relations between objects that are changed and repositioned, at its heart observing legal issues connected to sample clearing (McLeod and DiCola, 2011). As previously stated, Creative Commons license acts as an integrator and enabler of collective creativity, based on reliance on a poll of resources that undergo reproduction and progressive growth on the basis of existing material. The formal licensing is grounding of the reciprocity. As a result, an object mediates the creative relationship between artists, and quite often they do not know the names nor identities of their collaborators. Uploaded objects are either entirely new creations or made from existing ones. At the same time, re-mixed and re-created objects become items of networked authorship, forming pyramidal property relations. This completely changes the positionality of the object as compared to traditional copyright (Carruthers and Ariovich, 2004), as well as frees constraints that are visible in the remix of copyrighted material (McLeod and DiCola, 2011).

Contemporary culture has adopted collage as a technique of merging elements that do not seem to fit together. Sound is another domain for this type of work. Sound remix takes different forms, from simple joining music tracks (mixtape) to professional sound design, based on creative blending and merging sound to generate non-obvious, artistic creations of imagined, or otherwise not accessible phenomena, for instance time travel or nuclear bomb explosion. Sound design often translates to artistic identity, embedded in workflow but also relevant to the aesthetics of production and components used in production. As the next passage shows, a music producer, who also designs sound processing applications, uses open content as material for experimentation that is otherwise not affordable and rarely available through commercial channels.

> The classical choice you have when working on sound is: either you buy it or have to make it yourself. And I've always felt it's not right. So, somehow doing work using components that I find online helps me, I feel like I have a connection to that material, also there is ethical side: none of that

is stolen, it might sound weird but I feel like every track is a contribution of hundreds of samples that someone made to be shared. (...) I could never feel this way buying sound packs, I would need too many of them, and they are too generic for my kind of work.

music producer, France (1)

Open licensing not only broadens the availability of different types of objects but also provides an opportunity for their mass sourcing for certain needs. This producer emphasises a connection that he sees in open sound. He also understands his participation in FreeSound as a form of collective collaboration based on availability of components for his production. Interpreting sound pieces in a similar way to raw material permits understanding their role in the production process. Samples, like raw material, are extracted and given use-value, however at the same time their origins and background are valuable for the artist.

Even though there is no formalisation of control beyond the management of platform providers, there are tacit dynamics of social control at the foundation of this form of digital commoning.

I have actually always considered FreeSound as a community of fellow nerds who have a bit different understanding of sound. So I have a bit different sensitivity [to sound] (...). I have always liked FreeSound because it is the only platform with sole focus on content. Not loops, not birds, not heavy metal, not sales of advertisement but content is at the heart of it. (...) And so this way I followed users, by just pure following of people's work, and in a dozen cases, I know who these people are. I don't know them in person, some of their profiles I have checked out and I recall, but I know that they are the same as me, and I know it because I know their content. And the only way to do something with them, is by just using their content, which I think makes it a completely superior deal. [French music producer, interview]

The first part of this informal control is lack of artistic anonymity. As the respondent outlines, creators often treat their profiles as their brands. The passage concentrates on usage of content and the role of copyleft in fostering collaborative relationships between creators. Even though there is no obligation to contact the original owners of works, there is such a possibility, and this respondent shows that in some cases collaborations are established in this way. By providing a framework for pre-programming the future usage of content, copyleft influences the relationships between creators in part by removing them from the market and limiting intermediation. While often not knowing the personal details of the creator, the profile linking enabled by licensing creates an opportunity for self-promotion. This occurs in a similar way to traditional modes of collaboration between musical artists. According to one of the respondents:

> Giving my own sound away does not seem abnormal; I would say it is natural for the creative industries [...]. People have always done it, but by sharing it through the internet, it really crosses all [geographic] borders and [music] genres. Creative Commons just regulates the way how you do it. And there is an entire universe of people fulfilling different needs through it. [...] I do it for free loops, mostly drums, [...], and for some exposure.
> experimental music producer, Italy (2)

Increasing the supply of content might be regarded as a natural part of the distribution of creative works, with the CC providing a legal path for sharing and re-creating content. This creator emphasises the diversity of needs and interests in CC. Similarly, some other artists perceive the CC as the foundation of a community established through use-value relationships and shared awareness of a common interest. For instance: "I am taking, so I give; it is all part of the transparency that this framework creates [refers to CC]. I like seeing my work re-created; I also take other's work. I think everybody [using CC] shares this belief and respects other community members (music producer, USA (1))". The collective orientation also reflects broader trends, based on growth and development supported by the community of fellow users.

Quite often users do not respond to messages and follow-up on their content. However, user profile and history often can be used for verification. The key function of FreeSound is the possibility of establishing collaborations while verifying the potential collaborator through the content. This could be done, for instance by examining previous uploads, looking at profile info (which often contains information about the creator's background). Additionally, some of the creators receive direct feedback from other users. Some users share the belief that building a reputation, measured in the online activity on a page, may be a factor for future professional engagements: "I receive at least a few messages a month with propositions of sales or collaboration. Even though I usually say no, I've done some interesting projects for museums and media companies" (6). Establishing community and the number of views or downloads, strongly embedded in for-profit platforms and contracts with music industry firms, is being reflected in the copyleft scene.

Users also embed their activity in FreeSound, using all parameters to screen content and creators. While Creative Commons content might be moved to other platforms (it is not tied to FreeSound), the additional information aggregated by the platform helps users to find content to remix and trace the original authors. Here a major role is played by metrics, such as download statistics, popularity and experience. Often, they also come up when discussing how reusing CC material requires copyright verification, which is needed to minimise the chances of potential infringement, for example if protected work was illegally uploaded under a CC license.

An additional protection in the domain of collaborative creativity is mechanism of attribution, more broadly addressed in the next chapter. With the exception of CC-0 (public domain) license, if a FreeSound sample is used for making a new work, the original author needs to be credited. The credit ties a work to the original creator as well as future re-creators, openly communicating the connection. Uniquely enough, attribution signifies that each portion of data is not anonymous and allows for tracking. To some artists, reference to a sample creator is a source of satisfaction: "Attribution works in a similar way to credits. I enjoy hearing melodies that I once made in entirely new tracks" (ambient music producer, UK (3)).

∴

This chapter has shown how Creative Commons are supporting alternative routes of production and placement of content in new context. The material has several important outcomes for understanding of how alternative licensing contributes to the transformation of the mode of production. Considering the dynamics of FreeSound, I have shown how CC-licensing acts as an integrator, based on a mechanism of replication and self-reference. Creative Commons establish a framework that is widely and universally understood by users, and whose participation in FreeSound depends on the license. Moreover, their activity, both in recording new sound, and remixing existing ones, unless commercialising content, usually draws them back to FreeSound, for either sharing the effects of the work or sharing the unused components. Here the role is played not only by the license itself, but also by the platform, that stores history of users and content, as well as increases their positionality by exposing content and user profiles from search engines. As a result, FreeSound generates interconnections between content, with FreeSound as a natural mediator of content.

Lack of selection based on the quality of content stimulates alternative approaches to production, based on openness to all types of uploads. Content properties, aside from the low entry requirements, are not constrained by the platform's administrative rules. This stimulates the dynamic of creativity, reliant on placement of content into new, often unexpected contents. The process is remarkably unpredictable, often based on cross-sectional adoption of content that otherwise, within classical copyright regime, would never be considered useful. This approach to experimentation is very unique, however it responds to the needs of production, either connected to the way in which authors work, their limited library, or programme of composition based on online content available for free and online. While the motivations of users remain unidentified, the licensing clearly places users into the highly advantageous situation of processing content, and tests its usability, with the potential of using it legally, both acknowledging the requirements of usage by original creator as well as the source. The democratic access to content and clear requirements of usage provides a democratic access to diverse content, much different from traditional sources of sound: sound packs or stock libraries.

The openness of content also establishes a new format of collaboration. Works by being shared are absorbed into the system of circulation of content. Any content is readily open to the varying degree of collaboration. Even though the depth of involvement is specified in the license, all sounds create a network that contains millions of objects that can be traced, reconfigured, placed in different contexts, and combined. This format, previously reserved to underground remix culture, provides a more solid foundation for any kind of creative activity. This way, content provides a collective source of creativity, and it is up to the author to use it or place it accordingly. This dynamic offers a stark contrast from other open licensing projects described in the literature. For example, open software creators work together to build a computer programme or an operating system. They organize with a shared goal of expanding, improving or upgrading portions of code. The main dynamic in these projects is collaboration within teams working towards the same goal: final, closed product. This organisation has a rigorous function of different members. In a hypothetical situation when a user participating in open-source software development gives up, usually there is a mechanism in the community to fill the gap.

The instance of FreeSound shows a completely different type of collaboration. Here, development of content rests in the hands of individual users. There is no commonality of projects. If a user decides to stop being active, it effectively means that the content that he supplies is not going to be published on the side. Every piece of content uploaded by user, is a finished project. And even though FreeSound has many of users, their activity is not directed, organized or project oriented. And even though among core users of FreeSound there exists a shared idea of commons and the shared goal, their participation in that community is only via content and only through their individual creativity. The vector of that collaboration is thus inverted and based on a different logic, fostering individual work and a dispersed type of creativity based on use value activation by placing content into context.

CHAPTER 6

Acknowledging Authorship
Attribution in the Market Context

>"1191_two_cows.wav" *by reinsamba* LICENSED UNDER ATTRIBUTION 3.0 UNPORTED (CC BY 3.0)
>>an exemplary attribution from Minecraft's in-game sound page (MINECRAFT, 2021)

⋯

>MALE THIJS LOUD SCREAM SAMPLE, COURTESY OF THANVANNI-SPEN, TAKEN FROM HTTP://FREESOUND.IYA.UPF.EDU
>>an exemplary attribution from the 2006 film *Children of Men*

⋯

>A simple artificial soundscape for a sewer, built by combining and editing the following sounds I have uploaded: "Stream, Water, C.wav", "Dripping, Fast, A.wav", "Dripping, Medium, A.wav", "Dripping, Slow, A.wav".
>>an exemplary attribution from freesound.org containing links to sound pages

⋯

These examples of attributions might seem similar to academic references. Creative Commons' Attribution follows the same principle: "citing", based on receiving recognition in another work, and "referring", based on placing a reference to the original work in one's own work. Scholarly literature, especially in the science studies, has given significant attention to the studies of application and the role of annotation (Gilbert, 1977; Leydesdorff, 1988; Merton, 1942; Nicolasien, 2003). This stream has shown that references act as rhetorical devices, specific to the conventions of disciplines and quite central in adjusting

© MIŁOSZ MISZCZYŃSKI, 2022 | DOI:10.1163/9789004504240_008

the message (Hyland, 1999; Swales, 1990). For instance, the use of contrastive, often contradicting references has been typical of the humanities but not in the natural sciences (Hellqvist, 2010). Some of the findings of these studies have later been extended into quantitative methodology of citation counting, lying at the basis of citation indexes, treated as a benchmark of academic excellence. In academia, the convention of referencing and the calculation of volume and quality of references is a central criterion of academic assessment, influencing prestige, salary and both the recognition of a scholar inside and outside of academia.

Attribution functions in a similar way to academic citation and referencing. Attribution is a commoning mechanism that propels generation of commons, increases visibility of platforms and authors and supports spreading content. The commons-based attribution has a similar format to citation. Simply put, it is a short line of text, following a standard format and containing a hyperlink to the original work. Like academic referencing, attribution's main role is to ensure that the content's original author is credited. Attribution this has a key role in generating reciprocity between the creator, who shared the work, and the reuser, who is obliged to cite the author. While academic citing is based in a convention of referring to all authors of the original thought, or quoted text, the presence of attribution is stemming from the license requirements. In other words, the convention of attribution is present and practiced in three types of licensing: Attribution (CC-BY), Attribution-NonCommercial-Sharealike (CC BY-NC-SA) and Attribution-NonCommercial-NoDerrivatives (CC BY-NC-ND). In other words, while attribution is linked to the originality and organisation of content, it is determined by the license and foregrounded in motivation and intentions of the author of the work.

Attribution in legal tradition is part of a broader doctrine known as moral rights. Moral rights touch cultural creations and are typically understood as composed of the right of attribution, the right of integrity, and the right of disclosure (Strauss, 1955). The standpoint of moral rights is enshrined in the spirit of "protecting the author's personal dignity and the human spirit reflected in her artistic creations" (Kwall, 1985; 2001, p. 67). In this context, the right of attribution secures the right of the author to be recognised as the author of the work (and to prevent others from claiming that recognition). The right of integrity is the representation of author's creative personality (and allowing misrepresentation). Finally, the right of disclosure, times the public dissemination of the work. In many legal contexts, moral rights are seen as a subset of copyright law, aimed at protecting authors-creators. In contexts such as American, the focus of legal construction is rather embedded in protection of interests of copyright holders (Dworkin, 1994; Kwall, 2002). The relationship of moral rights, copyright and creative commons, will be addressed in this chapter. As I will show the question of commons' license protection, as well as securing moral rights, are closely tied to the mechanisms of attribution, which often are violated. As a result, the Creative Commons licensing violations falls into the copyright domain, contradicting the often-shared idea of "freeing the content" held by the creators. Since Creative Commons are a mix of private ownership rights (copyright) and common property rights (Creative Commons), non-compliance with the license signifies falling into the property law domain. As I show, for creators this situation signifies lack of enforceability, usually due to the legal and time-related costs. As a result, creators often resign from attribution licenses and move to sharing content under CC-0 Public Domain license, requiring no attribution, and permitting full usage of content.

The main consideration of this chapter is the study of attribution practices from a theoretical and conceptual point of view. The findings suggest that that attribution, so providing link to the author, plays a parallel role in commoning to the way in which citations work in the academia. The chapter starts by describing the mechanism of attribution, functioning as a reference requirement to the original author. It sets off by showing instances of attribution's function, perceived as a form of courtesy and a mechanism of reputation building. The findings suggest that the prevalent understanding of this mechanism is linked to the industry exposure. Unlike referencing, it is not treated as an obligation and ethical standard, but often emerges as a technical and economic decision done by the copyright holder. As shown below, attribution establishes a barrier for users of content, who often are willing to negotiate attribution waving, based on a payment. In other words, original authors provide themselves with a possibility of converting Creative Commons content into standard copyrighted content, protected by proprietary licensing.

Attribution is thus interpreted as a commons-based tool of building reputation: the findings show that through attribution some creators not only get involved in direct selling of their sound but also in provide paid services of composition, mix and mastering services, or establish longer-term collaborations. Interviewees are familiar with situations when a potential collaborator, fan or client can approach a creator, for instance to pay for a custom-made composition or rearrangement of a musical track. A Russian producer describes his experience: "(...) so all of a sudden I learn that seven of my sound effects are part of a game that is on Steam. (...) They put me in the credits and somehow I really like their aesthetic (...)" (techno music producer, Russia). The described situation led to a permanent collaboration with the creator, who now works on sound in two of the studio's projects. Other users told similar stories of building a professional trajectory through exposure of content, and user profile. Moreover, the pyramidal relationships of sound, so remixing work, also provides a source of recognition from availability of the content that creators virtually co-produced. The next pages show that creators value the fact that CC does not exclude alternative ways of commodifying creations and allows for the sale of physical copies of music that are available within the networked creative production model or for charging for additional permissions beyond the non-commercial CC license. Not only can CC-licensed work be commercially reused, and the artist's name used in advertising campaigns or film credits, but a high number of attributions can also lead to the increased interest in creator's work. Within this domain, I argue that attribution emerges as a tool of commodification.

In considerations of the role of attribution in the market context I draw attention to the limitations in the protection of commons-produced content, which strongly materialises in the context of almost nonexistent protection of the attribution-licensed content and enforcement of attribution. While the idea surrounding adoption of attribution is idealistic, pragmatism and practices of the industry often violate the license by not meeting the requirement of the attribution. Whether intentionally or unintentionally, some of the creators not only abandon the requirement of attribution but even move to the public domain license, which opens content and severs the connection with the author. Moreover, this dynamic influences the relationships of the industry and the commons. Industry actors are careful when working with Creative Commons content, appreciating the quality and value of content but facing difficulties with its verification.

1   Attribution and Reputation

To understand the idea attribution, it is necessary to consider the linkage between the creator and content. Traditional copyright assumes that creativity is property. This assumption has been widely criticised for discouraging the creative progress and consumption of cultural resources (Elkin-Koren, 2005; Lessig, 2001), who later co-authored the Creative Commons framework. The prevailing idea of protection has been linked to the model of economy of copyright, guided by the speculation and driven by profit rather than by the idea of progress in creativity or innovation. Several works have documented the tension between copyright and technology and cultural advancement. Creative industries epitomise the disconnection between copyright and original author, for example "invisible" sectors that are not driven by popularity of authors. The sound industry is one such discipline, where most employees not only stay in the shade, but who often perform technical functions, such as recordist, sound designer, or sound engineer.

In Creative Commons, attribution is a basic tool signalling the relationship between the author and the original work. Its main purposes, like that of academic references is building recognition, preserving the work's source and connecting the author to the product. Attribution ties a work to the creator and to future creators, and it provides a mechanism for communicating this connection. To most creators, attribution also is a tool for establishing reputation.

> I was sharing my content using attribution license because I thought it was a very small cost for someone to attribute me, and it might be a valuable source of some new gigs or maybe even give me a new work opportunities sometime. And it actually brought results. I got a few clients for my work, also sold a few packages. And it came from the fact that people found me on FreeSound, found my sounds, liked them and wanted me to make them game sounds or something else, like voiceover or other sound-related work. Because they found my voice recordings, looked at my music and this is how I got a couple of jobs for it. It was not much but it was valuable to me. (35)

While attribution plays a central role in building reputation, this process is not unique to FreeSound. Some creators value the exposure that comes from linking and attribution published on other pages.

> All my stuff is on attribution licence. The reason for that originally was that I liked the idea and I still do, I like the idea of being able to search for the attribution, so that I can get links to what people have used my sounds for. There may have been a bit of vanity in that in the start, 'oh, look, they are using my sound' but not so much, but it's nice to hear. As I said, I wouldn't know they've been in this theatre, they've been in that and that, because once it is used in performances the attribution is in the programme and that's not accessible on-line. So I've learned that in situations like that people reach out and ask for permission, usually offering some payment, but very small. So actually attribution makes them let me know that they are using my sound and also makes them pay for it. I wouldn't know any of that if they hadn't replied 'I put some money on your PayPal and I've used it here'. You know, I never check up if they attributed or not. (28)

This user starts from describing that his reliance on attribution license was initially grounded in the decision to follow the content and be able to observe in what projects it is being reused, by relying on search engines and the uniqueness of his username. Many users follow this convention: they occasionally input their usernames and look up their content on major platforms (such as YouTube or SoundCloud), which following this search displays material containing attribution, which typically is placed in the description section. Attribution is so important that some users keep logbooks in a format of a spreadsheet or text file, in which they list all of the uses of their content in others' projects. For that reason, one of the users has even started a new account – with a more unique username that is easier to identify for web search engines. Attribution thus gives a greater control over the effects of labour of the creator and knowledge about the type and scoping of projects that the content was used in. And finally, It provides a possibility of paying the author. For instance, it can be done using a PayPal link on a user's page.

Many users are active in the sound industry. To them, attribution contributes to professional recognition. In most cases they are aware of the high quality of content that meets the most rigorous sound production standards. It is not uncommon to hear that a user was told at work or at music school that someone used their sample from FreeSound. Below a respondent outlines his experiences of hearing his sound in other productions without attribution.

> And in fact, a bunch of samples from FreeSound, I've actually heard used on television. There is an alien sound effect I've heard in the episode of [00:08:33] that I made. I hear my punch sound effects everywhere on YouTube. I think the Kings of Mayhem used that for a transition effect. Eric Andre used one of my anime sound effects in one of his episodes. Actually, two of his episodes and I was like freaking out because I was watching it on TV and I heard my sound and here's like 'what was that?'. It was like, it had the same delay and everything. So I knew it was my sound. It just blew my mind. (...)Very few people actually ask for permission or actually reach out to you asking for permission or actually pay attention to the Creative Commons licence. And I notice very few movies, I think 'Children of Men' was like one of the few media that actually properly credit FreeSound. So it's a little discouraging knowing that, oh yes, that's another thing. I've heard one another anime sound effect I did in a dubstep track and it had over a million view on YouTube and I was like 'that's cool that I kind of made the basis to the beat'. It's like I wish you know, there was a little bit more credit towards that but again, it just goes to show that I know I can produce holy content. But again, I love making

stuff for free but I also, you know, want to be able to have a career out of it as well. (39)

Similar stories surfaced told during the interviews: creators, usually people who were very discerning when it came to sounds, heard other creators' sounds in popular productions and notified the creators. They noted that often they did receive attribution, even if they had to contact a production company to get it.

The understanding of attribution's role and the problems of enforcement also persist with users who are employees in sound design. These jobs tend not to be mainstream industry jobs and they are on strict budgets. These users are trained to transform content, for instance by processing it, combining works and generating new quality. Quite often they rely on samples from FreeSound and combine them with their library. Users are torn between the goal of building reputation and problems with attribution, especially in commercial projects. For instance:

> The main reason for me to have attribution licensing is because I figured that if my name is out there, it's easier for people to find my sounds which can benefit both other users but also myself in case I ever get an offer to do something like this professionally. So it has been in some self-interest but I also realised, you know, as I get older, this is not like, this is what I'm going to do for a living and so why not make it easier for the users and ... Because I know, when I, the few times that I still look for sounds myself on FreeSound, when I don't design them myself, I'm always very happy if the sound I'm looking for has a public domain licence because I was saying, it's not always convenient to give credit. It's not a, you know, prestige things to me, it's just more sort of, it has been a matter of principle but now it's more like 'I don't think it's always convenient for let's say, someone who is starting out making animations or something'. And you know, then they have to do a whole video description with links to people from FreeSound for example. It doesn't look very professional, you know? So I don't want to slow people down. So that's why I'm thinking about changing the licensing, really. (51)

In this sense, artists use attribution to control the use of their content. It resembles prominence building, like academic citations (with no indexing or metrics). While the literature recognises that a key motivation of sharing content under CC is building professional credibility and achieving recognition, attribution is instrumental in the process. Moral rights, as mentioned above, are understood as decency and genuine interests of other users. This creator hopes that they are guiding actions of commoning and hopes that on this shared recognition of commons he can build his reputation. However, attribution often causes problems, making projects look unprofessional or being too just time-consuming to negotiate with clients.

2   Waiving Attribution

Attribution signifies that none of the data is anonymous and can be tracked. However, there are times when attribution is either impossible or the user does not want to contribute. Some situations or media types make attribution impossible: a theatre uses a sound sample and is unable to credit the author; the programmes might already be printed, there is no website of the play; or simply the director does not agree to any type of unconventional additions. In this situation, quite often sound designers negotiate not-attributing by approaching the original creator. In these cases, there is a convention when a potential collaborator, fan or client approaches a creator, perhaps with a proposal to pay for content without a Creative Commons license. At the same time, he discusses making changes in the original track. This possibility of content sale is a way of obtaining non-attribution usage permissions. This negotiation often starts on FreeSound, when user profiles with contact information are found. An author might receive a message with a request to agree to lack of attribution. According to my interviewees, this message often contains an offer of compensation. "A marketing agency offered me payment for using my sound in an advertisement. They wanted to pay me and I felt they were kind of desperate" (4). Similar descriptions have been reported by many core users. For creators, attribution is both a tool for reputation-building, and a tool for the commodification of content. Attribution allows content to be placed on the market and erects a barrier that needs to be overcome.

Most creators who have uploaded large volumes of content often face dilemmas over the negotiation of permissions – often they receive several emails every day with requests to authorise the commercial use of material without attribution. Yet, there are important reasons universally shared by the community. One respondent states that, for him, the release from attribution is the release of ties connecting content to himself. So, as a means of compensation, he offers users the possibility of buying the sound, with compensation as a token of gratitude for releasing the ties.

> [referring to attribution] Yes, well, it would probably be a copyright violation. I mean, most of the time I can't really be that strict about the

licencing really, because it's impossible to manage everything and to track down everything. It's just not worth my time, really. But there are a couple of examples where it was quite significant. So for example, that was a lot of, quite a while ago, couple of years, that there was a DJ artist, I don't remember his name but he had a music track which he got another third party to create a music video for it. And in that music video, they used one of my sounds without attributing it. And this was before I had offered people to buy an attribution free licence. That's really what triggered me to do it. And then the music video went on hundreds of millions of views and things. And still, they do not credit me to this day. I have tried to contact them, but sort of, I don't really want to be bothered to chase it up anymore, to be honest. (61)

This creator sees attribution is a minimal requirement, which is usually ignored. To him, attribution means that his part in the work is acknowledged. He also describes a situation of using sound in a new context, and a case in which the new creation was remarkably successful yet violating this basic principle. This author stresses the uneven power in this relationship – despite his attempts to contact the reuser he has failed to sanction this usage. Often creators say that they simply don't have means or time to follow any type of usage that's not following the rules of attribution.

The problem of attribution and negotiating, seen as problematic by some creators, is prized by users who actively seek collaborators with a musical background. This group is tends to experiment with content and to look for partners for composition or to stretch a tight budget. For them, the possibility of contacting the remix's author offers a possibility of acquiring composition components without a purchase or subscription. At the same time, it brings together creators with similar interests, opening them to collaboration. The following passage illustrates the e problems between traditional market institutions and the CC-based distribution of sound.

> It is a completely different game. (…) Long time ago we [refers to his music collective] took drums from [name of the band] and contacted Sony. The whole dynamic was just wrong as the price for using that sample was ridiculous, and they did not care about accommodating our needs. (…) I think this is why it is better to approach artists directly. But even if we went to [name of the band anonymised], they would tell us to go to Sony as they are signed there. So they would not be able to extract a single track or do anything for us because everything is controlled by the label. (…) So, to start with, I try to sample from the public domain or CC

songs, (...) If the recording works, but for some reason there is too much clutter [refers to too many instruments], I just email the guy and ask for a single track or start the conversation to ask him for that kind of help.
 hip-hop producer, Poland (2)

This model of distribution through attribution differs from the traditional market practices of music industry. Traditionally, in the case of sampled music, samples, and permissions to sample from a particular song are acquired through distributors who either hold copyrights to works or who represent the authors (McLeod and DiCola, 2011). In this case the exchange value is extracted by the intermediating institution and is often tied to the copyright holder. The model of open licensing uses a different route, not only by excluding intermediation but also by increasing reliance on the extraction of use-value rather than being conformed to commodification. Moreover, this convention treats content not as a closed commodity but as building blocks that could be adapted to the needs of the purchaser. The creators who have been able to monetise their CC-licensed work emphasise that this process relies on direct contact and the support of re-creators. As one of the loop creators mentioned: "I always am willing to help out a guy who wants to use my track commercially and pay for it. People who approach me always have a very positive attitude and are willing to make an investment [refers to making payment] into this relationship" (experimental music producer, Italy (2)).

The creators in this study who faced a volume of requests to resign from attribution, often adopt a binary model of distribution that is based on both engagement within the traditional creative industries and on the fulfilment of distribution of content using open licensing. Ideally, their model of distribution removes intermediation and its associated mechanisms, conforming to the idea of de-intermediation. As a result of this removal, copyleft produces new structures of distribution and collaboration. On the one hand, the structures enhance the use-value extraction from content distributed using a CC license. On the other, the CC is used as a marketing tool of content and the artist's labour. Commodification occurs through individual negotiation, based on the purchase of permissions and on the additional enhancement of the needed content. Those dynamics supplement the mechanisms of the music industry, usually by catering to less-professional actors who have much smaller budgets or no bargaining power with major intermediaries.

However, attribution has a recognition problem. Users often face problem of how to apply it. While it is easy in web 2.0, for instance on YouTube.com, it becomes complicated in performance arts or film, where the format does not use text, or where there is only a short time to show the credits. Users emphasise that the issue of attribution touches is especially serious for salaried sound designers. It is often difficult for them to display the rules of the license and the need of attributing. According to one professional sound designer:

> I think most users at the beginning choose license with attribution but then people relax the permissions more and often shift the choice to the public domain. Every time I look at attribution I think that I would need to tell to the say director or producer 'hey, well, there is no money for private libraries [in the project that they are both working] so I got them from FreeSound'. This is where I try to introduce them to Creative Commons and how cool is all that. And I have tried to get the point across many times of like 'well, you know, some of the sounds I'm going to use, have an attribution licence meaning that somewhere you need to mention the author, well, you need to do a proper attribution'. And yes, lots of them didn't do that which kind of bothered me because it's like 'mate, you're doing a low-budget thing, you're getting me, I'm doing a good job and I'm telling you OK, no need to spend more money in private libraries, which you don't have any way; I will be able to provide a cool sound, mixing and design but you know, I'm using four or five sounds that need attribution, that doesn't look like a sacrifice'. Yet, the dynamic is that sometimes they didn't do it, because well, I remember a director who said she would do it and then, at the very end she didn't and said 'well, you know, I've been looking at movies and they don't have that kind of stuff in the end credits'. And I was like 'yes, the movies you watch cost millions. The one was done with 40k and I'm saving your money'. So yes, they rarely do it. I don't think, it looks more kind of a passion niche thing, the people enjoying a community based on copyleft concepts. (55)

For this respondent, the struggle is often budgetary; Creative Commons sound can lower the cost. However, as he points out, clients either misunderstand or deliberately ignore attribution. Even him, as a person responsible for the technical side of sound, cannot influence some of the clients, and often faces ethical dilemmas. In that case, argues for public domain, so license not requiring attribution, is a much better and safer choice for such projects. He also believes that lower budget productions could be more accommodating to attribution, for instance by having longer credit sequences (containing attribution) but at the benefit of financial savings.

The requirement of attribution complicates the process of production. On the user side, users of content requiring attribution often struggle with keeping track of original authorship and license requirements. FreeSound's forum, creators' inboxes and comments on sound files often contain questions about how to attribute content, or how to format and display the attribution. One user describes how he adds attribution to computer games:

> So, actually in college, I wrote a piece of software that could just create like from the file on you FreeSound, if you left them alone, it could pull out their sound IDs and auto generated attribution list for you that you could put in your movies and stuff. (…) I haven't really been maintaining it so I don't know if it works anymore, but yes. So in a game, typically, I would put it into the credits page or the 'Read me'. But yes, often like the games I'm doing are just sort of like for a little jam, so I might just put it in like the description of the game page or just like in a credit file or something inside of the game folder. That's sort of like just a quick thing. But yes, I was especially for Creative Commons attribution and I was involved in the site, I would always tell people 'hey, like make sure you're using into other stuff'. And I wrote like a little guide of how to attribute but I think that might still be part of the site. So thank you for asking about attribution. (47)

This respondent has several ways of enabling attribution, for example by placing the credits in the menu section of the game, or with the game's files. Other strategies, for instance in the performance arts, include posting attributions on websites or including their list in physical copies of music albums. A major tension, however, stems from the chronic problem of lack of attribution.

3   Violation of Creative Commons License

> I'm sure it's happened [referring to violation of attribution]. You know, because some of my sounds have tens of thousands of downloads or whatever and they must, presumably some of them, have been used somewhere, but I can't really tell. I told you that there were some people who have contacted me and said for whatever reason, 'the nature of my project doesn't allow me to place an attribution' or whatever, 'there is no place to do that'. And I've always told them 'just go ahead and do it' [refers to using it without attribution]. I suspect that there is a whole bunch of users out there that I don't know about and who are not crediting. The one thing I notice is that there are sites (…) and they aren't always necessarily

crediting the original you know, there is kind of building a whole sound inventory of their own but they don't bother to credit anybody. (29)

The opening passage of this sub-section notes the de-intermediation caused by Creative Commons: lack of their governance and its tools. This user again distinguishes two important elements that touch the issue of violating of attribution. The first, 'free riding', is the inability to credit and the deliberate use of content with attribution, usually for profit. The depth or type of violating the license varies, for instance from using it without correct attribution or by placing non-commercial content in commercial projects, to deliberate usage of content with no attribution, on sites such as YouTube.com.

Creative Commons licensing does not have the same institutional support that is embedded in regular copyright, meaning that there is no watchdog organisation for the correct usage of licensed content and. The official licensing site states that: "This license and the rights granted hereunder will terminate automatically upon any breach by You of the terms of this license" (Creative Commons, 2021). According to Creative Commons, in a situation when an attribution license is not followed, the license "terminates automatically", meaning that it is no longer shared using the CC framework. In practice it means that a person violating the license has no right to use the content, the Creative Commons license no longer applies but traditional copyright law does. In enforcing compliance with the license and acting against the violation, the site recommends to "consider contacting the person and asking them to rectify the situation and/or (...) consider consulting a lawyer to act on your behalf" (Creative Commons, 2021). The literature shows examples from multiple legal systems that show how courts rule, accepting the importance of attribution in open licensing, for example *Jacobsen v. Katzer,* where the United States court ruled that "there are substantial benefits, including economic benefits, to the creation and distribution of under public licenses that range far beyond traditional license royalties" (West, 2008: p. 911–914). Analyses of licensing show similar interpretations; in a situation of infringement (e.g., distribution without attribution), a court would likely reject reliance on Creative Commons, interpreting the license as terminated due to noncompliance. However, at the same time, regular copyright will take place of Creative Commons.

The realities of Creative Commons are dire. Many of the interviewed creators have stated that they are certain that the conditions of their content shared under attribution license have been violated. Their observations are associated with very high numbers of content downloads (and the inability to find their attributions) or being notified by other users that their content had appeared on other platforms or projects. In this case, the understanding of attribution requirement is seen as being of small importance to the system of copyright. For instance, "I will not go to the court with somebody who did not attribute me. This would be a big waste of time and I don't think anyone cares but me. I don't choose Creative Commons to fight in courts" (39). For creators, attribution is tied to the idea of building a reputation in the industry, with the hope that one day it might bring benefits. In this case the risks and tensions stemming from violations might be problematic, for instance because some of the sound might be identified as belonging to the person who re-uploaded it. And as this interviewee states, litigation is considered time-consuming and onerous.

Aside from copyright violation removals available on most content platforms, the main source of control of licensing takes place inside the commons. Individual authors are sensitive to their own reputation, quite often they verify content before remixing it. This tendency is strong among music producers, for whom growing recognition and the trust of collaborators, clients and audiences signifies professional development. The main mechanism from within the commons is the community, which plays an active role in identification and counteracting violations of copyright, for instance when the track uploaded to the platform is not owned by the uploader. "[referring to commoning activity] This also happens sometimes, when someone just rips a track of mine (...) I either get notified or can file a removal request. I need to do it purely to protect myself and others" (electronic music producer, Poland 2). Similar attitudes arise among all musicians involved in the cc. Easy access to data influences the creative process by changing the way in which the author perceives his/her own position, both in relation to other authors and to the whole network. As one of interviewed creators pointed out: "you don't have to ask, you don't have to think, you just take it and put it in your track – everybody already agreed you can do it. (...) But don't try to mess with it or pretend it's yours – nobody will like that" (hip-hop producer, Poland 1). The process of creation propels the development of data, and creators are diligent in protecting and sorting it.

This bottom-up mechanism of control of licensing remains visible with sounds of *Minecraft*, which uses many tracks from FreeSound (Minecraft, 2021). Some of the original creators of sounds that were placed in the game have been suspected of ripping original *Minecraft* sounds. Similarly, creators often get notified of their sound being used in a composition by other users, who, while being discerning, can tie it to content on FreeSound: "I got told about my samples being placed in YouTube videos but I did not do anything about it, I don't see any point or profit in doing that" (37). Similar mechanisms of human-based protection are the only mechanisms that govern the commons and the only path that creators selectively take is sending emails to users who have violated the license.

Paradoxically, the creators of high volume of content often ignore reports on license violation. They fear that interventions in any content violation disputes might involve them personally, or even financially. Several creators that I interviewed have remarked on the issue of finding and negotiating penalty for illicit usage of their content:

> I was actually on YouTube looking at something totally unrelated and I had like a YouTube recommends, down the site and there was a dark web, unboxing video and I was like 'oh, that sounds kind of random, I will click on it' and I'm watching the video and it's like 6 million views or something like that, then I'm watching it and again, kind of some of the Channel 4 thing, I was like 'I recognise this, surely', and I go in and I click in the 'more'. I think 'oh, he probably attributed me' but I wasn't listed. (…) So I reached out to the guy, and the way I'm talking to you just nicely, I said 'look, I really like your video, this is really cool but I see you've claimed that's yours. I'd rather you put my name on it or take it down completely'. And then he kind of panicked and kind of offered me a sum. I said 'look, I'm not asking you to offer me anything but whatever you feel comfortable with would help me actually get some equipment'. So we came to an agreement and he started using then and then commissioned me for another one. (15)

The most notorious violation took place in the early years of FreeSound, when a user appropriated a big part of FreeSound's content and re-uploaded it to YouTube.com.

> There used to be guy who stole sounds from Free Sound and shared them on YouTube pretending it is his; and this guy earned some dollars on it; there were quite a lot of them and it was a scandal on Free Sound. They [the creators] fought with him. What they achieved was him removing the attribution ones. He ended up only leaving the ones with public license [refers to CC-0]. Bu still, it was unfair because he claimed to be the author and he can only distribute. I think he was a Canadian. (32)

Another user set up a YouTube channel that contained sound effects that had been sourced from FreeSound. This case revealed several problems facing the commons. On the surface, many of these sounds were shared using attribution and/or non-commercial license (CC BY NC), and this user neither attributed nor made the sounds non-commercial (advertising was displayed). This uploader thus violated the license policy, was highly unethical, and users found it inexcusable but also difficult to sanction. On FreeSound's forum, this even raised questions surrounding the defence of author's rights to publish within the Creative Commons framework. As one of the users who had experienced license violation describes:

> Maybe it is not a big issue but one that I faced, it was actually sounds being used without attribution. Up till today there are several YouTubers that release sound packs, so to speak, they would include sound from FreeSound without attribution. I know, I don't think there are major legal issues as a result of that but I know several of mine were pouched so to speak. I never really did anything about it, because Google makes their legal process for that little complicated, at least for just few sound effects. So I don't really actively seek them out, so to speak. (4)

Another problem is connected to mechanisms of platforms, intended to protect copyright of works. For instance, the case of YouTube (owned by Google), is illustrative, since the platform uses an algorithm which interprets the first uploader, associating the uploader the ownership of the file. In some cases, users can generate a "content ID", which automatically detects and block possible violations. This mechanism was developed to support the work of labels uploading copyrighted music, which for instance share videoclips on the site. In the sound industry, this situation is more complex. For instance, this protection might mean that videos containing a sound licensed as Creative Commons, might have the soundtrack blocked (even though their owners attribute properly), or at worst, have an original creator who cannot use the original sound on the platform. As the respondent above mentions, many creators are unwilling to resort to litigation, as the stakes are often too low and the dispute takes time.

The creators note that linking with FreeSound and their profile is accompanied by extended support for the site, elevating its position on the internet.

Exposure of attribution on sites such as YouTube, provides links to users' profiles, generating more interest in their content. Additionally, exposure of user profiles in attribution promotes FreeSound on other platforms. Another respondent remarks on the advantages and disadvantages of the attribution license:

> I mean I don't mind about any of that, but the reason, the other reason legally was this guy who just listed all the sounds and put them with

money on them, with the price tag on them. I'd hoped that having an attribution sound, because he didn't attribute anything. All sounds just ended up there and you didn't know where they're from. [It seemed like] They were his, you know, there was no mention of anything. And that was against the copyright. I didn't like it and therefore I chose that I kept that license and didn't want to change it, exactly in the hope of stopping people like that. But as I said, Bram [FreeSound creator and first administrator] took a very, as I understand that he took a very to the side view, he didn't really want to do it [intervene], which I've certainly come to understand. Yes, so I use the attribution. But the other thing, I think the attribution is good also guessing but I would think it's good for FreeSound. (...) It makes a network of connections between FreeSound, the sounds that are on there, and the people who are downloading and using them. And that has got to be good for FreeSound. So that's another reason why I think it's a good thing to have the attribution. The CC-0 sound, I can go with that, but again for those couple of reasons, I would have thought for a FreeSound is more useful to have attribution and for the copyright thing, you can still hope that it's going to have some effect, but I'm skeptical. (28)

This respondent noes that FreeSound.org could be take more aggressive action against violation. His expectation of license enforceability is linked to the platform's administrators who at that time could not help him. He also indicates that the site benefits from attribution as the linking to content in attribution, also automatically generates links to the site. This linking makes the sound more visible to search engine's algorithms calculating the ranking of websites.

Lastly, some users accept violation as part of commoning and adopt a view embedded in the *laissez faire* approach to freeriding, often giving up monitoring and reacting to attributions. The common explanation of this approach is embedded in no understanding of licensing by the users who free ride and violate the license. One of the users hypothesised: "The name of the site is FreeSound.org and I think that it confuses users who by looking at the name think that they can take content for free, it's all theirs. People really don't read any statements or licenses. And that's fine, I've accepted it" (37). The claim is confirmed by other users with long experience in creative industries. One of them described working with business clients who often violate the terms of the license out of a lack of understanding:

> FreeSound is used by large advertising agencies that do international adds for global markets. In my experience they are often not aware of

Creative Commons licenses and in fact that they violate them. I tell them often – you don't want to have problems, use only commercial stocks, because it is clearly described there, because as someone, you know, on Free Sound there is even no verification of anyone who uploads what, no one is able to check. At least from a legal point of view. But despite everything, I can still see that a lot of people in advertising agencies who deal with sound who do not know about it [refers to licensing] at all. They will find something for free, because the boss did not give any budget for it and this is because FreeSound is often treated as a portal with free photos and that you can do whatever you want with it. (23)

The same user describes his experience with CC BY NC sound and the legal negotiations that often fail.

At least once every few days, someone wants to use my sound commercially and writes to me if they can, and so on. Well, use it, if you can't spare two bucks or a dollar on stocks, use it. And I had one such situation, that someone used one sound of mine, that was on Free Sound and then it was in some kind of a song, well-known in America, I forgot what this genre is called, something a la hip hop there was. Big Sean the name of this rapper, and they even wrote to me that they wanted to sign a contract about using this sound and so on. But the contact died off at some point, I was up to that. And then I looked, someone wrote to me that they recognized my sound in some song that was normally played at their concerts and he sent me a video link on YouTube, where the stadium was full of people and they played that song, and there my little distorted sample was literally in this song. (23)

Users who have more experience interacting with commercial actors often justify copyright violations. For example: "I guarantee you with my own head that in sound industry nobody gives a shit about copyright. I can tell you that 90% of projects are done with zero amount of thinking about copyright. I have stocks, packs but if I need a specific sound, I go to FreeSound. And this is how everyone is doing it. Nobody cares about CC, because there is no punishment" (71). This user, a sound designer working in the film industry, cites the lack of institutions guarding ownership and profits of copyright holders to sound, not attributing it to commons, but stating that the industry standard is based on ignoring it. Creators' other arguments include justifications, for example connected to the time of credits or technical issues of attribution. For example:

> Yes, I mean they've got 30 seconds to put all the major players in and you know, I'm lucky if I get to put my own name [refers to being put in credits as a sound designer]. So you know, that could potentially be dozens of the creators, if I was exclusively using FreeSound, but there just isn't time for that. And as for documentary and for commercial, there often is no credits at all. (7)

Similar experiences, as well as professional work in creative industries result in users being sceptical of any sanctioning of violation. As a result, professional users are turning to public domain (CC-0) tool.

4 Public Domain (CC-0) as a Response to Limitations of Protection

The obstacles to correct attribution, lack of protection and difficulty with detecting fraud are all reasons for uploaders' abandonment of attribution-based licenses. Attribution causes a barrier, both on the side of commodification, since commercial actors prefer either paying for it or ignoring it, and on the user side, often causing problems with enforcement of the license. Instead of following attribution license, creators increasingly participate in the commons based on public domain tool (CC 0), which donates uploaded content to the public. This license poses no limitations to using sound and any user can modify, copy and commercially use content. A respondent shares his thoughts about the decision use public domain.

> Yes, at the level of films that I'm doing that's definitely not going to be a concern ever. And not to mention just the way that copyright law works. There is not a system to actually catch things like that [refers to violations]. I'm generally only flagging copyright problems to directors and producers if it's pulled from a radio station or a television station or actual popular piece of music. But generally speaking, sound effects-related things, no one would ever catch it, no one would ever enforce it. That's also a big part of why, you know, as you probably saw, all of the sounds that I upload are Creative Commons 0, because I don't even bother [observing others] crediting me. No one credits anyone on these sound effects. You know? And no one should, it's way too much tedium. That's not the spirit of the things. The spirit of things is just that 'here is some stuff, use it'. I only upload my own things because, for two reasons. One and primarily because I'm interested in the idea that I can help make other projects sound better, really doing anything, you know? Once

> I upload the sound if it's a quality thing and people want to use it and some of these sounds have been downloaded like over 5000 times. Just knowing that it's been you know, that positive for that many projects and good, you know? But then also, there's a little bit of hope that there is at least one job that comes from there, you know? (20)

This respondent rejects attribution, but refers to building reputation, even though not attribution-driven, but still reliant on sharing and dissemination of content. Other experienced users adopt the same approach; they work with content professionally understand the problematic nature of attribution.

A result of negative experiences with attribution is acceptance of greater openness of content. Creators adopting CC-0 state that public domain license directly excludes them from making profit based on selling permissions and also prohibits the promotion of their activities through attribution. Yet, many of them find attribution-waiving requests more trouble than they are worth: "it is impossible to work this way, I just end up saying to people, take it, I agree to use it with no attribution" (71). Lack of attribution also signifies less knowledge of where the work has been used, which with attribution can be found using search engines. Yet, CC-0 sound offers similar surprises. One user describes the outcome of hearing content that he uploaded using CC-0 license in a computer game that he was playing.

> Another really funny occurrence of hearing one of my sounds was I was at the friend's house and they were playing a video game and then the character died and then the scream was my scream, literally my sound on FreeSound. I was like 'oh my God' [laugh]. But it just blew my mind because that was my voice coming from the video game. And so yes, I always love hearing where my sound is shown up. While the lack of credit is annoying, it's still cool to know that I've been able to produce professional content that other people have used for their projects. So like if I ever wanted to like professional pursue like a sample CD, or you know go professional, I really think I could do it. So if anything FreeSound has just been re-affirmation of that. (39)

Similar accounts of CC-0 sound in the context of re-usage indicate that CC-0 offers easier access to re-uploaders, looking to commodify the content: "I don't think that if my sound had attribution it would be placed in the film (30)". This creator refers to a documentary that extensively relied on his nature sounds and he was notified by the producer about this usage.

This rejection of attribution and movement to the public domain is the most visible among professional sound designers. One respondent explains his reliance on CC-0 licence and another instance of the professional usage of sound. He argues that his activity in several creative industries convinced him to pursue a non-commercial path in some of them.

> I don't really care about getting credited. Maybe that's part of the introversion. I mean, I don't care if people say 'oh, hey, you recorded it'. I don't care. I mean, it's the sound. I mean like it's just a sound designer. You know, I always understand like say, my music composer peers having organizations in different countries registering their composed work and giving royalties from it. And it's just not the same with sound design. I mean, like how do I prove that it [refers to a sound effect] was used? So I mean, it just doesn't matter to me. It's all question of money and altruism. You know, so if you feel like sharing: great; if you can make money of it, well, it's something to aspire; but you know, it's not quite the case of sound effects. So I just prefer to share it and try to make money of it in a different way. Maybe have like fewer people, you know, find me using the sound in the first place [refers to lack of attribution].

This creator outlines the specificity of sound design work and limitations stemming from protection of that work. He points out that there are no organisations that protect creators. He repeats an often-hears argument in the sound industry: lack of institutional governance. This author uses CC-0 license, partially to avoid problems of protecting attribution. He also commodifies his content using other means than attribution. He mentions altruism as central for commons. To him, his profession is unlike the mainstream creative industries, and an essential differentiator is the limited protection of copyright.

Some respondents produce both musical and non-musical sound and are active on platforms other than FreeSound. For them, the division also occurs through separation of activities. One respondent works on musical projectsand produces sound effects and samples. He considered the two activities separate. Officially, he follows the traditional way of making money in the music industry. However, at the same time, under a pseudonym, he participates in the commons to form a few collaborations.

> I've actually been thinking that I might switch all my current sounds over to public domain. There is a lot of people who contact me and sometimes they even send me direct messages, asking for permission to use my sounds and then they ask how to give credits and stuff. And I think that's

wonderful. I think it's wonderful that people respond to that licence with respect and professional courtesy. However, I also know that when you're a small it is difficult, so my idea is you know, provide sounds that might be useful for content creators of other kinds of media. So in that sense for FreeSound, for my audio production is opposed to my music production, I'm completely versed in the CC licensing aspect and I appreciate it very much. I appreciate the concept. So the question regarding royalty or any kind of payment for my sounds has to be answered with a strong no. I simply don't have a good model for that. I mean, I could imagine myself selling sounds to video games or movies, this has happened, but not something that I've already licensed as public domain.

This respondent's money-making model follows the logic of services. His career is based on no engagement or payment for content. Instead, he focuses on his salaried work and professional music career, with sound being secondary.

Many users are disillusioned with attribution. What matters most to them is easy and license-free access to content. The position of one respondent evolved when he became a sound designer in a game company.

In the moment that I started relying on the sounds published under the CC-0 license at work, I just felt how valuable it was [refers to lack of attribution]. It is very precious to someone who may not want to just waste money on commercial libraries. Because I could do it, yeah and say [to the project manager] that this is the cost of my work, I must have these libraries. But it also goes somewhere contrary to my philosophy of openness and of using free licenses wherever possible and free software and free culture. So I thought to myself that I don't need this exposure from these attributions anymore. Anyway, if someone does not care, they will use these sounds without attribution anyway, and I know that it happens so often and it is unenforceable. A couple of times I found someone who used my sound and didn't put an attribution anywhere, I had to intervene. As a result of both [work experience and violations], I decided that I wanted all my sounds, I don't know how many of them were there, I think there are over 800, I want to change the license to the CC-0 license, so that someone like me (...) has resources that are ready to use. So that this person can get these resources for free and that doesn't have to worry about negotiating with his employer or anybody else. So I thought to myself, I got a lot of sound that belongs to the others so I will change this license just to give more, to expand this unique global library of sounds. (35)

Similar experiences with violations have made users pragmatic about the content and more supportive of commons-based production.
– Honestly? I've just gone for the basic thing all the time, because legally this goes way of my head. I'm not good with that, so I will give it a cursory glance and pick the easiest option, probably.
– So you wouldn't care if it's used commercially or non-commercially?
– Well, I might block commercial usage. But wait I am not against people using it in films, but I am certainly against dishonesty and the theft of intellectual property. Those things are bad. Like that [popular artist name] record, whoever produced that, probably made the bunch of money of it, but used my sample without accreditation. That's a shame. I would like to get a couple of bucks out of that but it's not going to happen and as I said earlier, prosecuting the cause would be way too expensive. So I would like to have done more about that and how it works and figure it out.

Some creators describe the problems associated with relinquishing their rights to a work.

> When I was younger, I cared about it a lot because you know, I produced that content, you know, yes, I created, I released it under Creative Commons licence but the reason why I did that was that I would like to have a little bit of the attribution, knowing that I help create that sound. So yes, there is going to be always a little bit of like, 'I wish I had credit on that'. But on the flipside, we are dealing with sound effects that, as I'm sure you're aware, it tends to have a grey area in terms of copyright. So I'm also accepting the fact that these are sound, you know, they are going to duplicate no matter what because they're free. So you've got to take what you can get. You know? And what's the phrase, you know, take the good with the bad. And so, is it that they don't listen to Creative Commons? Absolutely. Is it a deal breaker? No, because that's to be expected. (39)

5 Conclusion

Attribution exemplifies the dilemma of governance of commons-based production in creative industries. An important factor to start commoning is a decision to follow the alternative route of distribution of their content due to the problems that creators perceive in traditional copyright and institutions guarding it. The ideological dimension of commons tackles problems with intermediaries, limitations to usage of cultural material or constraints of traditional model of the industry. Instead, as exemplified in the sound industry, the digital commons support alternative circuit of content and give the possibility of new ways of collaborating. Yet, at the same time, the reality of commons is not as it appears at first glance. While the Creative Commons framework gives full autonomy and enables circulation with no legal barriers, its separatism causes it to force parallel frictions and challenges to traditional copyright in the creative industries. While the model of attribution belonging to the Creative Commons framework offers potential new routes of collaboration and commodification of content, it has an intractable problem with enforcement and consistency.

The creators studied here understand attribution as a source of reputation, tied both to their works and to their profile on FreeSound. To them, the distribution of Creative Commons content is a showcase for their skills, interests and projects in a way that is comfortable for them. Yet, the decision to share content with the attribution license by many of them causes problems with enforcement of the license. These creators often accept the fact that the license is not obeyed, suspect industry problems in adopting this requirement as well as admit no trust in protection of their content. At the same time, they express a lack of trust in any governing bodies that regulate copyright, often by referring to the resource-consuming nature of any potential disputes, either on platforms where the content is distributed or in courts. The only effective mechanism used by these authors is direct messaging to the creators or the Digital Millenium Copyright Act (DMCA) removal, available on the major platforms. These findings confirm that in practice Creative Commons is an extension of traditional copyright frameworks and in problematic situations can be solved by the institutions guarding it. Paradoxically, the resource available to protect artists who reject traditional copyright is traditional copyright.

Parties involved in Creative Commons which have a strong interest in protecting the commons have sought solutions to the problems discussed in this chapter. There is a strong governance issue that this material illustrates and at the centre of it lies reputation, built on both content properties, such as uniqueness and quality of the audio file; as well as through creator's exposure, for instance through creators' profile visibility. They are all important elements influencing the dynamic of value extraction. Moreover, users with a potential interest in the commercial use of sound, face problems with the verification of ownership, which often proves impossible outside of platform algorithms. One idea of governance that has recently entered the discussion has been the development of a digital ledger reliant on blockchain technology, based on tracking every use and reuse of content and tying the work to its original creators. In this hypothetical scenario, the technological layer would ensure the obedience of the rules and tie the works together. Yet, at the base of this solution would be the question of technological administration and funding of such an approach to protection.

Lastly, the controversy around attribution and the easy approach to the violation of this license points at an additional fact: low harm and acceptance of these practices. None of the core creators has ever pursued violation of the license aside from emailing the reuser. A few stories described how a lengthy exchange of emails ended up in very little, or no financial gratification. Several times, contacting the violators has been upsetting due to the lack of contact and no results. One of the conclusions stemming from these stories is the argument that most of core users do not release content with a commercial activity in mind. Usually, the exchange value to these users is secondary, so they are willing to ignore the consequences of violation. The decision to upload is often associated with a hobby, curiosity, fun or the desire to preserve the content. In this scope, a violation results in their absence next to the work, but it does not conflict with the primary purpose. For that reason, and to maximise the use value of content, many experienced users move to CC-0 public domain, which ensures full use value extraction and with no limitations.

CHAPTER 7

Art for Art's Sake? Commodifying the Commons

How do works uploaded to FreeSound become commodities? How do business actors translate content into commercial activities? What is the role of sound on the market? This chapter focuses on activities driven by the idea of studying and extraction of exchange value by actors who participate in FreeSound. While commoning, they perform market activities by building business models based on content shared using the Creative Commons license.

The commoning literature offers observations of free/open-source software commons, where communities deliberately isolate from market activities, and then to their surprise face commodification of their projects, termed in the literature as "project hijacking" by commercial actors. Hijacking is based on usage of commons-developed code for commercial purposes, separated from the community. The literature is rich in examples of project hijacking, exemplifying the misuse and abuse of open source by private entities. Many of these examples stem from a controversy over governance, for instance causing a schisma of community, known as forking (Nyman, 2014). Examples are the Open Office project, which forked to LibreOffice (Nyman and Lindman, 2013); or the VLC player and the placement of a 'fake download' button (Fauvet, 2015). Hijacking can also result from the unscrupulous modification of software, for instance by imposition of a new proprietary platform (Lagace, 2000). However, these software commons are different from FreeSound due to their organisation, composed of numerous users that work and coordinate their production. The creative industry's specificity is much different, and based on individual, independent activity, that is uncoordinated on the commons-level, with governance reduced to administration of the site and filtrating content that might not be owned by users or that might be harmful.

The case of FreeSound differs in the domain of content commodification, providing a rather industry-focused model of commoning, which positions the commons in a direct linkage to creative industries. Unlike free/open-source software, the commons generated on FreeSound supplement professional activity and for many creators and content consumers they foster professional collaboration. Among the interviewed core users there was no clear rejection of commercial activity, typical of other types of commons, deeply tied to the hacker ethos (Chapter 2). Previous chapters have reflected on FreeSound's role in fostering a community oriented on use-value composed of a spectrum of creators interested in sound, from sound professionals and hobby recordists using top-quality equipment to amateur musicians and children looking for sound for their school projects. Cited material and passages from creators have reflected the accent on networked value and collaborative spirit in establishing the commons, showing parallels with other forms of commons-based production.

This chapter examines the actions deliberately aimed at the commodification of the commons. In this chapter, I consider commons-based business models, examining their specific functions related to the process of value generation by the commons. Considering the functions of a business model, my analysis focus on the value-related aspects, following the discussion of digital business models (Chesbrough and Rosenbloom, 2002; Demil and Lecocq, 2010; Martins et al., 2015; Roome and Louche, 2016). I outline "the core logic and strategic choices" (Casadesus-Masanell & Zhu, 2010, p. 3) of the for-profit actions inside the commons, assuming that all these activities rely on or relate to the commons-based production, which produces a specific ecosystem, or value network, linking suppliers and consumers of content and commons. As I show, the right of commercial usage, legitimised by the appropriate licensing (CC-0 Public Domain, CC BY), is the key mechanism at the heart of today's and tomorrow's business models. Under the traditional intellectual property framework, obtaining rights of usage was realised through market transactions and nearly any commercial usage of content has required costly and time-consuming negotiations. By opening up the content, open licensing changes this practice by transforming the process of obtaining rights of usage, in part by removing them from the market and excluding intermediation. Studying commons-based business models requires concentration on three aspects, typical of considerations of sustainability of business models (Bocken et al., 2014): the unique value proposition produced for the users, mechanisms of value creation and delivery, and the mechanisms of capturing exchange value.

The actions of users pursuing for-profit activities rest on the distinctive conditions of the sound industry. The sound industry has the same dynamic of production and distribution as the music industry and uses similar equipment and infrastructure. However, the sound industry has no protection of copyright, partially because of its much smaller revenues and size. While music industry has generated powerful watchdog institutions that guard copyright holders: royalty collecting societies, music labels and distributors protect access to music and use technology to create new tools for protection of content. In addition, the market for sound is dispersed and, most importantly, has no efficient mechanisms of sanctioning sound usage. All decisions and actions are made by original authors who are often notified about their content's presence in YouTube videos, films, and TV shows.

This chapter concentrates on the process when use value generated by the users of FreeSound is transformed into exchange value. As an outcome, sounds from the commons become commodities, being sold or used as a way of for-profit work. The format, quality, and approach to commoning on FreeSound is closely aligned with creative industries, with the platform functioning as a non-profit repository of sound that is open for usage. Even though the commons lack some of the properties of commercial libraries, such as standardisation of content and metadata, in some domains it is an important resource for for-profit activities. An important indicator of the integration with for-profit creative industries is the license preference of FreeSound users. Most the content is not licensed using the copyleft model of Creative Commons, propagating the adoption of the same license and requiring the use of Creative Commons licensing by derivatives, as reflected in the official numbers, reported by FreeSound (2021b). The site's hosted material is dominated by the CC-0 Public Domain (61%), followed by copyleft licenses: Attribution (23%) and Attribution-NonCommercial (16%). This means that only 16% of available content is not available for commercial usage, but, as I noted in Chapter 6, many adopters of the Attribution licenses are willing to "open" the content upon request. This leaves a negligible fraction of the entire repository with no permission to be commodified.

Users whose activity is located at the intersection of commoning and commodification often comment on the lack off protection of sound effect usage, often being disappointed or explaining that it is impossible to respect licenses given the way in which media agencies and the market works. As a result, a significant portion of efforts drifts towards reputation building and networking. In business model development, a shared view is the symbolic role of FreeSound. Notably, many of the interviewees have reflected that work shared on FreeSound has been used in commercial works and authors were either credited or later commissioned to collaborate with producers. The symbolic connection between high-budget blockbuster productions and the community of FreeSound is therefore instrumental in defining the model of understanding of business and commoning.

1   Symbolic Unity of Creative Commons and Creative Industries

The intertwining of commons and industry is most pronounced in the narratives about the contents of FreeSound's library. One of the most common reference points for the community, present both in the interviews, but also on the user forum, concerns the uses of content in the industry productions. The content from the commons, resurfacing in Hollywood films, popular music, productions by popular artists is often seen as a remarkable indicator of both quality of the content and skills of the commoners, whose abilities match the tough requirements of media production. To the FreeSound community, the most important example, is the 2006 film *Children of Men* which had an estimated budget of $76,000,000 (https://www.imdb.com/title/tt0206634/) and starred the Hollywood actors Clive Owen and Julianne Moore. The film's credits contain a reference to FreeSound. Many users have seen this reference without seeing the film as the screenshot containing the information about the source file is widely circulated on the forum and by sites writing and mentioning FreeSound.

I have interviewed the author of the original sample, who is a sound professional and specialises in sound design and works part-time at the School of Music and Technology at the Utrecht University of the Arts. In the interview he reflected on his FreeSound Activity, particularly the unexpected usage of his sound by the producers of the film.

> I was most active at FreeSound around the starting period of FreeSound. I used it in the non-professional projects, but I was very happy with the initiative that I thought 'oh, actually I also have quite a lot of samples, different stuff which maybe people could use'. So I put many of it online and some of these samples were used quite a lot. I realised like 'OK, there is apparently interest in it, maybe people can reuse it'. So it was funny. (...) I don't know if you know that like the 'Children of men' film? (...) [About the sample used in the film] I can send you the link [to the sample] if you want because actually it's really funny. It wasn't recorded very professionally because it was more like an interactive theatre play. We just recorded it on the location itself, so I had like this tiny microphone which we would normally use for minidisc field recordings, it's not a very good quality, mono. And we were doing a couple of screaming and shouting takes for like you know, voices to have in the theatre play. And a friend of mine wanted to demonstrate like 'no, no, it should be more like this', you know, and he was just doing this fragments. It's actually also clipping a little bit et cetera. So quality-wise it's a very dirty sample. But I like a lot how it came out, so I also made a competition with it, you know, like with all these different transformations or you know, like sound sculpturing, you could say. I also shared a couple of sounding music blocks or sounding building blocks from this composition. So these transformations are also shared with then also explanation like 'I did this from that sample'. (9)

This passage is a powerful example of how a spontaneous upload decision ended up in the soundtrack of a blockbuster production. This creator insists that that the recording was technically flawed and mentions that its production was coincidental; it happened during another artistic project. Besides talking about the film, he also talks about other reuses and applications of the content. Even though, this creator did not obtain renumeration for that sample (the license was CC-0), this instance has tied the commons very closely to the mainstream media and resonated in many interviews.

The same user mentions another instance of his sound being recognised by the mainstream industry. This time, he talks about being approached by the producers of the Grammy-winning rock group the Eagles:

> This band called The Eagles and they contacted me, like 'can we use this and that sample of yours?' Of course, I always say 'yes' and I didn't realise it was like this band, The Eagles from 'Hotel California', you know? So that was really funny that after a couple of months, maybe even a year, the same person sent me a message like 'yes, we would like to send you a sales block', you know, 'for your contribution'. And I didn't know what sales block was actually, so they sent me this huge frame with couple of CDs in it and also presented because of over 40 million copies sold worldwide. It was like 'what?' That's funny, I like. (...) It was also an interesting one, because actually they used two samples, but let's focus on the one sample that it's like a church bell. In the Netherlands we have like these, we have this tradition of tunes church bells. And I recorded a couple of churches also back in my studies. And I decided I can share it with the world. They were really popular and the good, clear recordings. (9)

This sample describes a spectacular incorporation of commons-based content into mainstream popular culture. The author of the sample was surprised that his sound was used, and that he received a tangible form of recognition. The volume of sales and the professionalism with which the interaction was conducted point at the value of this content for cultural production that followed all conventions of the industry.

These examples, though anecdotal, allow contributors who participate in commons-based peer production to see that their work, next to that of other users, has the potential for exposure to the mainstream industry. Similar stories help users to see that with persistence and skill, it is possible to contribute to major projects. Even unauthorised use can foster the belief that the professional sound designers representing a variety of creative industries are on FreeSound, looking for pieces to add to their productions. The exposure of violations likewise shows the potential of the commons. One user found his sample on a TV series.

> Yes, the firm I think is TNT, it's a massive film maker. And the show was *Falling Skies*, (...). I quite liked it, it was quite good. It was the penultimate, to the end of the season when they finally see these kind of, the overloads on the planet and I kind of set the scene with my, in this kind of weird, alien landscape with my chanting. It was quite kind of epic. And yes, I just can't believe it, because I was just, you know, by chance. And they are heavily featured in the scene. In a way I was coming like quite exciting saying 'well, it's quite cool' but then I was also like 'well, hang on, that's a serious company, that's kind of naughty'. So there's another site to this. Actually a lot of it it's just trust, because I have been fool for this. (12)

Creators whose content has been used in mainstream productions concur that FreeSound benefits from these instances, and that the community benefits from the popularisation of the site and its content.

> I remember there was a big deal, several years ago, it wasn't mine, but someone's sound effect was used in a Hollywood movie, if I remember correctly. And so, there was a lot of really good publicity for FreeSound. And I know my sound being used in Ken Burns' documentary, I think that speaks volumes on the quality of what FreeSound has to offer. But at the same time, it's also kind of pick and choose. Not that the sound designers, I think it also takes sound designers that might already be aware of FreeSound, because I feel like as far as the film industry, you know, they have a lot of resources so it takes, you need the designer who is kind of searching out of the box, maybe to come across FreeSound, but I think as more people are aware of it, and there's more people using it, you know, FreeSound can become a resource they will take into their professional lives. (4)

This user emphasises the fact that FreeSound has a unique value proposition: content that is "out of the box", and tremendous potential to be used professionally.

These are only three examples among thousands of uses of sound samples in popular culture, theatre plays, museums, podcasts and YouTube videos that have been viewed tens of millions of times. While most creators focus on high-quality and unique content, some of them also express concerns about the site's credibility building. Improvement of the reputation of the site (and content) is essential to tightening the relationships with the industry. A core user, working in a large American media house, remarked: "My production assistants use FreeSound because it is the fastest and easiest. But we don't want to mess with verification of ownership so most of that stuff gets replaced by stock library samples before it gets published" (71). These observations are shared by Frederic Font, FreeSound's developer and administrator. In an expert interview he commented:

> We've seen this case for example in video games where people told us or sent the message that 'yes, we use FreeSound for all these purposes, but then in the later stage we will replace all the sounds with sounds from another library for which we own the rights and we know we can just go without problem'. So it's with that for example, one clear example that we've seen. Well, I mean they don't know if, because they found this sound on the Internet and yes, it's Creative Commons licence but maybe they are not sure what happens if someone tells this sound was stolen or they don't have a document which says 'yes, I can use it here'.

Major commercial actors, who take legal responsibility for works such as films or advertisement campaigns in the descriptions of users approach content cautiously, as the use of potentially illegal content might bring detrimental consequences.

A result of this suspension between commons and the industry is a set of practices that I present in later further subsections. They all contain approaches to commodification of the commons, that contribute to the business models applied to FreeSound. All of them use the networked value of content to create exchange value, for example promoting unique content or the services of a creator. Their value capture is embedded in the commons ecosystem of value, for example in the form of comments, reuses and volume of coherent content, which assists with the legitimacy of the creator who relies on this credibility to develop the unique value proposition. In addition, they provide a range of levels of engagement with the commons: from very peripheral, occasional presence in the commons, to large-scale participation and reliance on volumes of material. This is especially relevant to the controversy of commodification and questions over the for-profit use of the commons, for instance to advertise one's own content, or to forage for free content for commercial projects. Several models within the commercial sphere use the commons as a central resource. Rather than focusing on the operational side, my analysis concentrates on providing descriptions relevant to business model representations (e.g., Amit and Zott, 2002; Tapscott et al., 2000) to draft the value relationships between the commons and commerce. It is hence limited to key value-related considerations.

2   Multiple Channel Content Sales

For the creative industries, technology has traditionally been used to create, bundle and distribute information and entertainment (Schumann and Hess, 2000). Cultural products have been tied to specific devices; for instance, music was accessed strictly for radio or records; film was available only in cinemas or on television. However, information technology and the internet have generated a new dynamic based on integration of new ways of creating, bundling, and distributing content. The way of accessing it has been transformed, often integrating all previously used equipment into a single device. Suddenly, in the 21st century, consumers could access content using inexpensive and simple personal computers, smartphones or even digital TVs connected to the internet. Similarly, production was easier due to both technological advancements, such as better cameras for less money, but also proliferation of user-made media. Part of that process have been stock libraries, a simple concept based on paid databases of media, available either in the form of price-tag store (you pay for every bit and the prices differ) or based on a flat subscription that allows constant access to that media. Stock libraries usually contain a variety of media, scoping digital pictures, sound, music and video. Naturally, stock libraries were instrumental in distributing the content that was royalty-free and non-exclusive, saving creators the cost of hiring models and booking studio time.

Several creators active on FreeSound participate in regular production of sound, recording a variety of sound effects, and often relying in their work on others' sound, also produce sound, which often is uploaded to stock libraries. In this sense, the most common and most traditional way of commodifying user creations is the marketisation of content in which FreeSound is a means of marketing, promotion, and experimentation. In this model of exchange value extraction, creators upload content to FreeSound, often using a non-commercial restrictive license (BY-NC); and sell a copyrighted license through stock libraries or other distribution channel. In most cases they rely on intermediation of stock websites which also screen content and certify its copyright. The sales occur in several ways, such as through stock pages where they have their content, on CDs or directly.

One of the users who has been most successful with this model is RobinHood76 who has also uploaded an impressive number of audio tracks to

FreeSound. He has shared his experience as a content creator, and explained the role of FreeSound in professionalising his sound-making activity:

> I started on Free Sound around 2008 and it was when I started having fun [recording sounds] because I had a recording studio. And my activity then was doing sound for various clients in the studio. But then on FreeSound I once saw that someone asked if anyone had sound similar to the link to a commercial stock. I clicked on the link and thought "nothing special". I remember my impression was that there are sounds that are not better than mine. And people pay for it. So I uploaded a couple of my sounds to that site. They accepted them and that's how it started. Well, let's say after two weeks, when I put there maybe 50 sounds, I earned my first dollar. (...) Then my energy shifted a bit to this commercial stock, it was probably iStock Audio then. And there I started regularly uploading there. I was at the point when I earned maybe 10–15 dollars a month, I was happy, even though I was earning much more from my regular work. (...) And so it developed slowly, (...) within maybe 4 years I found that I could give up these concerts [refers to working as an audio engineer], because I had quite nice money. In addition to work in the studio, I had these sounds. And now I don't know how many of all my sounds I made, probably like 25,000. They really sell on these different stocks, I have to say honestly, so I can only live from making sounds at this point. (23)

FreeSound was a factor in this user's decision to engage generate sound for stock libraries. RobinHood76 had prior experiences with the site, as well as extensive recording experience, and observed that his technical knowledge allowed him to start uploading his content to stock libraries – in the same way as he was doing it to FreeSound. His discovery, as well as consistent work on his content extending the library of authored sounds has gradually evolved into a full-time activity. He describes how the market for stock sound is becoming more saturated and challenging than ever.

> My biggest competition are such commercial libraries, for example Hollywood Sounds. They bought the rights to the tapes from the movies, and from there they can rip those sounds. We have no chance with them, because they are big corporations with 500,000- 1 million sounds. They're flooding these libraries now. (...) Acting as a one-person firm, I can say I do okay in this market, the key is to be persistent and consistent. Though starting now it would be very difficult to make any income from it because it already takes thousands of sounds in different places

> [refers to different stock libraries] for it [the business] to work. (…) I think stocks work in the same way as Free Sound: making useful sound available. So the key is to make it as useful as possible that no nonsensical sounds would end up there. I could be more active [on FreeSound], but I don't want to share that many sounds there, because then I could be unfair to those who buy them [on stock sites], so I usually put up some older sounds [to FreeSound] every now and then. (23)

RobinHood76 notices that these platforms are starting to be dominated by more powerful, media corporations which have greater resources and production power at their disposal.

FreeSound has an intriguing position in RobinHood76's activity. He uses FreeSound in his production as an enabler. It supported and introduced him to working on libraries of sound, provided a gateway to information about stock sites as well as trained him in maximizing the use value. He notes that the rules of the stock sites are similar and based on an ability of predicting and producing sound that might have as broad a spectrum of applications as possible. While the business idea originated from FreeSound's forum post, the role of the platform remained important to this user. He remains active on the platform, sharing on FreeSound sounds that have a lower commercial potential, or have aged; at the same time, he supports the community. RobinHood76 continues this activity, but FreeSound is only one of the outlets through which he shares his productions.

For some users, commoning is a way of reputation building. Their activity is also tied to sales of works using different channels, but they use their FreeSound account as a catalogue of their content, skills and industry experience. According to one user:

> When I negotiate the contract [refers to content sales and production], I always link the client my FreeSound account. This just shows them that I have a volume of sound, they can see what I've done, that some of that has few thousands of downloads. (…) I even got a few clients who sent me a DM [direct message] that they saw my work on FreeSound. (23)

As this respondent argues, his FreeSound history and activity, helps him build reputation and history which is useful for seeking clients and expanding his commercial activity. This history also helps to demonstrate an author's credibility, also given the fact that many commercial actors are suspicious of online content: "My account is the best business card I could have. Anyone can see that I am doing that from 2008 and I am really careful in crafting my sound for different projects, also on stocks and as a full-time sound designer" (23). Attitudes aimed at protecting the community and propagating the idea of open licensing arise among all stakeholders involved in the CC; however, there are serious obstacles connected to obtaining rights of usage through the CC license. As this respondent shows, long history and reputation facilitates these relationships.

Users who diversify their sales rely on non-commercial licensing to build interest in the content, and then monetise it using individual negotiations or stock sites. For example:

> My samples published as Creative Commons have a NC [non-commercial] license ... Let's say you are a company and would like to use my sound in your production, you need to come to me and pay me for signing a commercial contract. I have over 4000 sounds put up on-line and three hard drives of them in my catalogue. I assume what's on-line is just a demo (...). [Non-commercial] users download it and use it anyway, I don't care. What I get is good ratings and interest. But [commercial] businesses are too afraid to use it [for commercial products] without authorisation and I am a beneficiary of that. I make the content and I take all the responsibility for the fact that my content is credible.
> sound effect and music producer, Germany (3)

> There were really many such strange stories. Or a gentleman from an advertising agency from Poland calls and says – Sir, please save me. – But what's going on? – Well, because we used your highway sound in some commercial, which is on TV, but we have no permission and here Zaiks is picking on. Will you write us a permission to use it? – Cool, but why didn't you write to me first, before you used it commercially? I don't have the satisfaction of bullying someone, I wrote it to them, but they could write anything that would recognize my highway sound in some add. (23)

The respondent describes the alternative valorisation of creative labour. When uploading sound using a non-commercial licence, this creator increases the quantity of resources available for download and usage by users who will not use it commercially. This allows for the extraction of use-value, which increases his reputation and visibility. But the exchange value extraction, in other words, making money off this content, is possible only through direct engagement with this creator. There are groups of producers who do nothing but make samples for music composition or multimedia, such as sound effects and field recordings. Their way of labour valorisation is supported by the CC, which acts as a channel for promotion and free distribution. These creators use CC licensing to build their reputation, seeking possible collaborations or contacts by the creation and development of free-to-use portfolios. Even though they are never sure what use and exchange value their content might have, copyleft plays a key role in the distribution.

Sales using multiple distribution channels are a common strategy among users who connect their non-commercial commoning with sales embedded in traditional copyright law. This model of value extraction relies on the traditional distribution of closed content, occurring via platforms of stock sites. In this model, the varying degree of commoning fulfils different functions. On the one hand, it gives the creator a homepage as a reference point for future and existing customers. On the other hand, it confers a specific artistic identity. Even though the commoning activity might only be supplemental, the long-standing tradition of commoning, and embedding the roots of creator activity in open licensing, helps the creators to find common ground. Quite often the business model of content sales is also performed as a one-person activity – for that result many creators are seeking networking and linking within the industry.

3   Freemium Mode of Sound and Related Products

A similar model of commodification is built around the idea of freemium, used in software to denote a model of sales, based on offering a basic software version for free, and charging for additional features, functionalities or goods that complement the basic version. In the sound industry, the freemium model of distribution means that the free, open version is distributed inside the commons, offering a framework for sharing content that can be circulated and reused. The commercial, paid, part of the distribution is distributed in the form of extended content that complements the content available in the commons – for example as part of a bigger volume of content of the same time, more liberal license permissions or extended support and documentation of the media.

A project that depends on this adaptation of the commons-reliant freemium model is the Versilian Community Sample Library (VCSL). This project of Versilian Studios LLC., a virtual instrument development company based in Connecticut, has played a vital role in the commons, with 3163 samples of instruments by March 2021, recorded on studio-level equipment and suitable for professional production and uploaded to FreeSound with CC-0 Public Domain license. Versilian Studios provides samples of recorded instruments and sample-based software (in the form of plug-ins) that are "affordable, quality virtual instruments for students and professionals alike" (https://vis.versilstudios.com/, accessed 4.02.2021). Versilian studio's strategy is part of the tradition of commoning. Its first project, Versilian Studios Chamber Orchestra (VSCO), was based entirely on open content that was uploaded and shared on FreeSound. It was followed by VSCO 2, a commercial project of instruments sample library, characterised as "a celebration of the diversity of musical instruments and the people who play them; students, teachers, musicologists, and collectors- performing on everything from modern professional instruments to rare antiques" (https://vis.versilstudios.com/vsco-2.html, accessed 4.02.2021). This library is based on recordings of instruments which have been played in such a way that users of this library can compose songs and treat them like virtual instruments. Importantly, this product is offered as a free (Community Edition) version (1,952 samples), Standard Edition (9,254 samples – $99) and Professional Edition (23,000 samples – $229). The Community edition is available on FreeSound where it is shared under CC-0 Public Domain license.

In an interview, the creator of Versilian Studios, remarked on the development of the company, which started as a free project aimed at development of a sample library.

> I was getting started composing music, all I could have and this is back in like 2009, 2010, all that was available online were sound files, you know, like a 3 megabyte sound file that's supposed to have all the sounds of the orchestra. And you know, these are things that were probably originally recorded in the 90s and released on various hardware samplers that were limited to like you know, 4 to 8 megabytes of sample memory. And it's like we've come so far since then, why isn't anyone making new free sound libraries? And I was going through this process sort of around 2013, 2012 and I started putting together the original VSCO 1 which is now discontinued which was freeware and had no commercial component. And that was just piece together with little, it wasn't even sampled intentionally. It was just like 'here's a session I had of someone playing violin that I had recorded and had all the permissions too. Let me cut out those long notes and call it a violin'. And so that was kind of the first iteration of that and like the minute I put it out there, I was like I need to actually do this properly. And then I started on VSCO 2 and that was originally freeware. It was going to be a freeware from the beginning and then it featured creeps, like crazy. There was originally going to be like 3 gigabytes and like 12 instruments. And it ended up being like 20 gigabytes and 90 instruments by the time we finished recordings. It took like 2,5 years and cost a lot of money. Even though it was, I mean, at the end of the day I ended up

recording, personally playing about a third of the instruments to try to keep the cost down. (53)

This creator comments on the growth of the library and the emergence of a consistent strategy of recording and structuring the process. He mentions how the formation of a business model supported the growth of the library and the emergence of new products. He adds that the maintenance of production and management of the project are costly.

> (...) So yes, we ended up eventually having to say there is no way that you know, if I release this as freeware, I'm basically going to go into debt, because I've invested a lot of money into this. We made the commercial version kind of for that reason and that's actually that commercial version is what mainly spares on all of our development now, which includes the freeware. I pay about 150 to 200 dollars a month just in a bandwidth. Mostly for the freeware products that we self-host in order to keep these things accessible in formats like VST, as well as fortunately we have stuff like FreeSound and GitHub where we can keep the wav files themselves as well for people to really experiment and work with. I mean, almost all the freeware we make I release as Creative Commons 0, because I really believe it's just we have to get the stuff out there and we really need kind of this baseline framework there, so people can go to one place and get a great sounding start to music. (11)

The same respondent described his approach to sales of sound and his consumer base, which is similar to the audience of FreeSound, which consists of professionals, semi-amateurs and hobbyists.

> It's mostly composers. So mainly at the particular price point which is around 200 dollars, it's mainly intermediate composers or we get a fair number of students and we do offer like a student discount, too. But we will get some very diverse people. Like I have a number of customers who have bought it, who do like rock music and they like having, orchestra metal is a popular genre and they like having some of the orchestral instruments in there. A good number of people are doing stuff like video games going. I think that's probably one of the more prevalent areas. But there are definitely also some hobbyists who have it also. (64)

Commons provide access to sound that is useful but that also cross-fertalises production with components suitable for professional production. The variety of applications of the content and the emphasis on the quality are similar to the industry dynamics, and their reflection in the commons.

This respondent outlines the role of the community in the generation of ideas and in benchmarking the content demand. He cites an instance of software developed by his company and remarks on the parallels between the dynamic on FreeSound and the market for his products.

> I used to get emails like all the time of people leaving comments like 'oh, I used this in my game' or 'I used this in this project'. It's just so, you know, that kind of thing is exciting. And I've done that sort of thing too with the orchestral samples. So like Tubular Bells, for some reason, I guess no one has, except for us, has like really, I guess we've kind of cornered the Tubular Bells market, because I mean that was our first commercial product, I made a 10 dollar VSD plugin of tubular bells and it's sold like hundreds, I think it sold over 500 copies which is a little crazy, but yes, we have some TUBULAR BELLS on FreeSound and I think those have downloaded a tonne or two. But sometimes it will be like a weird thing, like I will be scrolling down and I will just feel like 'oh, this one sound from this one thing, like this one vibe slap sample is super popular or something'. It's like four times as many downloads as everything else. (05)

This respondent's experiences show that the market for his software, and for sound packages sold by the VSCO is similar to the dynamic on FreeSound. Commoning thus parallels the practices of this niche of the industry.

The instance of VSCO allows identification of the link between content production, networked value and commoning. FreeSound and the commons are a propagator of the products, while incorporating a high volume of high-quality sounds. The contribution of VSCO is very high, given the costs of the production process and the liberal licensing of the sound. Yet, at the same time commons offer networked value, which is important role in the distribution of content and accompanying information about its source as well as products offered by VSCO. Even though users of VSCO are not necessarily involved in commoning, the freemium model offers high exposition of the product range and enhances the online visibility of the content.

4   Exclusivity of Access and Intermediation

While in two previous models of commodification commons was the disseminator of content, another type of a business model relies on intermediation.

In this model, commons capture and lock users or content in exclusive deals. This model is based on extraction of value based on examination of content and creators' potential to generate profit and buying their content for exclusivity or hiring them to generate exclusive content. Organisations that apply this model emulate the work of labels, trying to capture filtered creators or content. This process follows the trend known as reintermediation of content, which occurs after de-intermediation caused by the proliferation of the internet and the emergence of new, alternative distribution based on direct sales and end-to-end commerce (Carroll, 2006). Reintermediation responds to the process of the highly needed fulfilment of commercial transactions, bringing benefits of scale, bargaining power and time and attention savings to the creators. At the same time, reintermediation causes tensions, stemming from industry's adoption of conventions emerging with removal of intermediation, such as pay-per-track or broadcasting model (Fox, 2004; Swatman et al., 2006). They result in the emergence of new types of access and intermediation models, attacked for unfair distribution (Marshall, 2015) and work to the advantage of powerful industry actors, solidifying their position in media (Braxton, 2016).

In the creative commons, intermediation captures value by identifying and legally closing unique content so that it can be offered at a premium price. In the traditional music industry, labels scout artists and sign exclusivity deals with them. In an ideal model, artists benefit from representation and access to more generous budgets and professional studio capabilities. The labels are able to commodify the works that the artists have produced under the contract. While the label model of intermediation survives due to labels' marketing power, the sound industry differs, typically with presence of intermediaries in the form of stock libraries that do not engage with the commons.

However, FreeSound users experience the activity of intermediaries. Many of the interviewed core users had been contacted through Freesound's messaging system with a proposition to sell content. Even though these propositions were occasional, most of the core users who shared content with attribution licenses have obtained propositions of content buyers. Typically, they were offered payment to obtain sound for resale. The interested buyers do not always mention the purpose of their projects, but creators said that they included commercially sold sound packs (sound effects were traditionally sold this way) or newly created subscription-based services (which lacked content). The interviewees have sporadically sold the sound as both the payment and the purpose of usage. One respondent expresses his experience with intermediaries:

> This is not worth it because that's not the main point of commoning. I get emails every couple of days with offers, sell me your stuff. But quite frankly most of the times, I think it is spam. I mean, you can't get rich making sound effects. People offer payments like 2 quid for a single sound. That just does not work for me. The administration of such payments, as well as communication with clients who would want to buy it would just not pay off. (36)

This creator, whose library is shared using attribution license, observes that the intermediation model does not offer him sufficient payment for content and that he ignores all single-sound intermediation offers.

The process of obtaining access to content and securing exclusivity is approached differently by one of the core users who works for an American media company that distributes sound and sound effects to broadcasters and studios. In the interview, he mentioned that the commons are a useful channel of recruiting users to produce content, which due to the volume also increases the revenue for creators.

> I mean, I've very pro Creative Commons. When I got hired we mostly worked with sound designers whom we hired for particular jobs. The number of sounds that typical media firm needs is not really as big as it seems. (…) And for the past ten years I think that I got a good model of building relationship with designers and checking their credibility. So pretty much it's all about finding people who have a volume of sound and can either sell it or can produce it for us. And it is about specialization, so if I see that you have good dog sounds, or nature more generally, I may ask you to produce me a hundred or so of them. (…) I know that when you're a small creator you know well you need to provide sounds that might be useful for creators of other kinds of media. So in that sense FreeSound really trains people in that, and then we later work with them. (67)

This path relies on securing rights and creators' work to provide services in the industry that are entirely separated from the commons. In this sense FreeSound's prominence-building process and the dynamic of the commons foster the capture and commodification of content.

A similar strategy, reliant on Creative Commons, but aimed at the commodification of music, was taken by Jamendo, a Luxembourg-based company that acts like a music label. The company contracts musicians who publish their work using Creative Commons, so without relying on traditional institutions, such as collecting societies or standard labels. Jamendo's revenue relies on selling rights of usage to content and providing services of background radio licenses to shops. Jamendo's offer is attractive due to lower costs: it does not depend on content handled by intermediaries or collecting societies and the distribution is online. By signing contracts with these publishers, artists gain the possibility of obtaining income from Jamendo. These distributors thus intermediate similarly to traditional copyright institutions, such as music labels and collecting societies. Jamendo's model parallels the standard model of intermediation. In 2017, the content manager of Jamendo commented on the firm's strategy of intermediation:

> I think there is a lot of the clients are just independent video makers that are like not necessarily professionals. They are just making videos. So they just need a track to put the video on YouTube and not be bothered. So there are a lot of those people and then there are like more professional video makers that then you know, are making commercial videos or videos that are monetised. And so they are aware that they need something really legal and they use Jamendo because it's cheaper and they find a lot of interesting music for great prices. And then you have like a smaller group of like bigger clients, like brands who would use Jamendo on the regular basis, because they produce a lot of content, a lot of videos or I don't know, like podcasts or stuff like that. So it's a lot of that and it's a lot of, like I guess most of their music for sync is used in videos that are like either corporate videos or like presenting the product or just like online TV series of like, I don't know, for bikers or cookies, YouTube. And then, for the in-store, it's the same structure. You have a lot of like very small shop owners or like bar owners, restaurants and then the small proportion of like really big brands that have like huge chain stores, like we work with Ikea or Burger King or Zara, you know, like really big retailers. They are using like, sometimes it's just for, in one country. Sometimes it's more global that they are using the Jamendo in-store solution for you know, cheaper prices rather than paying the local collecting society that you know, has blanket fee, blanket yearly fee that is just so much more expensive than what we offer.
>
> Jamendo interview

Jamendo's strategy is based on an advanced model of intermediation. Not only does this model rely on continuous signing of artists but also, depending on the popularity and usage of sound, it renumerates artists proportionally to the popularity and usage of content. The model follows the standard of royalty distribution in the music industry. It is thus reinstating the intermediation and ensuring continuous commodification of content in a similar way to traditional labels and publishers.

5 Curation and Automated Integration

Commons contain many sounds that are annotated by users who input metadata and describe the sound to facilitate searches by other users. However, one of the main problems of FreeSound, and of many other media platforms, is the process of finding suitable content. The last model of commodification relies on the idea of facilitating of user experience through processing, analysing and filtering. This process is based on a unique design of search tools, such as sound analysis algorithms. Search engines are a forerunner of this process. As Creative Commons uses a Resource Description Framework (RDF) for describing its metadata, the data shared using this license is visible to search engines (both the license and the data content). For example, in 2005, yahoo .com has allowed searches for media using Creative Commons' filter of licensing framework.

However, in the models employed by FreeSound there have been conversations about how to design and create a business model, based on automatic matching of content with search, aggregating content or creating catalogues at the top of those services or delivering services based on open content. One of the interviewees, a software developer and sound designer, shared his thoughts:

> Imagine a system which allows you to search for sounds in a very intelligent way and to know what you are looking for, like a Google of sounds if you want, right? And this is one of the hardest things you ever could do. I imagine that you can have two very, very close sounds, one to the other, but a musician will tell you 'this is crap' and 'this is wonderful'. (…) Even so, so all technology, sound technology proved amazingly helpful, because this Shazam for example, it's the application which really knows to recognise songs for far, even on a very hard hearing conditions. It amazes me all the time, again. But I still think that the world of sounds as a world of humans is so rich in so many aspects, that it's very hard really to organise it much better than what you got with FreeSound. I think you have a lot of discipline there for keywords, things that people add, usually how to create the sound, you have free text search, you can search by user.
>
> It's hard for me to imagine much more you can do. I would call it 'cows' but it's creative 'cows' and I think it depends also very much what you are looking for. If you have a certain video project and you look for certain

> sound, let's say a bell sound or whatever, you will find your bell sounds, it's not a problem. You will see maybe 100 on your page and 3, 4 will already be of your interest. It's so rich, it's amazing. It can be almost any kind of bells you can find in FreeSound, just as an example. You have to invest time, you have to search but I could hardly imagine, maybe I don't have enough background, technically how this could be much more improved, which is a very good idea, because it helps people to save time. (3)

This user exemplifies the need: a user wants to obtain sound that is matching the expectations. At the same time, he stresses the problem with sound's specificity, so the fact that sound is more difficult to be compared or analyzsd as relative to music, which has melody and more components than a sample. For that reason, the building of an ecosystem allowing for browsing Creative Commons sound has been discussed among users and in the literature. According to Blacc, Manta and Olson (2015): "Imagine an iTunes- or Spotify-type interface through which music programmers could look up songs and specific prices for various uses. (...) Commercial music purchasers may select songs and know individual prices with virtually the same ease that they currently enjoy in making their programming selections. This would allow for much more variety of music use and distribution than we currently have." (p. 48). Similar promises, relevant to the shifting role of the new type of circulation of media, based on analysis, cataloguing and tagging, have emerged in the industry.

A significant effort in building of such an ecosystem has been the AudioCommons initiative, led by the creator of FreeSound, Xavier Serra. This project, comprised of academic and business partners established an ecosystem of open sound that bridges the content of FreeSound and other sites (Jamendo, Europeana sound), to create tools for creators. The project included Waves, one of the largest developers of sound software plug-ins for Digital Audio Workstations. The software producer built commercial software for enhanced browsing and searching of open sound. In an interview, a manager of this project described his involvement with FreeSound, where content was to be accessed through application programming interface (API):

> What I like in our part of the project is that we are building the tool that can actually make a big change, it's a "music Google" that will allow people to search with the music criteria to find stuff and content inside this free content. (...) Because usually people are going to search for music content on Google.com [refers to the website], they are going to insert or type few keywords and look for the content. They might get all kinds of different content from all over. This could be articles on the meanings

of the words or whatever. It's not necessarily the music. And well, talking about my "music Google" it's like I'm a musician and I'm looking only for audio content. I don't want articles, I don't want anything else. I am concentrated on the musical content only and I really would like to make my search not based on only words but based on other search criteria like the scale and tone and all other stuff like BPM, because this is the terms that I'm used to work with when I'm creating the music inside the studios.
o6-expert interview

This developer describes the typical user issue. Calling his product "music Google", he argues for a better tool for browsing and searching content.

In the same interview, another member of Waves team outlined the user experience connected to the process of sound and music editing. He claimed that a chronic problem was the amount of time spent browsing content, for instance when working in a rented studio:

So if I am like someone who is working in the studio and I'm looking for, I'm in the middle of the session and I'm looking for some drum sample and I really need it now because it costs me money, this time in the studio, then I can open the plug[-in] and just find myself a bunch of samples and try them and use this one right now. So this money [in the studio] for me is valuable and also in my creation process. I could be another user like say someone who is just, as a habit, not a pro and he is looking for making video or whatever and he is looking for samples for his video. So he has just opened the browser and made his searches and can find the simple piece of audio to use in his video clip. There could be a lot of types of users, from not very professional to the professionals. (15)

The value proposition given by Waves thus relies on facilitation of search, redirection to content providers, such as FreeSound, and easy access to content.

At the same time, the discussion of automated curation and sorting drifts to the management of copyright within the commons, often connected to the process of securing rights. As one user stated: "I would stick to Public Domain CC-0 license but sometimes the stuff that you need is exactly attribution and we need systemic solutions to that, that's why I am working on an updated tool for my DAW" (expert 12). This user argued that his project is based on development of a computerised system of automatized attribution, similar to scholarly citation, thus making reused material easier to track. As one of the CC activists explained in one of the forums, "in those plans, attribution and modification will be inscribed into the sound file, creating a form of watermark stored in the metadata" (CC activist, UK). FreeSound now lists all downloaded files and licenses on a user's account, simplifying the attribution process. In the past there were tools that matched the unique sound identifier with author's credentials and license. However, none have managed to develop a commercial project. As the CC activist phrased it: "In the future the downloads and exchanges will be traceable in an easier way and that's the only way to make any money on the process of attribution" (expert 12). Furthermore, there have been conversations about the development of a contract-tracing system for open sound, like a digital ledger or blockchain technology.

6 Conclusions

These four models of value transformation lead to the observation that commons undergo an evolution that uses established models of sound and music industries. This phenomenon is based on the commodification of open content, seeking creative talent, making exclusive deals and reinstating intermediation. This overview of the process of value extraction differs from the "project hijacking". This term, drawn from the free/open source software context, denotes usage of commons data in order to achieve profit, usually separately from community and maintaining no connection to the original roots of the project (Ciffolili, 2004; Dahlander and Magnusson, 2008). Unlike hijacking, which is when a corporation uses portion of codes and turns it into a commercial product, the commodification of creative commons follows the rules of the industry and takes on a form of more granular sorting of content that contains exchange value.

The commodification of the commons works to the benefit of the commoning authors, who by value extraction often generate interest in their work, or sometimes even secure minor jobs. In a way, this process relies on the networked value of content, which permits extensive linking of content that might be used commercially with original creators, who are often believed to be capable of generating more content of good quality. Commons thus provide an easy path, if use value of content is very high, there is a possibility of transformation of this use value to exchange value, if not of content, then through salaried work of the creator. Paradoxically, when talking about commons to creators, some of them have explicitly mentioned that they were more than willing to follow any industry opportunities stemming from commoning. Commoning in the case of sound thus has rarely excluded commodification. Instead, its primary logic rested on the idea of freedom of creation and building portfolio, to the benefit of independent production and supporting the new forms of intermediation. Moreover, commodification is also beneficial for the commons. Any approaches to cataloguing, sorting, processing, and improving access to the content have influenced and repositioned the commons. The increased interest and traffic enhance usage rates, and the visibility of creators. In this sense, Creative Commons opens a window of opportunity to platform, but also benefits from widespread dissemination and free circulation of content. This content is open to remix and possible to use in creative projects and allows for experimentation. As a result, this process fosters creativity and experimentation. Even though large platforms are enhancing the search process, they pose no direct threat to the commons.

This chapter shows that even though commons in the sound industry are very closely aligned with creative industry, they do not reject its models or conventions. Instead, commons support independent entrepreneurship and cater to independent creative industries, usually characterised by smaller budgets and a more precarious position than mainstream creative industries. At the same time, the creators working within this sphere are actively seeking and supporting this process, often rejecting idea of commodification due to low profits, and continuing production and activity within the commons as part of their artistic activity. To them, the path to commodification is not necessarily connected to the payment but more to the application of content, for instance in a blockbuster film, instead of a Hollywood sound design studio.

Conclusion

The Art of the Creative Commons

The title of this book, *The Art of the Creative Commons,* describes the mechanism of artistic production based on open licensing. The case described in this book is an instance of commons that consists of creative content. These commons are built by a community pursuing a goal of artistic exchange and collaboration, and following a unique production method and organisation, that so far has not been broadly described in the literature. This book's main objective has been to propose a theoretical perspective on the shifts caused by the open licensing model of the Creative Commons license in the creative industries. The book posits that open licensing in creative industries serves a dual function: it proposes an alternative approach to intellectual property protection, thereby playing an important role in resisting current copyright practice, and more importantly, it enables new mechanisms of peer production, fosters new ways of achieving artistic innovation, mediated by the digital environment, and creates a path for new, commons-based business models. In other words, this project has identified how the open licensing model contributes to the changes in the ways in which cultural production and distribution occur, which in studies of creative industries so far has not received the same sustained attention as the resistance thesis. Focusing on the sound industry and its potential to cross-subsidise the value of audio/music to emerging industry needs, this project focused on the practices of users of the largest repository of sound licensed under the Creative Commons license, FreeSound.org, which contains almost 500.000 works shared by the authors in more than 15 years of existence.

Open licensing is taking significant steps in the direction of delivering transformational and universal impact on science, technology and society. As the management and social sciences literature lacks clear conceptualisations of its role in the creative industry, this project is intended to fill that niche by describing key spheres in the organisation of production, labour of artists, networked nature of objects, ways of collaboration driven by it and emerging monetization strategies. All these topics reflect the general opening of organisations in management and organisational studies. These works have shared findings showing that openness influences numerous spheres, touching open business strategies and operations, creating new participatory cultures within capital and production, as well as influences public policy in the domains of public data, governance and scholarship. The findings of this book add a voice to the debate, showing how openness transforms traditional creative production. The practices described in this book show an interconnected model that conceptualizes and identifies the communication and interaction between the commons, content creators, content users and mainstream industry. These findings help us to learn more about the context of open media to build a base of understanding of the role and mechanisms of the commons in the creative industries.

Below I conclude this book by addressing the main spheres to which my work contributes, shortly summarising the main arguments relevant to academic debate.

1 Creative Commons and the Opening of the Creative Industries

This book bridges theoretical arguments on the ongoing opening of industries, caused by a new paradigm of openness by depicting their intersection with creative production and the changing dynamics in the practice of creative production. Creative industries have traditionally used copyright as a closure mechanism, protecting rights to creative works and to regulate the economic reproduction of those works in a capitalist society. Understanding copyright began with the mechanisation of creative industries, when new inventions permitted broad circulation of recordings (phonograph), or film (cinematograph). These breakthroughs revolutionised the way in which mechanically reproduced cultural creations are interpreted (Benjamin, 1998). This dynamic has created a market for usage rights rather than for the product itself, thereby establishing the copyright trade. In effect, this process has accelerated the commodification of creations, changed the way in which the institutions of the industry operate and causing the emergence of a powerful structure of governance and sanctioning of the system, shaping copyright law and supporting the growth of collecting societies that act on behalf of signed artists (Boldrin and Levine, 2002; 2008).

The literature places a strong accent on the crisis of copyright and creative industries caused by the popularisation of technology. Several arguments have been advanced to highlight the legal system's inability to prevent unauthorised use and reuse of cultural products and its lack of suitability for the needs of production of the digital era (Marshall, 2005; McLeod and DiCola, 2011). Technological advancements ushered in a shift in the way consumers and producers viewed intellectual property, as they began, intentionally or unintentionally, violating copyrights by sharing work to which they had no rights. Some works trace it back to the popularity of home recording equipment, which has transformed the ways in which music and video have been consumed and produced since the late 1960s (Lopes, 1992). This shift resulted in problematic applications of copyright, such as bootlegging and home copying of music (Marshall, 2004; 2005).

An effect of digitalisation, miniaturisation and decrease of production costs, technology of recording and production became available to anyone, especially in wealthier economies. Devices such as smartphones became entry lines to video production, sound recording or even editing of content and purchasing semi-professional equipment did not require as enormous financial means as it had a couple of decades earlier. This popularisation of technology, along with the opening up of distribution channels, such as digital platforms and sites hosting content, spawned a new generation of creative hobbyists and entrepreneurs, who independent of old industry actors, such as mainstream media (radio, television) and publishers, gained audiences and have started to publish regularly. This discrepancy was so big that they were often completely marginalised by traditional media and unknown to their audiences. FreeSound is a production model that is also independent of dominant internet actors owning the platforms, like Google or Facebook. The model that these creators take places an accent on technical quality, and often at its heart it has an aspiration to be suitable for the production and sharing in the old types of media. The content made available through FreeSound is also accessed by the new creative class, who uses it in YouTube productions, computer games and independent creative projects.

I have commented on one of the ways in which creative production occurs, being inscribed in the opening of creative industries. By using FreeSound as a case study, I have identified the mechanisms guiding a peer-to-peer model of commons-based production that operated using alternative copyright framework: the Creative Commons license. The model described in this book is different from earlier descriptions of cultural production, such as sampling (McLeod and DiCola, 2011), as it approaches cultural production from another angle. Instead of violating copyright, participants in production use a framework that is based on a set of permissions, enabling other creators to use their content to produce other works, for instance by remixing sound, compiling it and finding alternative uses for content in their own creative projects. This commons-based model is separate from traditional intermediaries, such as music labels and collecting societies.

This book provides a theoretical interpretation of the changes in creative industries that have accompanied the proliferation of technology, based on the emergence of commons-based production model. It gives insight into a vibrant community that fosters creative projects and a variety of works, from elementary school plays to exhibitions in the Smithsonian or multimillion-dollar Hollywood films. Taking up the perspective of the creative workforce involved in production and collaboration, permits understanding the rules of production that follows an alternative model of production. The theoretical foundation of this book is that a thorough study of Creative Commons requires the researcher both to examine the contents and suitability of the licensing to different contexts, and to concentrate on the work and production relations as well as organisational patters, which as I demonstrate, add an important dimension to the analysis of creative production and sharing. The main argument rests on the assertion that creative producers are facing challenges connected to structural limitations that arise from both the traditional nature of creative industries, such as low-pay and precarious work conditions, and from the outcomes of technological revolution that have changed the distribution, production and quality of work in the industry. I show how these two types of limitations affect the organisation of commons, leading to the creation of mutual dependencies between the Commons and the industry.

This book adds a new perspective to creative workers as participants in the global labour market: workers who cannot defend their social well-being in the market context and who by participating in the commons extensively involve, or depend upon, their other domains of livelihood, investing their efforts in enriching the commons. This type of involvement neither fits the traditional idea of cooperation, nor is a solitary activity; it should be recognised as a significant part of a new model of production. By including this model of participation in this analysis, this book demonstrates another type of a Polanyian struggle, one that is understood as a response to the commodification of social existence (Burawoy, 2000; Polanyi, 1944). Therefore, this analysis supplements the critical literature concerning the global exploitation of the workforce (Seidman, 2007; Webster et al., 2011) and studies that have addressed technological reliance on low-skilled employment, low wages and how this process translates into the progressive degradation of employment practices. This literature notes that since the 1970s, the quest for lower production costs has intensified, exacerbating the power imbalance between local workforces and industrial producers. None of the literature has, however, explicitly identified the role of the commons in this process. This book does.

Open licensing is having a transformative impact on science, technology, and society. Because the management and social science literature lacks a clear conceptualisations of its role in the creative industry, this project discusses the key spheres related to production organisation, artist labour, the networked nature of objects, collaborative methods driven by it, and emerging monetisation strategies. All these topics, which fall under the sub-disciplines of organisational studies and work and employment studies, have the potential to add a significant voice to the debates. Transforming the traditional linear valuing system could break the traditional linear value chain of media, in which content is delivered from producer to consumer, to a fully interconnected model that conceptualizes and identifies the communication and interaction between all stakeholders. It is also necessary to learn more about the context of open media to comprehend its dissemination.

2 Networked Value and the Commons

This book gives insight into the mechanisms of production inside the commons. A key theoretical concept that enhances our understanding of this production is networked value – a mechanism that structures work in the commons and generates an appeal to publish inside them. Using the example of FreeSound I have shown how network value works in the context of sound sample sharing and processing. In short, users use the platform to share content and activate its value within the network. This content usually has no value to them, for instance if they were production components that were not used in an abortive project. Yet, these users see a potential to reveal this content's use value inside the network within the commons, for example when other users place a drum sample inside their songs. Creators often try to enhance the content, making it easier to use, for example processing it so that the sound can be easily placed in a new composition. This practice is often connected to a careful model of frugality: users do not want to delete content that might be of value to others; or that are motivated by sharing their work's life, which can find exposure in others' work. The uses and configurations of such content are unlimited, and to many creators this connection to the network is an exciting opportunity to contribute to creative production, which otherwise would not have been possible.

The networked model of value might be similar to the process of clothes donation: we clear our closets but think that someone else might want the clothes that we no longer wear – thus we donate the garments to thrift stores. However, I will never find out who is now wearing what had been my favourite military jacket. Unlike the process of clothes valuation, the commons-based production offers a simple legal requirement of attribution that allows for tracking of usage. Networked value is central in establishing indirect collaboration, mediated by the digital environment and content. While creators rarely establish any longer-standing relationships with users of their content, they monitor attributions, receive messages informing them about the uses of content as well actively seek uses of their content, for instance by typing in their usernames into popular search engines of platforms hosting content.

Networked value plays a vital role in building reputation, which is characteristic of the commons. User metrics, such as the number of sounds and downloads, as well as history of activity on the site, support assessing credibility of other users. This assessment is important in situations when the verification of content's ownership is central – for example if a user wants to use a sound sample in a project of a client and is legally responsible for confirming the source and permission of using the content. Users with many similar sounds, possessing long history of uploads have a higher reputation and naturally attract more users. Within this network there is also an elite of users, whose handles are broadly recognisable, who have specialised in uploading specific types of sound, and some of whom have also entered commercial circulation, for instance providing services or selling content.

The network within the commons recognises the contribution of the authors and sanctions all violations of license. FreeSound's core users are experts in sound, capable of remembering and recognising other users' sound in media projects, often identifying violations or reporting uses to the original creators. At the same time, the site's platform tracks authorship. Since uploaded content is tied to the uploader, it has a date and time of upload as well as license information. This evidence is especially helpful when authorship must be verified, as I have illustrated with *Minecraft*. When a popular computer game has used content without attributing original users, these users have been accused them of posting sound from the game. When this happens, mapping sound sources and evidencing original ownership, supports greater transparency and management of copyright ownership.

3 Artistic Work through Commons-Based Production

My work has also outlined the specificity of creative peer-to-peer production. The model of this production was embedded in an approach that no work is at the end of creative process. This approach to content allowed for continuous iteration of any type of work, allowing for new creative combinations, based on sound processing, mixing and mastering and placing content in the new context. While traditional remixers have typically sourced musical pieces, sometimes placing some elements of speech (known in hip-hop as 'cuts'), the interviewed creators who use others' sound have processed and used the full spectrum of sounds for the purpose of their sound design. The mode of production that the commons have opened has been much different from old music and sound industry's way, partially because of the scale and easy access of others' content. As a result, production inside the commons, has crossed the boundaries of production, fostering a new type of creativity, often supported by recognised creators, such as mainstream music makers Skrillex or C418, who are popular and well-known artists.

The multitude and diversity of content has influenced the way in which content is produced. Users of content have emphasised that they rely on FreeSound's content, placing it in their prototypes of soundtracks, often replacing or looking for the sample that fits the needs of production, or the aesthetics of work. To the benefit of the creators, FreeSound's library contains sound that is often non-standard, offering other qualities than commercial libraries, and through providing these unique components, influencing the shape and final outcomes of the creative production. Openness fostered by this model creates a situation in which any user can upload any original, non-musical sound of any quality. While some parts of the community focus on providing content of superior technical quality, recorded on professional equipment, the users often value diversity and depth of sounds, arguing that technical quality is secondary to what the sound depicts. With the possibility of relying on the commons, creators can use more material that is more unique and is distinctive from the many of the standard databases, with overutilised sounds that are recognisable, like the BBC seagull. Enrichment of media with new, independently produced sounds expands the variety.

FreeSound confirms the credibility of the commons. While users often begin uploading content with more restrictive licenses (NonCommercial, Attribution), with time and experience their approach to licensing changes and they often move to complete openness of content (licensing using CC-0 Public Domain). This progression is tied to the efforts of maximalisation of the use value of content, but also is tied to trust in the platform. Users who release sound using CC-0 are voluntarily giving up content that they have produced. They tie the upload to FreeSound and usually see it in terms of contribution to the commons (rather than giving up all rights). To them, FreeSound guarantees the continuity of the commons, but also reflects the spirit of creativity and openness that they identify with. It is notable that FreeSound has a long history as a non-commercial, university-administered portal that has never used commercial advertising or membership fees.

The result of this trust in the platform is an approach embedded in enrichment of the commons that makes making FreeSound's database as comprehensive as possible. While users are not governed aside from content moderation – aimed at filtering out content violating copyright, there are community-built mechanisms aimed at the generation of content for the commons. They are mostly unorganised, uncoordinated, individualised and separated from any form of coercion. Some users however have their strategies that are based on maximalisation of their efforts to fill in niches of content, actively browsing content, looking for underrepresented types of sounds or participating in competitions that promote and expand the content of the commons.

This model of production at its heart has not only generation of content, but also its annotation and building of metadata. This reflects the broader technologisation of creative industries. Since the production of content relies on components from different sources, creative activity is also influenced by cataloguing. The interviewed core users have mastered metadata generation, using specific keywords, often building an identity using them, and controlling the quality of other users' tags. This exemplifies the transformation of production, where annotation and different parameters of content facilitate and shape production. The study has also shown that there have been efforts to expand the quality of metadata, for instance by developing software that analyses and automatically catalogues the data, which could improve production and facilitate the use of the components.

4 Creative Commons in the Political Economy of the Creative Industries

The literature recognises commons-based production as a third way of producing: neither anti-capitalist, nor aligned with capitalism, but its effects bring productive resources exploited by capitalism (Bauwens, 2005). FreeSound shares this interpretation but takes a more nuanced view of the industry.

FreeSound's life, even though non-commercial, is closely tied to the industry. Interviewed users placed an emphasis on the professionalisation of contributors, arguing that the material is often of professional quality. Core users have worked in media and creative industries, or in IT-related professions. The interviews have shown that despite their professional involvement with the creative industries, it often remained separate from their commoning activity. However, all these creators valued the proximity of the commons to the industry, often citing uses of their content in high-budget films, popular computer games, documentaries or music albums. Commons were described in symbolic proximity to, yet separate from, mainstream creative industries.

The narratives of the core users FreeSound emphasise the elitist character of the site. Many core users fondly recalled the early days of the internet, and the site's simplicity, lack of advertisement and design. At the same time, the collaborative spirit, embedded in the idea of meritocracy and level of contribution,

CONCLUSION   183

helped creators feel committed to the site. Although they adopted the commoning model of production, they understood it as aligned with the mainstream industry. The form of collaboration offered by the licensing model and the platform allowed participation in a community that shared a similar interest in sound, knowledge of the equipment and recognition of licensing. Even though most users have never met a fellow FreeSounder (or even established any longer ties), the identities tied to the site and the community have endured and many users felt committed, donated to the site's maintenance and hoped for its growth and prosperity.

Yet the choice to participate in this model of production and distribution was opposed to the model of the creative industries. Creative industries have traditionally rested on a power imbalance between individual creators and gatekeepers. In the music industry, creators had always faced structural limitations arising from both the surplus of work and the artists, and from the business strategies of the intermediaries. Consequently, few musicians become popular and found financial success and sustainability in the creative industries. This work has demonstrated an alternative, inclusive model of creative industries, based on no rejection of content. Many interviewees emphasised their engagement in the commons, and the popularity of the content remains a rewarding and exciting opportunity. This perspective produces a picture of creative organisation that goes beyond the workplace and traditional networks of mainstream actors, and it is crucial for the study of similar communities, engaged in independent production, often fuelling mainstream industry with content and labour. The exponential growth of content on FreeSound is an important case study, where content creation, sharing and recreation coincide with progressing application of the commons in the industry and commodification of formerly non-marketed spheres of creative production. This approach also shows how creative production produces what Nancy Fraser has termed 'the social-reproductive contradiction of financialised capitalism' (Fraser, 2017, p. 22). The findings of this book allow for further consideration of the ethics of the commons in the context of unpaid labour.

Despite the limitations in protection, this book has identified several mechanisms of commodification of the commons, typical of FreeSound. These models rely on the network of participants and/or the network value of content. In the multiple-channels sales and freemium model, I have shown how creators translate their work to the commons, to reach the broadest audiences and maximise the use value of content, while demonstrating their products and offering a commercial product, either based on the extension of licenses or a bigger library of sound. Two other models, depend on the network, based on the acquisition of talent and content to secure exclusive rights, as well as on the commons-based model of generation of services. These models either extended the commons, contributing to their production, or improved their operations, by offering new, alternative ways of accessing and using it.

The Creative Commons framework is unprotected; violations of the terms of license are rarely sanctioned. The creators interviewed here described many instances of violations and none of them initiated a legal dispute with the violator. Creative Commons content remains protected by a standard copyright but given the lack of profitability they lack institutions to ensure correct usage. The music and film industries have grown in the environments within which their closed content is monitored by external agents, like collecting societies. For them, any form of reuse is treated like a business loss, so extensive monitoring for any kind of presence of content, from coffeeshops, to digital platforms and peer-to-peer sharing networks. Yet, some industries fail to protect the creations. In that domain, commons enhance ethical production without the violation of copyright and, by building the networked value and reputation, also support commercial production. However, this study has shown that no mechanism allows for sanctioning of Creative Commons violations.

5   Future Research on the Art of the Commons

This research identifies several new spheres that require more attention from the creative industries. A key aspect occurs in the domain of production, which will soon undergo a dynamic change. The normalisation of the digital collage in artistic production requires closer examination, tied to specific markets and industries. In the future digital technologies will be indispensable in supporting content reuse in unprecedented and unexpected ways, such as procedurally generated soundtracks, benefiting content creators and content users and erasing the boundaries between them. There are strong efforts to reinforce the application and popularisation of open data by institutional actors, but more research will need to address both the legal status and technological solution in production of cultural works relying on remixed works.

Creative Commons framework is reaching a peak of recognition, which implies that any content shared using this license will be exponentially expanding, enriching not only creative products but also other domains of socioeconomic life. Future research needs to concentrate on the activities of commercial actors that use such content in innovative ways, including the described annotation, access, transformation and licensing. While open licensing models have been identified as a key aspect of the Digital Agenda for Europe (see IP/10/581, MEMO/10/199 and MEMO/10/200) and recognised as a key driver to develop content markets in Europe, the research needs to consider additional aspects of such transformation that are relevant to business strategy, operations and marketing research tied to this new form of production and distribution.

In addition, the change ushered in by CC has changed the status of creative products, the objects of labour. Opening them up to the public has created a set of objects which could become available to an unlimited number of users who comply with the terms of the license. These types of objects under classical copyright regime were either sold as niche products or excluded from the market and thus were not easily accessible for creative work. Having millions of objects available has influenced the ways in which creative production occurs, replacing permission seeking with content seeking and filtering, in parallel to the popularisation of licensing which has increased the importance of metadata and annotation.

Lastly, there is a need to study the relationships between objects. This book assumes that the works have unique qualities that place them in a new context of remix and recreation, driven by openness in artistic innovation and freedom of collaborations when they are licensed under the CC framework. Future research should explore these relationships, monitoring their properties and any changes in those properties. These property relations will permit an enhanced understanding of the new artistic production and improve the understanding of how commons support the art of the commons.

Bibliography

Adorno, T. & Horkheimer, M. (1979). *Dialectic of enlightenment*. London: Verso.

Afuah, A. & Tucci, C.L. (2012). Crowdsourcing as a solution to distant search. *Academy of Management Review, 37*(3), 355–375.

Ågerfalk, P.J., & Fitzgerald, B. 2008. Outsourcing to an unknown workforce: Exploring opensourcing as a global sourcing strategy. *MIS Quarterly 32*(2): pp. 385–409.

Agrawal, A., Catalini, C., & Goldfarb, A. (2014). Some simple economics of crowdfunding. *Innovation Policy and the Economy, 14*(1), 63–97.

Alexander, P.J. (2002). Peer-to-peer file sharing: The case of the music recording industry. *Review of Industrial Organization 20*(2): 151–161.

Allison, T. H., Davis, B. C., Short, J. C., & Webb, J. W. (2014). Crowdfunding in a prosocial microlending environment: Examining the role of intrinsic versus extrinsic cues. *Entrepreneurship Theory and Practice*. doi:10.1111/etap.12108*.

Altunay, M., et al. (2010). A science-driven production cyberinfrastructure – the Open Science grid. *Journal of Grid Computing, 9*(2), 201–218. doi:10.1007/s10723-010-9176-6.

Amsterdam Call for Open Science (2016) accessed online at: https://www.government.nl/binaries/government/documents/reports/2016/04/04/amsterdam-call-for-action-on-open-science/amsterdam-call-for-action-on-open-science.pdf (date of access September 16, 2020).

Andrades, L., & Dimanche, F. (2014). Co-creation of experience value: A tourist behaviour approach. In M. Chen & J. Uysal (Eds.). *Creating experience value in tourism* (pp. 95–112). London: CABI. doi:10.1079/9781780643489.0095.

Antelmann, K. (2004). Do open-access articles have a greater research impact? *College & Research Libraries, 65*(5), 372–382.

Apache.org (2020). Apache License, Version 2.0, accessed online: https://www.apache.org/licenses/LICENSE-2.0 (10.04.2020).

Apache.org (2020a). Community-led development "The Apache Way", accessed online: https://www.apache.org/foundation/ (9.04.2020).

Apache.org (2020b). Briefing: The Apache Way, accessed online: https://www.apache.org/theapacheway/ (22.09.2020).

Appelgren, E. (2018). An illusion of interactivity: The paternalistic side of data journalism. *Journalism Practice, 12*(3), 308–325.

Arazy, O., Morgan, W., & Patterson, R. (2006). Wisdom of the Crowds: Decentralized Knowledge Construction in Wikipedia. *SSRN Electronic Journal*. doi: 10.2139/ssrn.1025624.

Attard, J., Orlandi, F., Scerri, S., & Auer, S. (2015). A systematic review of open government data initiatives. *Government Information Quarterly, 32*(4), 399–418.

Baack, S. (2015). Datafication and empowerment: How the open data movement re-articulates notions of democracy, participation, and journalism. *Big Data & Society*, 2(2), 2053951715594634.

Baack, S. (2018). Practically engaged: The entanglements between data journalism and civic tech. *Digital Journalism*, 6(6), 673–692.

Baden, T., Chagas, A.M., Gage, G., Marzullo, T., Prieto-God-ino, L.L. and Euler, T. (2015). Open labware: 3-D printing your own lab equipment. *PLoS Biol*, 13(3): e1002086. DOI: https://doi.org/10.1371/journal.pbio.1002086.

Baldwin, C. Y., & Clark, K. B. (2006). The architecture of participation: Does code architecture mitigate free riding in the open source development model? *Management Science*, 52(7), 1116–1127.

Barley, S. R., & Kunda, G. (2001). Bringing work back in. *Organization Science*, 12(1), 76–95.

Baucus, M. S., & Mitteness, C. R. (2016). Crowdfrauding: Avoiding Ponzi entrepreneurs when investing in new ventures. *Business Horizons*, 59(1), 37–50.

Bauwens, M. (2005). The political economy of peer production. *CTheory*, 12–1.

Bauwens, M. (2009). Class and capital in peer production. *Capital & Class*, 33(1), 121–141.

Bauwens, M., & Pantazis, A. (2018). The ecosystem of commons-based peer production and its transformative dynamics. *The Sociological Review*, 66(2), 302–319.

Belanger, V., Thornton, J. (2013). Bioelectricity: A quantitative approach -Duke University's First MOOC.

Belleflamme, P., Lambert, T., & Schwienbacher, A. (2013a). Crowdfunding: Tapping the right crowd. *Journal of Business Venturing*, 29(5), 585–609. doi:10.1016/j.jbusvent.2013.07.003*.

Belleflamme, P., Lambert, T., & Schwienbacher, A. (2013b). Individual crowdfunding practices. *Venture Capital*, 15(4), 313–333. doi:10.1080/13691066.2013.785151*.

Benjamin, W. (1998). The work of art in the age of mechanical reproduction. Accessed on-line: Marxists.org.

Benjamin, W (2008) *The work of art in the age of mechanical reproduction*. London: Penguin.

Benkler, Y. (2002). Coase's Penguin, or, Linux and "The nature of the firm". *Yale Law Journal*, 369–446.

Benkler, Y., & Nissenbaum, H. (2006). Commons-based peer production and virtue. *Journal of Political Philosophy*, 14(4), 394–419.

Benkler, Y. (2014). Between Spanish huertas and the open road: a tale of two commons?. In B.M. Frischmann, M.J. Madison and K.J. Strandburg (Eds.), *Governing knowledge commons* (p. 69). Oxford: Oxford Scholarship Online.

Benkler, Y. (2017). Peer production, the commons, and the future of the firm. *Strategic Organization*, 15(2), 264–274.

Benlian, A., Hilkert, D. and Hess, T. (2015). How open is this platform? The meaning and measurement of platform openness from the complementors' perspective. *Journal of Information Technology, 30*(3), 209–228.

Berger, P. L., & Luckmann, T. (1966). *The social construction of reality: A treatise in the sociology of knowledge*. New York: Anchor.

Berger, S., & Gleisner, F. (2009). Emergence of financial intermediaries in electronic markets: The case of online P2P lending. *BuR Business Research Journal, 2*(1), 39–65. doi:10.1007/BF03343528*.

Bergquist, M., Ljungberg, J., 2001. The power of gifts: Organising social relationships in open source communities. *Information Systems Journal 11*(4), 305–320.

Bergvall-Kåreborn, B., & Howcroft, D. (2014). Amazon Mechanical Turk and the commodification of labour. *New Technology, Work and Employment, 29*(3), 213–223.

Berinsky, A. J., Huber, G. A., & Lenz, G. S. (2012). Evaluating online labor markets for experimental research: Amazon.com's Mechanical Turk. *Political Analysis, 20*(3), 351–368.

Berne Convention (1979). Full text: http://www.wipo.int/treaties/en/text.jsp?file_id=283698.

Berry, D.M. (2008). *Copy, rip, burn: The politics of copyleft and open source*. London: Pluto Press.

Bertot, J. C., Jaeger, P. T., & Grimes, J. M. (2010). Using ICTs to create a culture of transparency: E-government and social media as openness and anti-corruption tools for societies. *Government Information Quarterly, 27*(3), 264–271.

Beyers, J. (2004). Voice and access: Political practices of European interest associations. *European Union Politics 5*(2), 211–240.

Bharwani, S., & Jauhari, V. (2013). An exploratory study of competencies required to co-create memorable customer experiences in the hospitality industry. *International Journal of Contemporary Hospitality Management, 25*(6), 823–843. doi:10.1108/IJCHM-05-2012-0065.

Bhattacharjee S, Gopal RD, Lertwachara K, et al. (2007). The effect of digital sharing technologies on music markets: a survival analysis of albums on ranking charts. *Management Science 53*(9): 1359–1374.

Birkinbine, B. J. (2018). Commons praxis: Toward a critical political economy of the digital commons. TripleC: Communication, capitalism & critique. *Open Access Journal for a Global Sustainable Information Society, 16*(1), 290–305.

Birkinbine, B. J. (2021). Political economy of peer production. *The Handbook of Peer Production*, 33–43.

Bitzer, J., & Schröder, P. J. (2005). Bug-fixing and code-writing: The private provision of open source software. *Information Economics and Policy, 17*(3), 389–406.

Bitzer, J., Schrettl, W., & Schröder, P. J. (2007). Intrinsic motivation in open source software development. *Journal of Comparative Economics, 35*(1), 160–169.

Blacc, A., Manta, I. D., & Olson, D. S. (2015). A sustainable music industry for the 21st century. *Cornell L. Rev. Online, 101,* 39.

Bocken, N. M., Short, S. W., Rana, P., & Evans, S. (2014). A literature and practice review to develop sustainable business model archetypes. *Journal of Cleaner Production, 65,* 42–56.

Boldrin, M. & Levine, K. (2002). The case against intellectual property. *American Economic Review: Papers & Proceedings 92*(2), 209–212.

Boldrin, M. & Levine, K. (2008). *Against intellectual monopoly.* Cambridge: Cambridge University Press.

Bollier, D., & Helfrich, S. (2012). Introduction: The commons as a transformative vision. *The wealth of the Commons: A world beyond market and state.* Amherst, MA: Levellers Press, 8–19.

Bollier, D., & Helfrich, S. (Eds.). (2015). *Patterns of commoning.* Commons Strategy Group and Off the Common Press.

Borg, J. (2007). Protecting investors and the integrity of capital markets, *Journal of Investment Compliance 8*(2), 49–51.

Boudreau, K. J., & Lakhani, K. R. (2009). How to manage outside innovation. *MIT Sloan Management Review, 50*(4), 69–76.

Bouncken, R. B., Komorek, M., & Kraus, S. (2015). Crowdfunding: The current state of research. *International Business & Economics Research Journal (IBER), 14*(3), 407–416.

Boyle. J. (2004). A manifesto on WIPO and the future of intellectual property. *Duke Law and Technology Review 9,* 1–12.

Brabham, D. C. (2009). Crowdsourcing the public participation process for planning projects. *Planning Theory, 8*(3), 242–262.

Brabham, D. C. (2013). *Crowdsourcing.* MIT Press.

Braxton, E. (2016). Youth leadership for social justice: Past and present. In J. Conner & S. Rosen (Eds.), *Contemporary youth activism: Advancing social justice in the United States* (pp. 25–38). Westport, CT: Praeger.

Bromley, D. W. (1992). The commons, common property, and environmental policy. *Environmental and Resource Economics, 2*(1), 1–17.

Burawoy, M. (1998) The extended case method. *Sociological Theory 16,* 4–33.

Burawoy M. (2000) *Global ethnography: Forces, connections, and imaginations in a post-modern world.* Berkeley: University of California Press.

Cabiddu, F., Lui, T.-W., & Piccoli, G. (2013). Managing value co-creation in the tourism industry. *Annals of Tourism Research, 42,* 86–107. doi:10.1016/j.annals.2013.01.001.

Cahir, J. (2004). The withering away of property: The rise of the internet information commons. *Oxford Journal of Legal Studies, 24*(4), 619–641.

Campos, A.C., Mendes, J., Oom do Valle, P. & Scott, N. (2015). Co-creation of tourist experiences: A literature review, *Current Issues in Tourism,* doi: 10.1080/13683500.2015.1081158.

Carroll, M. W. (2011). Why full Open Access matters. *PLoS Biology, 9*(11), p.e1001210. doi: 10.1371/journal.pbio.1001210.

Carroll, M.W. (2006). Creative commons and the new intermediaries, *Michigan State Law Review, 45*(13), 124–146.

Carruthers B.G. & Ariovich, L. (2004). The sociology of property rights. *Annual Review of Sociology 30*: 23–46.

Casadesus-Masanell, R., & Ghemawat, P. (2006). Dynamic mixed duopoly: A model motivated by Linux vs. Windows. *Management Science, 52*(7), 1072–1084.

Casadesus-Masanell, R., & Zhu, F. (2010). Strategies to fight ad-sponsored rivals. *Management Science, 56*(9), 1484–1499.

Casadesus-Masanell, R., & Zhu, F. (2013). Business model innovation and competitive imitation: The case of sponsor-based business models. *Strategic Management Journal, 34*(4), 464–482.

Cecere, G., & Rochelandet, F. (2013). Privacy intrusiveness and web audiences: empirical evidence. *Telecommunications Policy, 37*(10), 1004–1014.

Chamakiotis, P., Petrakaki, D., & Panteli, N. (2020). Social value creation through digital activism in an online health community. *Information Systems Journal*.

Chan, W. C., Chen, P. C., Hung, S. W., Tsai, M. C., & Chen, T. K. (2017). Open innovation and team leaders' innovation traits. *Engineering Management Journal, 29*(2), 87–98.

Cheng, C. (2011). Dynamic service innovation capability, radical service innovation and open business models. *International Journal of Services Technology and Management, 16*(3/4), 229–242.

Chesbrough, H. (2003). *Open innovation. The new imperative for creating and profiting from technology*. Boston, MA: Harvard Business School Press.

Chesbrough, H. (2006). Open innovation: A new paradigm for understanding industrial innovation. In *Open innovation: Researching a new paradigm.* H. Chesbrough, W. Vanhaverbeke & J. West, Eds. Oxford: Oxford University Press, pp. 1–12.

Chesbrough, H.W. (2007). *Open business models: How to thrive in the new innovation landscape*. Boston, MA: Harvard Business School Press.

Chesbrough, H. W. (2007). Why companies should have open business models. *MIT Sloan Management Review, 48*(2), 22–28.

Chesbrough, H., & Crowther, A. K. (2006). Beyond high tech: Early adopters of open innovation in other industries. *R&D Management, 36*(3), 229–236.

Chesbrough, H., & Rosenbloom, R. S. (2002). The role of the business model in capturing value from innovation: Evidence from Xerox Corporation's technology spin-off companies. *Industrial and Corporate Change, 11*(3), 529–555.

Chu, P.-Y., & Chen, W.-C. (2011). Open business models: A case study of System-on-a-Chip (SoC) design foundry in the integrated circuit (IC) industry. *African Journal of Business Management, 5*(21), 8536–8544.

Ciffolilli, A. (2004). The economics of open source hijacking and declining quality of digital information resources: A case for copyleft. *First Monday, 9*. doi: 10.5210/fm.v9i9.1173.

Ciriacy-Wantrup, S. V., & Bishop, R. C. (1975). "Common property" as a concept in natural resources policy. *Natural Resources Journal, 15*(4), 713–727.

Clark, P. (2015). The invisible defense against music piracy. *J. Marshall Rev. Intell. Prop. L., 15*, i.

Clohessy, T., Acton, T., & Morgan, L. (2014, December). Smart City as a Service (SCaaS): A future roadmap for e-government smart city cloud computing initiatives. In *2014 IEEE/ACM 7th International Conference on Utility and Cloud Computing* (pp. 836–841). IEEE.

Coffey, A., & Atkinson, P. (1996). *Making sense of qualitative data: Complementary research strategies*. Sage Publications, Inc.

Communia Association (2021) COMMUNIA policy paper on the Directive proposal on Collective Management of Copyright. Accessed online: https://www.communia-association.org/wp-content/uploads/2013/01/communia_policy_paper_colsoc_directive.pdf.

Cooper, J. & Harrison, D.M. (2001). The social organization of audio piracy on the Internet. *Media Culture & Society 23*(1), 71–89.

Coriat, B. & Weinstein, O. (2011). Patent regimes, firms and the commodification of knowledge. *Socio-Economic Review 10*(2), 267–292.

Coriat, B., & Weinstein, O. (2012). Patent regimes, firms and the commodification of knowledge. *Socio-Economic Review, 10*(2), 267–292.

Corporations and markets advisory committee (CAMAC) (2014). *Crowd sourced equity funding – Report*. Australia: Commonwealth.

Crane, D. (1972). *Invisible colleges: Diffusion of knowledge in scientific communities* (1st ed.). Chicago: University of Chicago Press.

Creative Commons (2015) State of the commons. Available at: https://stateof.creativecommons.org/2015/ [01-05-2015].

Creative Commons (2021) Frequently asked questions. Accessed at https://creativecommons.org/faq/.

Cumming, D. J., Hornuf, L., Karami, M., & Schweizer, D. (2020). Disentangling crowdfunding from fraudfunding. *Max Planck Institute for Innovation & Competition research paper*.

Cumming, D. J., Leboeuf, G., & Schwienbacher, A. (2015). Crowdfunding models: Keep-it-all vs. all-or-nothing. *Financial Management*.

Cumming, D. J., Leboeuf, G., & Schwienbacher, A. (2020). Crowdfunding models: Keep-it-all vs. all-or-nothing. *Financial Management, 49*(2), 331–360.

Czarniawska-Joerges, B. (1992). Exploring complex organizations. Thousand Oaks, CA: Sage Publications.

Fisher, D. & Gould, P. (2012). Open-source hardware is a low-cost alternative for scientific instrumentation and research. *Modern Instrumentation, 1*(2), 8–20. doi:10.4236/mi.2012.12002.

Dahlander, L. & Gann, D.M. (2010). How open is innovation? *Research Policy, 39*(6), 699–709.

Dahlander, L. & Magnusson, M. (2008). How do firms make use of open source communities? *Long Range Planning, 41*(6), pp. 629–649. doi:10.1016/j.lrp.2008.09.003.

Dahlander, L., & Gann, D. M. (2010). How open is innovation? *Research Policy, 39*(6), 699–709.

David, P. (2005). From keeping 'nature's secrets' to the institutionalization 'open science'. In R. A. Gosh (Ed.), *CODE: Collaborative ownership and digital economy* (pp. 85–108). Cambridge, MA: MIT Press.

David, P.A. (2004). Understanding the emergence of 'open science' institutions functionalist economics in historical context. *Industrial and Corporate Change 13*(4), 571–589.

David, P.A. (2008). The historical origins of 'open science': An essay on patronage, reputation and common agency contracting in the scientific revolution. *Capitalism and Society, 3*(2), 1–116.

DCMA (The Digital Millennium Copyright Act) (1998), accessed online: http://www.copyright.gov/legislation/dmca.pdf.

De Angelis, M. (2010). The production of commons and the "explosion" of the middle class. *Antipode 42*(4):954–997.

De Filippi, P. (2015). Translating commons-based peer production values into metrics: Toward commons-based cryptocurrencies. In *Handbook of digital currency* (pp. 463–483). Academic Press.

de Rosnay, M. D., & Musiani, F. (2016). Towards a (de) centralisation-based typology of peer production. *Triple C-Communication, Capitalism & Critique, 14*(1), 189–207.

de Solla Price, D.J. & Beaver, D. (1966). Collaboration in an invisible college. *American Psychologist, 21*(11), 1011–1018.

Demil, B., & Lecocq, X. (2010). Business model evolution: In search of dynamic consistency. *Long Range Planning, 43*(2–3), 227–246.

Deschler, G. D. (2013). Wisdom of the intermediary crowd: What the proposed rules mean for ambitious crowdfunding intermediaries. *Louis ULJ, 58*, 1145.

Di Gangi, P. M., & Wasko, M. (2009). Steal my idea! Organizational adoption of user innovations from a user innovation community: a case study of Dell IdeaStorm. *Decision Support Systems, 48*(1), 303–312.

Di Gangi, P.M., Wasko, M.M. & Hooker, R.E. (2010). Getting customers' ideas to work for you: Learning from Dell how to succeed with online user innovation communities. *MIS Quarterly Executive, 9*(4), 213–228.

Di Pietro, F., Prencipe, A., & Majchrzak, A. (2018). Crowd equity investors: An underutilized asset for open innovation in startups. *California Management Review*, 60(2), 43–70.

Doshi, A. (2014). Agent heterogeneity in two-sided platforms: Superstar impact on crowdfuding (SSRN Working Paper No. 2422111). Retrieved May 15, 2014, from http://papers.ssrn.com/sol3/papers.cfm?abstract_id¼2422111*.

Doshi, A. (2014). Star impact on two-sided platforms: evidence from crowdfunding. Available at SSRN 2422111 (2014). http://papers.ssrn.com/sol3/papers.cfm?abstract_id=242211

Dougherty, D. & Conrad, A. (2016). *Free to make: How the maker movement is changing our schools, our jobs, and our minds*. Berkeley: North Atlantic Books.

Dowd, T.J. (2003). Structural power and the construction of markets. *Comparative Social Research* 21: 145–199.

Durst, S., & Ståhle, P. (2013). Success factors of open innovation: A literature review. *International Journal of Business Research and Management*, 4(4), 111–131.

Dusollier, S. (2006) The master's tools v. the master's house: Creative commons v. copyright. *Columbia Journal of Law & Arts* 29, 271–293.

Dworkin, G. (1994). The moral right of the author: moral rights and the common law countries. *Colum.-VLA JL & Arts, 19*, 229.

Ebner, W., Leimeister, J. M., & Krcmar, H. (2009). Community engineering for innovations: The ideas competition as a method to nurture a virtual community for innovations. *R&D Management, 39*(4), 342–356.

ECB (2015) Virtual currency schemes – a further analysis, https://www.ecb.europa.eu/pub/pdf/other/virtualcurrencyschemesen.pdf (accessed online 16.09.2020).

Economides, N., & Katsamakas, E. (2006). Two-sided competition of proprietary vs. open source technology platforms and the implications for the software industry. *Management Science, 52*(7), 1057–1071.

Eisenmann, T., Parker, G. and van Alstyne, M.W. (2009). Opening platforms: How, when and why? In A. Gawer (ed.) *Platforms, Markets and Innovation*, pp. 131–162.

Elkin-Koren, N. (2006). *Exploring creative commons: A skeptical view of a worthy pursuit: The future of public domain* (Lucie Guibault & P. Bemt Hugenholtz eds.). Berlin: Kluwer Law International.

Elkin-Koren, N. (2005). What contracts cannot do: The limits of private ordering in facilitating a creative commons. *Fordham L. Rev., 74*, 375.

Elmquist, M., Fredberg, T. & Ollila, S. (2009). Exploring the field of open innovation. *European Journal of Innovation Management, 12*(3): 326–345. https://doi.org/10.1108/14601060910974219.

Emanuel, E. J. (2013). Online education: MOOCs taken by educated few. *Nature, 503*(7476), 342.

Eraqi, M. I. (2011). Co-creation and the new marketing mix as an innovative approach for enhancing tourism industry competitiveness in Egypt. *International Journal of Services and Operations Management, 8*(1), 76–91.

European Union (2001). EU Directive 2001/29/EC, accessed online: http://eur-lex.europa.eu/LexUriServ/LexUriServ.do?uri=OJ:L:2001:167:0010:0019:EN:PDF.

Eve, M. P. (2014). *Open access and the humanities*. Cambridge: Cambridge University Press.

Fang, Y., & Neufeld, D. (2009). Understanding sustained participation in open source software projects. *Journal of Management Information Systems, 25*(4), 9–50.

Faraj, S., Jarvenpaa, S. L., & Majchrzak, A. (2011). Knowledge collaboration in online communities. *Organization Science, 22*(5), 1224–1239.

Farell, R. (2015). An analysis of the cryptocurrency industry. Accessed online: https://repository.upenn.edu/cgi/viewcontent.cgi?article=1133&context=wharton_research_scholars.

Fauvet, L. (2015). What happened to Sourceforge?. https://blog.local.com/2015/06/02/what-happened-to-sourceforge/ (12/02/2021).

Fecher, B., & Friesike, S. (2013). Open science: one term, five schools of thought. In S. Bartling & S. Friesike (Eds.), *Opening science* (pp. 17–47). New York: Springer.

Fecher, B., Friesike, S., & Hebing, M. (2015). What drives academic data sharing?. *PloS one, 10*(2), e0118053.

Feller, J., & Fitzgerald, B. (2002). *Understanding open source software development*. London: Addison-Wesley.

Feller, J., Finnegan, P., Hayes, J., & O'Reilly, P. (2010). Institutionalising information asymmetry: governance structures for open innovation. *Information Technology & People, 22*(4), 297–316.

Feller, J., Finnegan, P. & Nilsson, O. (2011). Open innovation and public administration: Transformational typologies and business model impacts. *European Journal of Information Systems, 20*(3), 358–374.

Feller, J., Finnegan, P., Fitzgerald, B., and Hayes, J. (2008). From peer production to productization: A study of socially enabled business exchanges in open source service networks, *Information Systems Research 19*(4), 475–493.

Firth, S. (2001). The popular music industry. In S. Firth, W. Straw, & J. Street, J. (eds). *The Cambridge companion to pop and rock* (pp. 26–52). Cambridge: Cambridge University Press.

Fisher, D. & Gould, P. (2012). Open-source hardware is a low-cost alternative for scientific instrumentation and research. *Modern Instrumentation, 1*(2), 8–20. doi: 10.4236/mi.2012.12002.

Fligstein, N. (1990). *The transformation of corporate control*. Cambridge, MA: Harvard University Press.

Fox, M. (2004). E-commerce business models for the music industry. *Popular Music and Society* 27(2), 201–220.

Frank, M., Walker, J., Attard, J., & Tygel, A. (2016). Data literacy: What is it and how can we make it happen? *The Journal of Community Informatics, 12*(3).

Fraser, N. (2017). A triple movement? Parsing the politics of crisis after Polanyi. In *Beyond neoliberalism* (pp. 29–42). London: Palgrave Macmillan.

Fredriksson, M. (2014). Copyright culture and pirate politics. *Cultural Studies* 28(5–6): 1022–1047.

Freedman, S., & Jin, G. Z. (2017). The information value of online social networks: lessons from peer-to-peer lending. *International Journal of Industrial Organization, 51*, 185–222.

FreeSound (2017). User survey, unpublished document.

FreeSound (2019) AudioCommons Initiative Survey on Creative Interaction with Audio Content [unpublished] – private access granted via Google Docs [access 1.03.2019].

FreeSound (2021a) 2020 in numbers, accessed online: https://blog.freesound.org/?p=1291.

FreeSound (2021b) Sustainability Report 2019 https://blog.freesound.org/?p=1206.

Frydrych, D., Bock, A., Kinder, T., & Koeck, B. (2014). Exploring entrepreneurial legitimacy in reward-based crowdfunding. *Venture Capital, 16*(3), 247–269. doi:10.1080/13691066.2014.

Füller, J., Hutter, K., & Faullant, R. (2011). Why co-creation experience matters? Creative experience and its impact on the quantity and quality of creative contributions. *R&D Management, 41*(3), 259–273.

Furgason, A. (2009). Afraid of technology? Major label response to advancements in digital technology. *Popular Music History* 3(2): 149–170.

Futurelearn (2013). Futurelearn launches, http://futurelearn.com/feature/futurelearn-launches/.

Galvagno, M. & Dalli, D. (2014). Theory of value co-creation: a systematic literature review. *Managing Service Quality: An International Journal, 24*(6), 643–683. https://doi.org/10.1108/MSQ-09-2013-0187.

Garcelon, M. (2009). An information commons? Creative Commons and public access to cultural creations. *New Media & Society, 11*(8), 1307–1326.

Gardler, R. (2013) Open Source and Governance. In N. Shemtov, & I. Walden (Eds.), *Free and open source software: Policy, law and practice*. Oxford: Oxford University Press.

Gasaway, L. N. (2013). Questions and answers-Copyright column. *Against the Grain, 25*(3), 26.

Gassmann, O., Enkel, E., & Chesbrough, H. W. (2010). The future of open innovation. *R&D Management, 40*(3), 213–221.

George, G., & Bock, A. J. (2011). The business model in practice and its implications for entrepreneurship research. *Entrepreneurship Theory and Practice, 35*(1), 83–111.

Georgiev, G.V., Sánchez Milara, I & Ferreira, D. (2017). A framework for capturing creativity in digital fabrication. *The Design Journal 20*. sup1, S3659–S3668.

Giannopoulou, E., Yström, A., Ollila, S., Fredberg, T., & Elmquist, M. (2010). Implications of openness: A study into (all) the growing literature on open innovation. *Journal of Technology Management & Innovation, 5*(3), 162–180.

Gibson-Graham, J. K., Cameron, J., & Healy, S. (2016). Commoning as a postcapitalist politics 1. In A. Amin & P. Howell (Eds.), *Releasing the commons* (pp. 192–212). London: Routledge.

Gil-Garcia, J.R., Pardo, T.A., & Nam, T. (2015). What makes a city smart? Identifying core components and proposing an integrative and com-prehensive conceptualization. *Information Polity, 20*(1), 61–87.

Github.com (2020). Open source license usage on GitHub.com, https://github.blog/2015-03-09-open-source-license-usage-on-github-com/.

GNU (2019). What is free software? accessed online: https://www.gnu.org/philosophy/free-sw.en.html#f1 (08.04.2020).

GNU (2020). What is Copyleft? https://www.gnu.org/licenses/copyleft.en.html.

Goldman, R. & Gabriel, R.P. (2005). *Innovation happens elsewhere*. Amsterdam, The Netherlands: Morgan Kaufmann.

Gonzalez-Zapata, F., & Heeks, R. (2015). The multiple meanings of open government data: Understanding different stakeholders and their perspectives. *Government Information Quarterly*, doi:10.1016/j.giq.2015.09.001.

Goss A.K. (2007). Codifying a commons: Copyright, copyleft, and the Creative Commons project. *Chi.-Kent Law Review 82*, 963–996.

Graber, C. B. & Nenova, M.B. (eds.) (2008). *Intellectual property and traditional cultural expressions in a digital environment*. Cheltenham: Edward Elgar.

Gray, J., Gerlitz, C., & Bounegru, L. (2018). Data infrastructure literacy. *Big Data & Society, 5*(2).

Green, C. H. (2014). *Banker's guide to new small business finance: Venture deals, crowdfunding, private equity, and technology*. John Wiley & Sons.

Grewal, R., Lilien, G. L., & Mallapragada, G. (2006). Location, location, location: How network embeddedness affects project success in open source systems. *Management Science, 52*(7), 1043–1056.

Grissemann, U. S., & N. E. Stokburger-Sauer (2012). Customer co-creation of travel services: The role of company support and customer satisfaction with the co-creation performance. *Tourism Management 33*(6), 1483–1492.

Griswold W (1981) American character and the American novel: An expansion of reflection theory in the sociology of literature. *American Journal of Sociology* 86(4): 740–765.

Guibault, L. M. (2006). *The future of the public domain: identifying the commons in information law 16*, Kluwer Law International BV.

Guibault, L., & Angelopoulos, C. Eds. (2011). *Open content licensing: From theory to practice*. City: Amsterdam University Press.

Haeussler, C. (2011). Information-sharing in academia and the industry: A comparative study. *Research Policy, 40*(1), 105–122. doi: 10.1016/j.respol.2010.08.007.

Hahn, J., Moon, J. Y., & Zhang, C. (2008). Emergence of new project teams from open source software developer networks: Impact of prior collaboration ties. *Information Systems Research, 19*(3), 369–391.

Hamari, J., Sjöklint, M., & Ukkonen, A. (2016). The sharing economy: Why people participate in collaborative consumption. *Journal of the Association for Information Science and Technology, 67*(9), 2047–2059.

Hann C (2007) A new double movement? Anthropological perspectives on property in the age of neoliberalism. *Socio-Economic Review 5*(2): 287–318.

Hardaway, D.E. & Scamell, R.W. (2012). Open knowledge creation: Bringing transparency and inclusiveness to the peer review process. *MIS Quarterly, 36*(2), 339–346.

Hardin, G. (1968). The tragedy of the commons, *Science, 162*(3859), 1243–1248.

Hardy, P. (2012). *Download! How the internet transformed the record business*. London: Omnibus.

Haring, B. (2000). *Beyond the charts: MP3 and the digital music revolution*. Los Angeles: JM Northern Media.

Harrison, T.M., Guerrero, S., Burke, G.B., Cook, M., Cresswell, A., Helbig, N., et al. (2011). Open government and e-government: Democratic challenges from a public value perspective. *Proceedings of the 12th Annual International Conference on Digital Government Research*. College Park, Maryland.

Hars, A. & Ou, S. (2002). Working for free? Motivations for participating in open-source projects. *International Journal of Electronic Commerce, 6*(3), 25–39.

Hauge, Ø., Ayala, C., & Conradi, R. (2010). Adoption of open source software in software-intensive organizations–A systematic literature review. *Information and Software Technology, 52*(11), 1133–1154.

Hautz, J., Seidl, D., & Whittington, R. (2017). Open strategy: Dimensions, dilemmas, dynamics. *Long Range Planning, 50*(3), 298–309.

Hazen, T. (2012). Crowdfunding or fraudfunding? Social networks and the securities laws – Why the specially tailored exemption must be conditioned on meaningful disclosure. *North Carolina Law Review, 90*, 1735–1769.

Healy, K. (2015). The performativity of networks. *European Journal of Sociology/Archives Européennes de Sociologie, 56*(2), 175–205.

Heipke, C. (2010). Crowdsourcing geospatial data. *ISPRS Journal of Photogrammetry and Remote Sensing, 65*(6), 550–557.

Hellqvist, B. (2010). Referencing in the humanities and its implications for citation analysis. *Journal of the American Society for Information Science and Technology, 61*(2), 310–318.

Henderikx, M. A., Kreijns, K., & Kalz, M. (2017). Refining success and dropout in massive open online courses based on the intention–behavior gap. *Distance Education, 38*(3), 353–368.

Hertel, G., Niedner, S., & Herrmann, S. (2003). Motivation of software developers in Open Source projects: an Internet-based survey of contributors to the Linux kernel. *Research Policy, 32*(7), 1159–1177.

Herzenstein, M., Dholakia, U. M., & Andrews, R. L. (2011). Strategic herding behavior in peer-to-peer loan auctions. *Journal of Interactive Marketing, 25*(1), 27–36. doi:10.1016/j.intmar.2010. 07.001*.

Hess, D.J. (2007). *Alternative pathways in science and industry: Activism, innovation, and the environment in an era of globalization* (p. 22). Cambridge, MA: MIT Press.

Hicks, C., & Pachamanova, D. (2007). Back-propagation of user innovations: The open source compatibility edge. *Business Horizons, 50*(4), 315–324.

Hielkema, H., & Hongisto, P. (2013). Developing the Helsinki smart city: The role of competitions for open data applications. *Journal of the Knowledge Economy, 4*(2), 190–204.

Hilgers, D., & Ihl, C. (2010). Citizensourcing: Applying the concept of open innovation to the public sector. *International Journal of Public Participation, 4*(1).

Himanen, P. (2001). L'etica hacker e lo spirito dell'età dell'informazione (Vol. 59). Feltrinelli Editore.

Hippel, E. V., & Krogh, G. V. (2003). Open source software and the "private-collective" innovation model: Issues for organization science. *Organization Science, 14*(2), 209–223.

Hirsch, P.M. (1972). Processing fads and fashions: An organisation-set analysis of cultural industry systems. *American Journal of Sociology 77*(4): 639–659.

Holm, A. B., Günzel, F., & Ulhøi, J. P. (2013). Openness in innovation and business models: Lessons from the newspaper industry. *International Journal of Technology Management, 61*(3/4), 324–348.

Holtgrewe, U. & Werle, R. (2001). De-commodifying software? Open source software between business strategy and social movement. *Science Studies 14*(2): 43–65.

Hossain, M. & Kauranen, I. (2016). Open innovation in SMEs: A systematic literature review., *Journal of Strategy and Management, 9*(1) pp. 58–73. https://doi.org/10.1108/JSMA-08-2014-0072.

Hossain, M., Islam, K., Sayeed, M. & Kauranen, I. (2016). A comprehensive review of open innovation literature. *Journal of Science and Technology Policy Management, 7*(1), pp. 2–25. https://doi.org/10.1108/JSTPM-02-2015-0009.

Howard, T. J., Achiche, S., Özkil, A., & McAloone, T. C. (2012). Open design and crowdsourcing: maturity, methodology and business models. In *DS 70: Proceedings of DESIGN 2012, the 12th International Design Conference, Dubrovnik, Croatia* (pp. 181–190).

Howe, J. (2006a). The rise of crowdsourcing. *Wired Magazine, 14*(6), 1–4.

Howe, J. (2006b, June 2). Crowdsourcing: A definition. Wired Blog Network: Crowdsourcing. Retrieved June 15, 2007, from http://crowdsourcing.typepad.com/cs/2006/06/crowdsourcing_a.html.

Howe, J. (2008). *Crowdsourcing*. New York, NY: Crown. https://www.gnu.org/philosophy/open-source-misses-the-point.en.html.

Hua, J. J. (2014). Construction of digital commons and exploration of public domain. In *Toward a more balanced approach: Rethinking and readjusting copyright systems in the digital network era* (pp. 175–199). Berlin, Heidelberg: Springer.

Hulme, M. K., & Wright, C. (2006). Internet based social lending: Past, present and future. *Social Futures Observatory, 11*, 1–115.

Huws, U. (2014). *Labor in the global digital economy: The cybertariat comes of age*. New York University Press.

Hyland, K. (1999). Academic attribution: Citation and the construction of disciplinary knowledge. *Applied Linguistics, 20*(3), 341–367.

IFPI (International Federation of the Phonographic Industry) (2017). Global Music Report 2017, http://www.ifpi.org/downloads/GMR2017.pdf [accessed: 07.11.2017].

Inauen, M. & Schenker-Wicki, A. (2012). Fostering radical innovations with open innovation, *European Journal of Innovation Management. 15*(2), pp. 212–231. https://doi.org/10.1108/14601061211220986.

Ingram, C., Teigland, R., & Vaast, E. (2014). Solving the puzzle of crowdfunding: Where technology affordances and institutional entrepreneurship collide. In *System sciences* (HICSS), 2014 47th Hawaii International Conference on, IEEE. (pp. 4556–4567). doi:10.2139/ssrn.2285426*.

Irwin, A. S. M., & Milad, G. (2016). The use of crypto-currencies in funding violent jihad. *Journal of Money Laundering Control, 19*(4), 407–425. doi:http://dx.doi.org/10.1108/JMLC-01-2016-0003.

Janssen, M., Charalabidis, Y. and Zuiderwijk, A. (2012). Benefits, adoption barriers and myths of open data and open government. *Information Systems Management, 29*(4), 258–268.

Jaszi, P., & Aufderheide, P. (2011). *Reclaiming fair use: How to put balance back in copyright*. Chicago: University of Chicago Press.

Jemielniak (2014). *Common knowledge? An ethnography of Wikipedia*. Stanford, CA: Stanford University Press.

Jones, S. & Lenhart, A. (2004). Music downloading and listening: Findings from the Pew Internet and American Life Project. *Popular Music and Society 27*(2): 185–199.

Juris, J.S. (2005). The new digital media and activist networking within anti–corporate globalization movements. The *Annals of the American Academy of Political and Social Science 597*(1): 189–208.

Kaartemo, V. (2017). The elements of a successful crowdfunding campaign: A systematic literature review of crowdfunding performance. *International Review of Entrepreneurship, 15*(3), 291–318.

Kafai, Y., Fields, D., & Searle, K. (2014). Electronic textiles as disruptive designs: Supporting and challenging maker activities in schools. *Harvard Educational Review, 84*(4), 532–556.

Kane, G.C., & Fichman, R.G. (2009). The shoemaker's children: Using wikis for information systems teaching, research, and publication. *MIS Quarterly 33*(1): pp. 1–17.

Kassen, M. (2013). A promising phenomenon of open data: A case study of the Chicago open data project. *Government Information Quarterly, 30*(4).

Kavanagh, D., Miscione, G., & Ennis, P. J. (2019). The bitcoin game: Ethno-resonance as method. *Organization, 26*(4), 517–536.

Kellner, D. (1995). *Media culture: Cultural studies, identity and politics between the modern and the postmodern*. London and New York: Routledge.

Kemp, R. (2009). Current developments in open source software. *Computer Law & Security Review, 25*(6), 569–582.

Khan, Z., Anjum, A., Soomro, K., & Tahir, M. A. (2015). Towards cloud based big data analytics for smart future cities. *Journal of Cloud Computing, 4*(1), 1–11.

Kirby, E., Worner, S. (2014). Shane crowd-funding: An infant industry growing fast. Staff, Working Paper of the International Organisation of Securities Commissions Research Department, SWP3/2014.

Kitchin, R. (2014). The real-time city? Big data and smart urbanism. *GeoJournal, 79*(1), 1–14.

Klijn, EH, Edelenbos, J, Kort, M, van Twist, MJW (2008) Facing management dilemmas: An analysis of managerial choices in 18 complex environmental public private partnership projects. *International Review of the Administrative Sciences 74*(2), 2.

Komninos, N., Kakderi, C., Panori, A., & Tsarchopoulos, P. (2019). Smart city planning from an evolutionary perspective. *Journal of Urban Technology, 26*(2), 3–20.

Konecki, K. (2000). Studia z metodologii badań jakościowych. Teoria ugruntowana. Warsaw: PWN.

Kostakis, V., & Drechsler, W. (2013). Peer production and desktop manufacturing: the case of the Helix_T wind turbine project. *Science, Technology, & Human Values, 38*(6), 773–800.

Kostakis, V., & Bauwens, M. (2020). Grammar of peer production. In M. O'Neil, C. Pentzold and S. Toupin (Eds.), *The handbook of peer production* (pp. 19–32). Hoboken, NJ: John Wiley & Sons.

Kostakis, V., & Bauwens, M. (2021). *Grammar of peer production. The handbook of peer production*, 19–32.

Kostakis, V., Niaros, V., & Giotitsas, C. (2015). Production and governance in hackerspaces: A manifestation of Commons-based peer production in the physical realm? *International Journal of Cultural Studies, 18*(5), 555–573.

Kretschmer, M., Klimis, G. & Wallis, R. (2001). Music in electronic markets: An empirical study. *New Media and Society 3*(4): 417–442.

Kromidha, E. & Robson, P. (2016) Social identity and signalling success factors in online crowdfunding, *Entrepreneurship & Regional Development, 28*:9–10, 605–629, doi: 10.1080/08985626.2016.1198425.

Kshemkalyani, A. D., & Singhal, M. (2011). *Distributed computing: principles, algorithms, and systems*. City: Cambridge University Press.

Ku, R. and Shih, R. (2002) The creative destruction of copyright: Napster and the new economics of digital technology. *University of Chicago Law Review 69*(1): 263–324.

Kuk, G. (2006). Strategic interaction and knowledge sharing in the KDE developer mailing list. *Management Science, 52*(7), 1031–1042.

Kunz, M. M., Bretschneider, U., Erler, M., & Leimeister, J. M. (2017). An empirical investigation of signaling in reward-based crowdfunding. *Electronic Commerce Research, 17*(3), 425–461.

Kuppuswamy, V., & Bayus, B. L. (2018). Crowdfunding creative ideas: The dynamics of project backers. In D. Cumming & L. Hornuf (Eds.), *The economics of crowdfunding* (pp. 151–182) [Douglas Cumming and Lars Hornuf]. Palgrave Macmillan, Cham.

Kwall, R. R. (1985). Copyright and the moral right: Is an American marriage possible. *Vand. L. Rev., 38*, 1.

Kwall, R. R. (2001). Author-stories: Narrative's implications for moral rights and copyright's Joint Authorship Doctrine. *S. CAl. l. reV., 75*, 1.

Kwall, R. R. (2002). The attribution right in the United States: Caught in the crossfire between copyright and Section 43 (A). *Wash. L. Rev.*, 77, 985.

Lagace, M. (2000). The simple economics of open source. Harvard Business School working knowledge. https://hbswk.hbs.edu/archive/the-simple-economics-of-open-source.

Lakhani, K.R. and von Hippel, E. (2003). How open source software works: 'Free' user-to-user assistance. *Research Policy, 32*(6), 923–943.

Lakhani, K. R., & Wolf, R. G. (2003). Why hackers do what they do: Understanding motivation and effort in free/open source software projects. Open Source Software Projects (September 2003).

Latour, B. (1986). Visualization and cognition: Thinking with eyes and hands. *Knowledge and Society. Studies in the Sociology of Culture Past and Present* 6: 1–40.

Lee, E., & Lee, B. (2012). Herding behavior in online P2P lending: An empirical investigation. *Electronic Commerce Research and Applications, 11*(5), 495–503. doi:10.1016/j.elerap.2012.02.001*.

Lee, K. and Cole, R.E. (2003). From a firm-based to a community-based model of knowledge creation: The case of the Linux kernel development. *Organization Science 14*(6), 633–649 and 754–755.

Leimeister, J.M., Huber, M., Bretschneider, U. and Krcmar, H. (2009). Leveraging crowdsourcing: Activation-supporting components for IT-based ideas competition. *Journal of Management Information Systems, 26*(1), 197–224.

Lerner, J., & Tirole, J. (2002). Some simple economics of open source. *The Journal of Industrial Economics, 50*(2), 197–234.

Lerner, J. (2013). *The comingled code: Open source and economic development.* Boston: MIT Press Books.

Lessig, L. (2001). *The future of ideas: The fate of the commons in a connected world.* New York: Vintage.

Leydesdorff, L. (1988). Problems with the 'measurement' of national scientific performance. *Science and Public Policy, 15*(3), 149–152.

Levy, S. (1984). *Hackers: Heroes of the computer revolution.* New York: Penguin Books.

Lindengaard, S. (2010). *The open innovation revolution. Essentials, roadblocks, and leadership skills.* Hoboken, NJ: Wiley.

Lindtner, S. (2015). Hacking with Chinese characteristics: The promises of the maker movement against China's manufacturing culture. *Science, Technology, & Human Values, 40*(5), 854–879.

Liu, Y., & Tsyvinski, A. (2018). Risks and returns of cryptocurrency (No. w24877). National Bureau of Economic Research.

Lloyd, R. (2014). Unauthorized digital sampling in the changing music landscape. *J. Intell. Prop. L., 22*, 143.

Lopes, P.D. (1992) Innovation and diversity in the popular music industry: 1969 to 1990. *American Sociological Review 57*(1): 56–71.

Luhmann, N. (1990). *Essays on self-reference.* New York: Columbia University Press.

Mach, T., Carter, C., & Slattery, C. (2013). Peer-to-peer lending to small businesses. Federal reserve system community development research conference. Retrieved March 19, 2020, https://frbatlanta.org/documents/news/conferences/13resilience_rebuilding_paper_Mach.pdf*.

Macht, S., & Weatherston, J. (2014). The benefits of online crowdfunding for fund seeking business ventures. *Strategic Change, 23*(1–2), 1–14. doi:10.1002/jsc*.

Madison, D.S. (2011). *Critical ethnography: Method, ethics, and performance.* New York: Sage.

Magalhaes, G., Roseira, C. & Manley, L. (2014). Business models for open government data. *Proceedings of the 8th International Conference on Theory and Practice of Electronic Governance (ICEGOV)*, ACM.

Maier, C. E. (2002). A sample for pay keeps the lawyers away: A proposed solution for artists who sample and artists who are sampled. *Vand. J. Ent. L. & Prac., 5*, 100.

Majchrzak, A. & Malhotra, A. (2013). Towards an information systems perspective and research agenda on crowdsourcing for innovation. *Journal of Strategic Information Systems, 22*(3), 257–268.

Makelberge, N. (2012). Rethinking collaboration in networked music. *Organised Sound 17*(1): 28–35.

Mallapragada, G., Grewal, R., & Lilien, G. (2012). User-generated open source products: Founder's social capital and time to product release. *Marketing Science, 31*(3), 474–492.

Marjanovic, S., Fry, C., & Chataway, J. (2012). Crowdsourcing based business models: In search of evidence for innovation 2.0. *Science and Public Policy, 39*(3), 318–332.

Marshall, L. (2004). The effects of piracy upon the music industry: A case study of bootlegging. *Media, Culture and Society 26*(2):163–181.

Marshall, L. (2005). *Bootlegging: Romanticism and copyright in the music industry.* London: Sage.

Marshall, L. (2015). 'Let's keep music special. F—Spotify': on-demand streaming and the controversy over artist royalties. *Creative Industries Journal 8*(2), 177–189.

Martins, L. L., Rindova, V. P., & Greenbaum, B. E. (2015). Unlocking the hidden value of concepts: A cognitive approach to business model innovation. *Strategic Entrepreneurship Journal, 9*(1), 99–117.

Mason, W., & Suri, S. (2012). Conducting behavioral research on Amazon's Mechanical Turk. *Behavior Research Methods, 44*(1), 1–23.

Mayer, K. (2015). Open Science – Policy Briefing, http://era.gv.at/object/document/2279 (16.09.2020).

McAndrew, S. & Everett, M. (2015). Music as collective invention: A social network analysis of composers. *Cultural Sociology 9*(1): 56–80.

McCourt, T. & Burkart, P. (2003). When creators, corporations and consumers collide: Napster and the development of on-line music distribution. *Media, Culture and Society 25*(3): 333–50.

McDermott, P. (2010). Building open government. *Government Information Quarterly, 27*(4), 401–413.

McDonagh, L. (2013). Copyright, contract, and FOSS. In Shemtov, N., & Walden, I., (Eds.) Free *and open source software: Policy, law and practice.* Oxford: Oxford University Press.

McLeod, K. & DiCola, P. (2011). *Creative license: The law and culture of digital sampling.* Durham, NC: Duke University Press.

McVeigh, M. E. (2004). *Open access journals in the ISI citation databases: analysis of impact factors and citation patterns: a citation study from Thomson Scientific* (p. 125). Philadelphia: Thomson Scientific.

Meijer AJ, Curtin D, Hillebrandt M. (2012). Open government: connecting vision and voice. *International Review of Administrative Sciences 78*(1):10–29. doi:10.1177/0020852311429533.

Merton, R. K. (1942). A note on science and democracy. *J. Legal & Pol. Soc., 1*, 115.

Milan, S. (2013). *Social movements and their technologies: Wiring social change.* New York: Springer.

Milan, S., & Van der Velden, L. (2016). The alternative epistemologies of data activism. *Digital Culture & Society, 2*(2), 57–74.

BIBLIOGRAPHY

Minecraft (2021). *Open source sound attributions*, accessed at: https://www.minecraft.net/zh-hant/attribution/.

Mirri, S., Prandi, C., Salomoni, P., Callegati, F., & Campi, A. (2014, September). On combining crowdsourcing, sensing and open data for an accessible smart city. In *2014 Eighth International Conference on Next Generation Mobile Apps, Services and Technologies* (pp. 294–299). IEEE.

Mollick, E. (2014). The dynamics of crowdfunding: An exploratory study. *Journal of Business Venturing, 29*(1), 1–16.

Mollick, E., & Kuppuswamy, V. (2014). After the campaign: Outcomes of crowdfunding (UNCKenan-Flagler Research Paper No. 2376997). Retrieved May 15, 2014, from http://papers.ssrn.com/sol3/papers.cfm?abstract_id¼2376997*.

Molteni, L. & Ordanini, A. (2003). Consumption patterns, digital technology and music downloading. *Long Range Planning 36*(4): 389–406.

Moon, M. J. (2002). The evolution of e-government among municipalities: Rhetoric or reality? *Public Administration Review, 62*(4), 424–433.

Moore, C. (2005). Creative choices: Changes to Australian copyright law and the future of the public domain. *Media International Australia Incorporating Culture and Policy, 114*(1), 71–82.

Moritz, A., & Block, J. H. (2016). Crowdfunding: A literature review and research directions. In *Crowdfunding in Europe* (pp. 25–53). Springer, Cham.

Morris, M., Schindehutte, M., & Allen, J. (2005). The entrepreneur's business model: Toward a unified perspective. *Journal of Business Research, 58*(6), 726–735.

Moscardo, G. (1996). Mindful visitors. Heritage and tourism. *Annals of Tourism Research, 23*(2), 376–397.

Nakamoto, S. (2008) Bitcoin: A peer-to-peer electronic cash system. [Online]. https://bitcoin.org/bitcoin.pdf.

Negus, K. (1998). Cultural production and the corporation: Musical genres and the strategic management of creativity in the US recording industry. *Media, Culture & Society 20*(3): 359–379.

Nehme, M. (2017). The rise of crowd equity funding: Where to now? *International Journal of Law in Context, 13*(3), 253–276.

Neumann, M. & Simpson, T.A. (1997). Smuggled sound: Bootleg recording and the pursuit of popular memory. *Symbolic Interaction 20*(4): 319–341.

Nicolaisen, J. (2003). The social act of citing: Towards new horizons in citation theory. *Proceedings of the American Society for Information Science and Technology, 40*(1), 12–20.

Nielsen, M. A. (2012). *Reinventing discovery: The new era of networked science*. Princeton: Princeton University Press.

Nigel Gilbert, G. (1977). Referencing as persuasion. *Social Studies of Science, 7*(1), 113–122.

Niyazov, Y., Vogel, C., Price, R., Lund, B., Judd, D., Akil, A., ... & Shron, M. (2016). Open access meets discoverability: Citations to articles posted to Academia.edu. *PloS One, 11*(2).

Norris, D. F., & Reddick, C. G. (2013). Local e-government in the United States: Transformation or incremental change? *Public Administration Review, 73*(1), 165–175.

Nyman, L. (2014). Hackers on forking. *OpenSym '14.* doi: 10.1145/2641580.2641590.

Nyman, L. & Lindman, J. (2013). Code forking, governance, and sustainability in open source software. *Technology Innovation Management Review, 3*(1), pp. 7–12. doi: 10.22215/timreview/644.

Oberholzer-Gee, F. & Strumpf, K. (2007). The effect of file sharing on record sales: An empirical analysis. *Journal of Political Economy 115*(1): 1–42.

ODI (2020) https://theodi.org/about-the-odi/our-vision-and-manifesto/our-mission/ accessed 18.09.2020.

OKFN (2020) Why open data? https://okfn.org/opendata/why-open-data/ (accessed 18.09.2020).

Olsen, T. & Carmel, E. (2013). The process of atomization of business tasks for crowdsourcing. *Strategic Outsourcing: An International Journal, 6*(3). https://doi.org/10.1108/SO-10-2013-0019.

Onnée, S., & Renault, S. (2016). *Crowdfunding: principles, trends and issues. In Research handbook on digital transformations.* City: Edward Elgar Publishing.

Ooi, C. (2010). A theory of tourism experiences: The management of attention. In P. O'Dell & T. Billing (Eds.), *Experiencescapes: Tourism, culture, and economy* (pp. 51–68). Koge: Copenhagen Business School Press.

Open Source Initiative (2007). The Open Source Definition, accessed online: https://opensource.org/docs/osd (08.04.2020).

opensource.com (2020). Open source licensing at GitHub, accessed online: https://opensource.com/life/15/7/interview-ben-balter-github.

Ordanini, A., Miceli, L., Pizzetti, M., & Parasuraman, A. (2011). Crowd-funding: transforming customers into investors through innovative service platforms. *Journal of Service Management, 22*(4):443–470.

Orlikowski, W.J. (2000). Using technology and constituting structures: A practice lens for studying technology in organizations. *Organization Science 11*(4): 404–428.

Orlikowski. W.J. & Baroudi, J.J. (1991). Studying information technology in organizations: Research approaches and assumptions. *Information Systems Research 2*(1): 1–28.

Orlikowski, W.J., & Scott, S.V. (2015). The algorithm and the crowd: Considering the materiality of service innovation, *MIS Quarterly 39*(1), 201–216.

Osterwalder, A., Pigneur, Y., & Tucci, C. L. (2005). Clarifying business models: Origins, present, and future of the concept. *Communications of the Association for Information Systems, 16*(1), 1.

Ostrom, E. (1990). *Governing the commons: The evolution of institutions for collective action.* Cambridge University Press.

Paolacci, G., Chandler, J., & Ipeirotis, P. G. (2010). Running experiments on Amazon Mechanical Turk. *Judgment and Decision Making, 5*(5), 411–419.

Papavlasopoulou, S., Giannakos, M. N., & Jaccheri, L. (2017). Empirical studies on the Maker Movement, a promising approach to learning: A literature review. *Entertainment Computing, 18,* 57–78.

Parveen, R., & Alajmi, A. (2019). An overview of Bitcoin's legal and technical challenges. *Journal of Legal, Ethical and Regulatory Issues, 22,* 1–8.

Paul, K. A. (2018). Ancient artifacts vs. digital artifacts: New tools for unmasking the sale of illicit antiquities on the dark web. *Arts, 7*(2) doi: http://dx.doi.org/10.3390/arts7020012.

Pearce, J. M. (2012). Building research equipment with free, open-source hardware. *Science, 337*(6100), 1303–1304.

Pearce, J. M. (2017). Emerging business models for open source hardware. *Journal of Open Hardware, 1*(1), 2–10.

Peled, A. (2011). When transparency and collaboration collide: the USA open data program. *Journal of the American Society for Information Science and Technology, 62*(11), 2085–2094.

Pereira, G. V., Macadar, M. A., Luciano, E. M., & Testa, M. G. (2017). Delivering public value through open government data initiatives in a Smart City context. *Information Systems Frontiers, 19*(2), 213–229.

Peters, G. W., Chapelle, A., & Panayi, E. (2014). Opening discussion on banking sector risk exposures and vulnerabilities from virtual currencies: An operational risk perspective. Available at SSRN 2491991.

Peters, M.A. & Britez, R.G. (2008). *Open education and education for openness*. Rotterdam: Sense Publishers.

Phelps, L., Fox, B. A., & Marincola, F. M. (2012). Supporting the advancement of science: Open Access publishing and the role of mandates. *Journal of Translational Medicine, 10,* 13.

Piller, F. T., Ihl, C., & Vossen, A. (2010). A typology of customer co-creation in the innovation process. Available at SSRN 1732127.

Pletcher C (2009) Are publicity rights gone in a flash: Flickr, Creative Commons, and the commercial use of personal photographs. *Florida State University Business Review 8*(1): 129–156.

Poetz, M. K., & Schreier, M. (2012). The value of crowdsourcing: can users really compete with professionals in generating new product ideas? *Journal of Product Innovation Management, 29*(2), 245–256.

Polanyi, K. (1944). *The Great Transformation*. New York: Farrar & Rinehart.

Poster. M. (2004). Consumption and digital commodities in the everyday. *Cultural Studies 18*(2–3): 409–423.

Powell, A. (2012). Democratizing production through open source knowledge: From open software to open hardware. *Media, Culture & Society, 34*(6), 691–708.

Prahalad, C. K., & Ramaswamy, V. (2000). Co-opting customer competence. *Harvard Business Review 78*(1): 79–90.

Priem, J., & Costello, K. L. (2010). How and why scholars cite on Twitter. *Proceedings of the American Society for Information Science and Technology, 47*(1), 1–4.

Raasch, C., Herstatt, C., & Balka, K. (2009). On the open design of tangible goods. *R&D Management, 39*(4), 382–393.

Ramaswamy, V., & Ozcan, K. (2018). What is co-creation? An interactional creation framework and its implications for value creation. *Journal of Business Research, 84*, 196–205.

Rayna, T. & Striukova, L. (2009). Monometapoly or the economics of the music industry. *Prometheus 27*(3): 211–222.

Raymond, E. (1999). The cathedral and the bazaar. *Knowledge, Technology & Policy, 12*(3), 23–49.

Remneland Wikhamn, B., & Wikhamn, W. (2013). Structuring of the open innovation field. *Journal of Technology Management & Innovation, 8*(3), 173–185.

Roberts, J. A., Hann, I. H., & Slaughter, S. A. (2006). Understanding the motivations, participation, and performance of open source software developers: A longitudinal study of the Apache projects. *Management Science, 52*(7), 984–999.

Robinson, D., Yu, H, Zeller, W. & Felten, E. (2009). Government data and the invisible hand. *Yale Journal of Law & Technology, 11*, 160–175.

Rochelandet, F. (2003) Are copyright collecting societies efficient organisations? An evaluation of collective administration of copyright in Europe. In W.J. Gordon, & R. Watt (eds.) *The economics of copyright: Developments in research and analysis.* Cheltenham: Edward Elgar, 176–197.

Rodgers, T. (2003). On the process and aesthetics of sampling in electronic music production. *Organised Sound 8*(3): 313–320.

Roggero, G. (2010). Five theses on the common. *Rethinking Marxism, 22*(3), 357–373.

Roome, N., & Louche, C. (2016). Journeying toward business models for sustainability: A conceptual model found inside the black box of organisational transformation. *Organization & Environment, 29*(1), 11–35.

Ruckenstein, M., & Schüll, N. D. (2017). The datafication of health. *Annual Review of Anthropology, 46*, 261–278.

Rufai, R., Gul, S., & Shah, T. A. (2012). Open Access journals in library and information science: The story so far. *Trends in Information Management, 7*(2).

Russi, G. (2011). Creative Commons, CC-plus and hybrid intermediaries: a stakeholders' perspective. *International Law and Management Review*, Spring.

Saebi, T., & Foss, N. J. (2015). Business models for open innovation: Matching heterogeneous open innovation strategies with business model dimensions. *European Management Journal, 33*(3), 201–213.

Samuelson, P. (2006). IBM's pragmatic embrace of open source. *Communications of the ACM, 49*(10), 21–25.

Santos, C., Kuk, G., Kon, F., & Pearson, J. (2013). The attraction of contributors in free and open source software projects. *The Journal of Strategic Information Systems, 22*(1), 26–45.

Santos-Vijande, M. L., Álvarez, B. Á., & Rodríguez, N. G. (2012). Internal marketing as a driver of market orientation and co-creation culture in the tourism sector. *African Journal of Business Management, 6*(13), 4707–4716. doi:10.5897/AJBM11.1717.

Saxton, G. D., & Wang, L. (2013). The social network effect: The determinants of giving through social media. *Nonprofit and Voluntary Sector Quarterly.* doi:10.1177/0899764013485159*.

Scacchi, W., & Alspaugh, T. A. (2012). Understanding the role of licenses and evolution in open architecture software ecosystems. *Journal of Systems and Software, 85*(7), 1479–1494.

Scherzinger, M. (2014) Musical property: Widening or withering? *Journal of Popular Music Studies 26*(1): 162–192.

Schlagwein, D. & Bjørn-Andersen, N. (2014). Organizational learning with crowdsourcing: The revelatory case of LEGO. *Journal of the Association for Information Systems, 15*(11), 754–778.

Schlagwein, D., Conboy, K., Feller, J., Leimeister, J. M., & Morgan, L. (2017). "Openness" with and without Information technology: A framework and a brief history. *Journal of Information Technology, 32*(4), 297–305. https://doi.org/10.1057/s41265-017-0049-3.

Schumann, M., Hess, T., & Hess, T. (2000). *Grundfragen der Medienwirtschaft* (Vol. 2). Berlin, Heidelberg: Springer.

Seidman, G.W. (2007). *Beyond the boycott: Labour rights, human rights, and transnational activism.* London and New York: Russell Sage Foundation.

Shahrokhi, M. & Parhizgari, A. (2019). Crowdfunding in real estate: evolutionary and disruptive. *Managerial Finance, 46*(6), 785–801. https://doi.org/10.1108/MF-10-2018-0492.

Shemtov, N. & Walden, I. (2013). *Free and open source software: Policy, law, and practice.* Oxford: Oxford University Press.

Sinha, R.K, Machado, F.S. & Sellman, C. (2010). Don't think twice, it's all right: Music piracy and pricing in a DRM-free environment. *Journal of Marketing 74*(2): 40–54.

Skarzynski, P., & Gibson, R. (2008). *Innovation to the core: a blueprint for transforming the way your company innovates.* Boston, MA: Harvard Business Review Press.

Skirnevskiy, V., Bendig, D., & Brettel, M. (2017). The influence of internal social capital on serial creators' success in crowdfunding. *Entrepreneurship Theory and Practice, 41*(2), 209–236.

Snowden, E. (2019). *Permanent record.* Macmillan: London.

Söderberg, J. (2002). Copyleft vs. copyright: A Marxist critique. *First Monday 7*(3). https://doi.org/10.5210/fm.v7i3.938.

Spellman, P. (2006). *Indie power: a business-building guide for record labels, music production houses, and merchant musicians*. Boston, MA: MBS Business Media.

Spithoven, A., Clarysse, B., Knockaert, M. (2011). Building absorptive capacity to organise inbound open innovation in traditional industries. *Technovation, 31*(1), 10–21.

Stallman (2020). Why open source misses the point of free software, accessed on-line: https://www.gnu.org/philosophy/open-source-misses-the-point.en.html (08.04.2020).

Stam, W. (2009). When does community participation enhance the performance of open source software companies? *Research Policy, 38*(8), 1288–1299.

Stangler, D., & Maxwell, K. (2012). DIY producer society. *Innovations: Technology, Governance, Globalization, 7*(3), 3–10.

Stanisz, A. (2018). Collecting sounds. Online sharing of field recordings as cultural practice. *Ethnologia Polona, 39*, 127–144.

Stol, K. J., Babar, M. A., Avgeriou, P., & Fitzgerald, B. (2011). A comparative study of challenges in integrating open source software and inner source software. *Information and Software Technology, 53*(12), 1319–1336.

Stol, K.-J. & Fitzgerald, B. (2015). Inner source – Adopting open source development practices in organizations: A tutorial. *IEEE Software, 32*(4), 60–67.

Stracke, C. M. (2017). The quality of MOOCs: How to improve the design of open education and online courses for learners?. In *International Conference on Learning and Collaboration Technologies* (pp. 285–293). Springer, Cham.

Strauss, W. (1955). The moral right of the author. *The American Journal of Comparative Law*, 506–538.

Styven, M. (2007) The intangibility of music in the Internet age. *Popular Music and Society 30*(1): 53–74.

Su, H. N., & Lee, P. C. (2012). Framing the structure of global open innovation research. *Journal of Informetrics, 6*(2), 202–216.

Suber, P. (2016). *Knowledge unbound: Selected writings on open access, 2002–2011*. Boston: MIT Press.

Surowiecki, J. (2004). *The wisdom of crowds*. New York: Anchor Books.

Swan, M. (2012). Scaling crowdsourced health studies: The emergence of a new form of contract research organization. *Personalized Medicine, 9*(2), 223–234.

Swales, J. M. (1990). *Genre analysis: English in academic and research settings*. Cambridge, UK: Cambridge University Press.

Swatman, P. M., Krueger, C., & Van Der Beek, K. (2006). The changing digital content landscape. *Internet research*.

Tapscott, D., Lowi, A., & Ticoll, D. (2000). *Digital capital – Harnessing the power of businesswebs*. Cambridge, MA: Harvard Business School Press.

Tavakoli, A., Schlagwein, D., & Schoder, D. (2017). Open strategy: Literature review, re-analysis of cases and conceptualisation as a practice. *The Journal of Strategic Information Systems, 26*(3), 163–184.

Teddlie, C. & Yu, F. (2007). Mixed methods sampling: A typology with examples. *Journal of Mixed Methods Research*, 1(1), 77–100.

Thompson, P., Parker, R. & Cox, S. (2016). Interrogating creative theory and creative work: Inside the games studio. *Sociology* 50(2): 316–332.

Tkacz, N. (2014) *Wikipedia and the politics of openness*. Chicago: University of Chicago Press.

Tolbert, C. J., & Mossberger, K. (2006). The effects of e-government on trust and confidence in government. *Public Administration Review*, 66(3), 354–369.

Tolbert, C. J., Mossberger, K., & McNeal, R. (2008). Institutions, policy innovation, and E-Government in the American States. *Public Administration Review*, 68(3), 549–563.

Toynbee, J (.2016). *Making popular music: Musicians, creativity and institutions*. London: Bloomsbury Publishing.

Troutt, D. D. (2009). I own therefore I am: copyright, personality, and soul music in the digital commons. *Fordham Intell. Prop. Media & Ent. LJ*, 20, 373.

Tu, K. V., & Meredith, M. W. (2015). Rethinking virtual currency regulation in the bitcoin age. *Washington Law Review*, 90(1), 271–347.

UK Digital Economy Act (2010), Full text: http://www.legislation.gov.uk/ukpga/2010/24/pdfs/ukpga_20100024_en.pdf.

Umney, C. & Kretsos, L. (2014) Creative labour and collective interaction: The working lives of young jazz musicians in London. *Work, Employment & Society* 28(4): 571–588.

Vaccaro, V. & Cohn, D. (2004). The evolution of business models and marketing strategies in the music industry. *The International Journal on Media Management* 6(1–2): 46–58.

Vaisnore, A., & Petraite, M. (2011). Customer involvement into open innovation processes: a conceptual model. *Social Sciences*, 73(3), 62–73.

Vallance, R., Kiani, S., & Nayfeh, S. (2001, May). Open design of manufacturing equipment. In *Proceedings of the CHIRP 1st International Conference on Agile, Reconfigurable Manufacturing* (pp. 33–43).

Van der Graaf, S. (2012). Get organized at work! A look inside the game design process of Valve and Linden Lab. *Bulletin of Science, Technology & Society*, 32(6), 480–488.

Van Houweling, M.S. (2010). Author autonomy and atomism in copyright law. *Virginia Law Review* 96: 549–642.

Vargo, S., & Lusch, R. (2004). Evolving to a new dominant logic for marketing. *Journal of Marketing* 68(1): 1–17. doi:10.1509/jmkg.68.1.1.24036.

VentilAid.com (2020) "Vision" Accessed online: https://www.ventilaid.org/ [27.03.2020].

Vetter, P., Fredricx, F., Rajan, G., & Oberle, K. (2008). Recommendations for a multi-service access architecture from the European MUSE Project. *Bell Labs Technical Journal*, 13(1), 11–28.

Vicente-Saez, R., & Martinez-Fuentes, C. (2018). Open Science now: A systematic literature review for an integrated definition. *Journal of Business Research, 88*, 428–436.

Vision, T. J. (2010). Open data and the social contract of scientific publishing. *BioScience, 60*(5), 330–331. doi: 10.1525/bio.2010.60.5.2.

Von Hippel, E. (1988). *The sources of innovation*. New York: Oxford University Press.

Von Hippel, E. (2005). *Democratizing innovation*. Cambridge, MA: MIT Press.

Von Hippel, E., & Von Krogh, G. (2006). Free revealing and the private-collective model for innovation incentives. *R&D Management, 36*(3), 295–306.

Von Krogh, G., & Von Hippel, E. (2006). The promise of research on open source software. *Management Science, 52*(7), 975–983.

Von Hippel, E. 2007. Horizontal innovation networks – by and for users. *Industrial and Corporate Change* 2(1): 1–23.

Von Krogh, G., & Spaeth, S. (2007). The open source software phenomenon: Characteristics that promote research. *The Journal of Strategic Information Systems, 16*(3), 236–253.

Vulkan, N., Åstebro, T., Sierra, M.F., (2016) Equity crowdfunding: A new phenomena. *J. Bus. Ventur. Insights 5*, 37–49.

Walsham, G. (1993). *Interpreting information systems in organizations*. New York: John Wiley & Sons.

Wang, W., Mahmood, A., Sismeiro, C., & Vulkan, N. (2019). The evolution of equity crowdfunding: Insights from co-investments of angels and the crowd. *Research Policy, 48*(8), 103727.

WCT (WIPO Copyright Treaty) (1996). Accessed online: http://www.wipo.int/treaties/en/ip/wct/.

Weber, M. (1958). *The rational and social foundation of music*. Chicago: SI Press.

Webber, A. (2007). Digital sampling and the legal implications of its use after Bridgeport. *John's J. Legal Comment., 22*, 373.

Webster, E., Lambert, R., & Beziudenhout, A. (2011). *Grounding globalization: Labour in the age of insecurity*. New York and London: John Wiley & Sons.

Weiblen, T., Frankenberger, K., & Gassmann, O. (2013). The open business model: Towards a common understanding of an emerging concept. Unpublished paper draft presented at EURAM Conference.

West, J., & Bogers, M. (2014). Leveraging external sources of innovation: A review of research on open innovation. *Journal of Product Innovation Management, 31*(4), 814–831.

West, J., & O'mahony, S. (2008). The role of participation architecture in growing sponsored open source communities. *Industry and innovation, 15*(2), 145–168.

West, J., Salter, A., Vanhaverbeke, W. & Chesbrough, H. (2014). Open innovation: The next decade. *Research Policy, 43*(5), 805–811.

Westbrook, S. (Ed.). (2009). *Composition and copyright: Perspectives on teaching, text-making, and fair use*. Albany, NY: SUNY Press.

Wintel (2017). Worldwide Independent Market Report 2017, http://winformusic.org/files/WINTEL%202017/WINTEL%202017.pdf [accessed: 07.11.2017].

WIPO (2020). Summary of the Rome Convention for the Protection of Performers, Producers of Phonograms and Broadcasting Organisations (1961), accessed online: https://www.wipo.int/treaties/en/ip/rome/summary_rome.html.

WPPT (WIPO Performances and Phonograms Treaty) (1996). https://wipolex.wipo.int/en/text/295477.

Wu, M. W., & Lin, Y. D. (2001). Open Source software development: An overview. *Computer, 34*(6), 33–38.

Yeong, C. H., & Abdullah, B. J. J. (2012). Altmetrics: The right step forward. *Biomedical Imaging and Intervention Journal, 8*(3), 1–2.

Young, S. & Collins, S. (2010). A view from the trenches of music 2.0. *Popular Music and Society 33*(3): 339–355.

Yu, A. K. (2006). Enhancing legal aid access through an open source commons model. *Harv. JL & Tech., 20*, 373.

Yuan, L., & Powell, S. (2013). MOOCs and disruptive innovation: Implications for higher education. *eLearning Papers, In-depth, 33*(2), 1–7.

Yuan, H., Lau, R. Y., & Xu, W. (2016). The determinants of crowdfunding success: A semantic text analytics approach. *Decision Support Systems, 91*, 67–76.

Yum, H., Lee, B., & Chae, M. (2012). From the wisdom of crowds to my own judgment in microfinance through online peer-to-peer lending platforms. *Electronic Commerce Research and Applications, 11*(5), 469–483. doi: 10.1016/j.elerap.2012.05.003*.

Yun, J. J., Yang, J., & Park, K. (2016). Open innovation to business model: New perspective to connect between technology and market. *Science, Technology and Society, 21*(3), 324–348.

Zeitlyn, D. (2003). Gift economies in the development of open source software: Anthropological reflections. *Research Policy, 32*(7), 1287–1291.

Zott, C., & Amit, R. (2002). *Measuring the performance implications of business model design: Evidence from emerging growth public firms.* Fontainebleau: INSEAD.

Zott, C., Amit, R., & Massa, L. (2011). The business model: Recent developments and future research. *Journal of Management, 37*(4), 1019–1042.

Zouni, G., & Kouremenos, A. (2008). Do tourism providers know their visitors? An investigation of tourism experience at a destination. *Tourism and Hospitality Research, 8*(4), 282–297. doi:10.1057/thr.2008.30.

Zuboff, S. (2015). Big Other: Surveillance capitalism and the prospects of an information civilization. *Journal of Information Technology, 30*(1), 75–89.

Zuiderwijk, A., et al. (2014). Special Issue on Innovation through OpenData: Guest editors' introduction. *Journal of Theoretical and Applied Electronic Commerce Research, 9*(2), i–xiii.

Index

advertisement   122, 134, 182
AlienXXX   98, 101
All Rights Reserved   6, 66, 74, 80
Amazon's Mechanical Turk   29–30
anonymity   18, 22, 36
   artistic   122
   digital   22
Apache Software Foundation   62
Arduino   40–41
attribution   14, 20–21, 49, 78–79, 118, 124, 127–51, 154, 172–73, 179, 181
   automatising   79, 172
   protecting   147

Benjamin   3, 176
Benkler   8, 19, 50–52, 60–62, 64
Berne Convention   67–68
Bridgeport Music, Inc v Dimension Films   65, 72
BSD license   2, 10, 58–59
Burawoy   16, 178

Caroll   5, 46, 167
Chesbrough   24, 27–28, 31, 153
collaboration
   asynchronous   61, 108
   collective   122
collecting societies   11, 21, 65, 71–72, 78, 80, 153, 168–69, 176–77, 184
commonality   52, 60, 90, 125
commons   2–3, 8–11, 19–21, 50–53, 57, 60–64, 106, 125, 128–30, 140–41, 144–45, 147, 149–50, 152–76, 178–85
commons-based production   8–9, 19–21, 60, 62, 64, 149, 153, 177, 179–80, 182
copyleft   57–58, 63, 77, 122, 136, 163
   licenses   58, 154
copyright   3–5, 11, 23, 25–26, 56–60, 65–76, 78, 80, 129–30, 140, 142–44, 147, 149–50, 153, 176–77
copyright intermediaries   2, 10, 80
Creative Commons   2, 6, 10–11, 14–15, 17–21, 49, 65–111, 123–24, 129–32, 137, 139–40, 142, 144–45, 149–50, 167–68, 170, 173–78, 184
   licensing   14–15, 49, 84, 139, 154

creative industries   2–4, 6–9, 11–12, 15, 18–22, 49, 60, 64–67, 69–71, 147, 149–50, 152, 154, 174–78, 182–84
crowd equity   35–36
crowdfunding   33–37, 41
crowdsourcing   25, 29–30, 33, 35, 46
cryptocurrencies   33, 36
cultural production   2, 4–5, 12, 15–16, 70, 72, 156, 175, 177

Dahlander   24, 27–28, 173
DiCola   4–5, 70, 72–73, 176–77

editing   85–86, 104, 115, 127, 177
Elkin-Koren   7, 66, 75, 130
enforcement   69, 72, 130, 133, 145, 150
equipment   73, 85, 93, 96, 110, 112, 116, 118, 141, 153, 159
Europeana Sound   81, 171
European Union   44, 68–69
exchange value   10, 83, 136, 151–54, 158, 163, 173
expiration of copyright   59
exploitation   69, 76
   commercial   76

field recordings   13, 82, 85–86, 93, 162
film   11–12, 15, 18, 114, 127, 136, 145–46, 149, 153, 155–56, 158–59
Firth   4, 70
Fisher   40
Fitzgerald   25, 30, 38, 40, 68
Font, Frederic   13–14, 16, 158
forum   41, 63, 96, 98–99, 111, 155, 172
FreeSound   13–14, 16–17, 81–82, 84–86, 90–104, 111–20, 122–25, 131–34, 137–38, 140–48, 152, 154–61, 163–66, 170–73, 177, 181, 183
   forum   137, 142

gaming   13, 53, 118, 129, 135, 138, 140, 166, 180
General Public License (GPL)   58, 74
governance   7–8, 10, 19, 28, 39, 43, 49–50, 139, 149–50, 152, 175–76
Grissemann   29
Griswold   3–4, 69–70

hackers 52–55
Hackerspaces 109
Hardy 5, 71
Haring 5, 71, 73
Harrison 5, 48, 71, 73

industries
    audio 7, 78
    changed 103
    cultural 6, 17, 66
    emerging 2, 12, 175
    entertainment 25, 72
    high-tech 27
    service 29
    technological 19
    tourism 29
    video 5, 15
InfoSoc Directive 68–69
innovations 3, 16, 19, 24–31, 39, 44, 101, 109, 130
    artistic 2, 12, 107, 175, 185
    community-guided 39
    corporate 40
    open 31
iTunes 5, 71, 171

Jamendo 7, 81–82, 168–69, 171
Jemielniak 40, 62–63

Konecki 15–16
Kostakis 8, 49, 55, 62–63, 66, 82
Kostera 15

labels 21, 72–73, 81, 135, 167
    major 6, 71–72
labour 7, 17, 30, 62, 83, 106, 132, 175, 183, 185
    artist's 136
    contractual 40
    creative 162
Lakhani 32, 38, 62
Latour 3, 69
laugh 91, 100, 146
law 3–4, 17, 56, 60, 69, 80
legal frameworks 37, 50, 52, 54, 63–64, 106–8
Lenhart 5, 71, 73
Lerner 2, 10, 63
Lessig 130

licensing 6–7, 14, 37, 75, 78–81, 123, 125, 128, 139, 143–44, 178, 181, 183–85
    CC-0 146–47
Luhmann 110

Maxwell 109
Mayer 44
Mayhem 132
McAndrew 105, 108
McCourt 5, 71, 73
McDermott 48
McLeod and DiCola 4–5, 70, 72–73, 176–77
McVeigh 46
media 60, 65, 87, 95, 159, 163, 167–68, 170–71, 177, 179, 181–82
    CC-licensed 90
    open 7, 176, 179
    popular 55
    social 34
    traditional 177
metrics 22, 46, 124, 133
music 3–5, 69–74, 80, 82, 98, 102, 107–8, 117–18, 121, 130–31, 159, 164–65, 168–69, 171–72, 177
    background 78
    classical 119
    copyrighted 142
    making 118–19
    producing 78
    rock 165
    sampled 71–73, 136
    selling 116
    sharing 71, 73
music producer 72, 107, 116, 119, 121, 123, 140, 162
    ambient 124
    dance 90
    electronic 119–20, 140
    experimental 116, 123, 136
    techno 129
music production 12, 71, 93, 108, 119, 148

networked value 8, 10–11, 21, 84, 153, 166, 179–80, 184

open access 24, 36, 44–47, 66
open innovation 19, 24–28, 30–31, 54–55
open production 24–25, 37–38, 40

open scholarship   26, 43–44
open science   26, 43–44, 46
Ordanini   5, 34, 71, 73
Ostrom   50–51

peer-production   8–9, 50–63, 83–84, 90, 105
    model of   9, 50, 84
    new mechanisms of   2, 175
peer-to-peer-lending   35
platforms   13–14, 16, 29–30, 32–33, 47, 77–78, 80–82, 90, 92–96, 99–103, 105–6, 114–15, 124, 139–40, 142, 161, 181
Polanyi   178
popularity   16, 36, 40, 58, 87, 97, 124, 130, 169, 176, 183
popular music   4, 70, 155
production   7–12, 14–15, 19–22, 37–38, 40–41, 48–49, 51–52, 60–65, 72–73, 82, 84–86, 92–93, 97–98, 108–10, 116–17, 119–22, 124–25, 155–56, 161–62, 174–85
    amateur   111
    big-budget   21
    blockbuster   156
    collaborative   52
    collective   64
    commercial   52, 184
    hip-hop   116, 136, 140
    professional   163, 165
professionalisation   109, 182
profit   12, 37, 54, 120, 130, 139–40, 144, 167, 173
property relations   62, 109, 185
protection   21, 23, 25, 56–57, 60, 67, 121, 124, 128, 130, 142, 145, 147, 150–51, 153–54
proximity   38, 182
    cultural   34
    geographical   34
public data   7, 48, 175
public domain   59–60, 74, 80, 118, 124, 135, 137, 145, 147–48, 151, 164
publishing   18, 24, 33, 44, 46–47, 73, 76, 116

qualitative methodology   16
quality myth   111

radio   12, 114, 159, 177
Ramaswamy   28–29
recognition   6–7, 60, 62, 66, 68, 74–75, 81, 127–28, 130, 133, 183–84

recording   13–14, 72–73, 78, 85, 96, 98, 100, 111–12, 115, 156, 159, 165, 176–77
RedHat   41
remix   15, 77, 79, 86, 111, 121, 124, 174, 185
reputation   55, 63, 123, 130, 134, 140, 150, 157, 161–63, 180, 184
resistance   5, 7, 35, 54–55, 71, 74, 109
    culture of   19, 52

sales   72, 75, 122–23, 130, 156, 159, 161–63, 165
samples   71–74, 85–86, 98, 101–2, 104, 119–22, 132–33, 135–36, 147, 149, 155–57, 162–64, 171–72
sampling   20, 67, 71–72, 74, 78, 116, 177
Scherzinger   4, 70
Schlagwein   24–25, 30
search engines   13, 42, 75, 77, 87–88, 124, 132, 146, 170
Serra, Xavier   13, 171
Shazam   170
Shemtov   6, 66
Snowden   54–55
software   32, 38, 40, 51, 57–60, 62, 65, 101, 116–18, 163, 166
    free/open-source   60, 62, 152
Sony Music   72
Soundcloud   81–82, 132
sound design   88, 102–3, 121, 133, 147, 155, 180
sound effects   11, 13, 80–82, 118, 120, 141–42, 145, 147, 149, 157, 159, 162, 167–68

tagging   13, 88–89, 92, 171
Thompson   108
Thornton   47
Tkacz   2, 5, 10, 71

Universal Music Group   72
Universitat Pompeu Fabra   13–14, 81
user profiles   123–24, 130, 134, 142
use value   9–10, 84–85, 87, 96, 101, 105, 110, 118, 154, 161, 173

Vaccaro   6, 71, 73
Vaisnore   29
value   8, 10, 12, 20, 36, 48, 64, 66, 82, 84, 105–7, 156, 158, 167, 179
Velden   43

INDEX

VentilAid   41
Versilian Studios   163–64
video games   12, 54, 146, 148, 158, 165
videos   4–5, 14, 78, 95, 141–42, 159, 169, 172, 177
violations   139–43, 145, 148–49, 151, 157, 180, 184
   counteracting   140
   identifying   180
   privacy   54

Warner Music Group   72
Waves   171–72
Wikipedia   40, 62, 77

yahoo   81, 170
YouTube   7, 78, 114, 132, 141–42, 144, 169

Zeitlyn   39, 63
Zendesk   14
Zuboff   48

Printed in the United States
by Baker & Taylor Publisher Services